CURRENT ISSUES IN HEALTH ECONOMICS

CONTRIBUTIONS TO ECONOMIC ANALYSIS

290

Editors:
B.H. BALTAGI
E. SADKA

United Kingdom – North America – Japan
India – Malaysia – China

CURRENT ISSUES IN HEALTH ECONOMICS

DANIEL SLOTTJE
Department of Economics, Southern Methodist University, Dallas, TX, USA

RUSTY TCHERNIS
Department of Economics, Georgia State University, Atlanta, GA, USA

Emerald

United Kingdom – North America – Japan
India – Malaysia – China

Emerald Group Publishing Limited
Howard House, Wagon Lane, Bingley BD16 1WA, UK

First edition 2010

Reprints and permission service
Contact: booksandseries@emeraldinsight.com

British Library Cataloguing in Publication Data
A catalogue record for this book is available from the British Library

ISBN: 978-0-85724-155-9
ISSN: 0573-8555 (Series)

Contents

List of Contributors

Patricia M. Anderson	Department of Economics, Dartmouth College, Hanover, NH, USA
W. David Bradford	Department of Public Administration and Policy, University of Georgia, Athens, GA, USA
James F. Burgess, Jr.	Department of Health Policy & Management, Boston University School of Public Health, Boston, MA, USA
Kristin F. Butcher	Department of Economics, Wellesley College, Wellesley, MA, USA
Resul Cesur	Department of Economics, Andrew Young School of Policy Studies, Georgia State University, Atlanta, GA, USA
Ryan Conrad	School of Public Health, University of California, Los Angeles, CA, USA
Carolina C. Felix	Department of Economics, Emory University, Atlanta, GA, USA
Jason M. Fletcher	Division of Health Policy, School of Public Health, Yale University, New Haven, CT, USA
Michael T. French	Department of Sociology, University of Miami, Coral Gables, FL, USA
David E. Frisvold	Department of Economics, Emory University, Atlanta, GA, USA
Jennifer Ghandhi	Harris School of Public Policy Studies, University of Chicago, Chicago, IL, USA
Michael Grossman	Ph.D. Program in Economics, City University of New York Graduate Center and National Bureau of Economic Research, New York, NY, USA
Gulcin Gumus	College of Business, Florida Atlantic University and IZA, Boca Raton, FL, USA
Chris M. Herbst	School of Public Affairs, Arizona State University, Phoenix, AZ, USA
Joseph G. Hirschberg	University of Melbourne, Melbourne, Victoria, Australia
Jenny F. Homer	Department of Sociology, University of Miami, FL, USA

Jeanette N. Lye University of Melbourne, Melbourne, Victoria, Australia

Sara Markowitz Department of Economics, Emory University and National Bureau of Economic Research, Atlanta, GA, USA

James Marton Department of Economics, Andrew Young School of Policy Studies, Georgia State University, Atlanta, GA, USA

Ian McCarthy FTI Consulting and University of North Texas, Dallas, TX, USA

Diane Whitmore Schanzenbach The School of Education & Social Policy, Northwestern University, Evanston, IL, USA

Cynthia S. Searcy Department of Public Management and Policy, Andrew Young School of Policy Studies, Georgia State University, Atlanta, GA, USA

Jasmina Spasojević Department of Economics, Trinity College, Hartford, CT, USA

Erdal Tekin Department of Economics, Andrew Young School of Policy Studies, Georgia State University, Atlanta, GA, USA

Introduction

In March 2010, President Obama signed into law the most broad and sweeping reform of health care in U.S. history. This was done at a time when aggregate medical expenses are significantly higher than they have ever been:

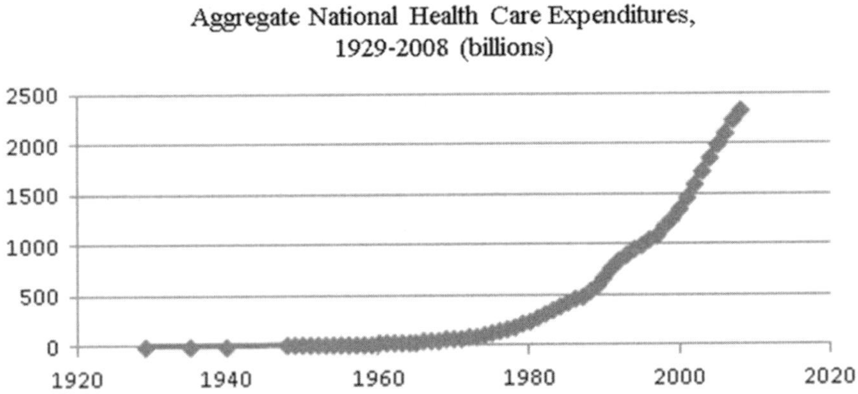

Sources: *Datapedia of the United States 1790-2005 2nd ed. Bernan, Lanham, MD.* Web. Accessed from http://www.mindfully.org/Health/Health-Expenditures-1929-1997.htm on July 22, 2010 and

Historical National Health Expenditure Data. Centers for Medicare and Medicaid Services. https://www.cms.gov/NationalHealthExpendData/downloads/tables.pdf Accessed July 27, 2010.

Decade (number of observations)	Average annual spending (billions)
2000s (9)	1,854.3
1990s (10)	969.4
1980s (10)	413.1
1970s(10)	128.9
1960s (10)	41.5
1950s (10)	18.0
1940s (3)	8.7
1930s (1)	2.9
1920s (1)	3.6

The average aggregate medical expenditure from 2000 to 2008 was 1.85 trillion dollars per year. In addition, the medical portion of the consumer price index (CPI) shows a higher price level of medical care than ever before. It is unlikely that quality of care has risen at the same rate (the medical CPI is almost eight times as high as it was in 1976), so it is very possible that consumers are paying more for each effective unit of medical care.

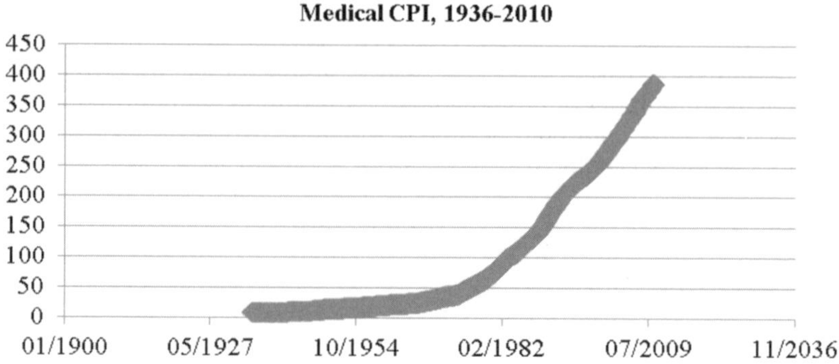

Source: *Databases, Tables, & Calculators by Subject.* United States Bureau of Labor Statistics. http://data.bls.gov/PDQ/servlet/SurveyOutputServlet. Accessed July 22, 2010.

The purpose of this book is to analyze the effect of policy on national health status and to expand the knowledge base regarding the economics of health care. Many of the issues pertaining to health care are fundamentally economic issues, from universal coverage and waste issues to aggregate supply of health care professionals and the pricing of pharmaceuticals. This book will provide, in one place, theoretical and empirical research on a wide variety of issues in medical economics.

In Chapter 1, Dr. Patricia M. Anderson of Dartmouth College, Dr. Kristin Butcher of Wellesley College, and Dr. Diane Schanzenbach of the University of Chicago collaborate to state that, given the large amount of time that children spend in school, public health policy makers tend to focus on schools as an important battleground in the fight against childhood obesity. The question of interest is whether the school environment is currently a contributing factor to the increase in childhood obesity, and whether changes in school policies could help curb the increase. It is important to realize that fundamentally, obesity is the result of an energy imbalance – more calories are consumed than are burned. It is possible for the school environment to have an effect on either side of this equation. Of interest, then, is whether being in school is beneficial or detrimental to children's weight outcomes overall, as well as identifying what policies may be affecting the energy balance equation. Discussion suggests that some school environments are worse than others – that is, that schools with lower quality lunches, more junk food, and more accountability pressure are likely to produce fatter children. It may still be the case, though, that being in school is better than being out of school – it will depend on what the alternative is.

In this chapter, Drs. Anderson, Butcher, and Schanzenbach review their (and other's) research on the role of school policy (and school in general) on childhood obesity. Their aim is to synthesize this literature and provide interpretation and context for readers new to the area of school policy and childhood obesity. Using the simple idea of energy balance, they simulate the impact of various policies, by making straightforward assumptions about the changes in activity levels or caloric intake implied by each policy. They implement a model of basal metabolic rate, and metabolic equivalent intensities of activity, and then use the fact that an excess of 7,500 calories adds a kilogram of weight, to simulate the potential effect of a range of policies. Seemingly, small changes in policy may well result in noticeable changes in the weight distribution of children.

In Chapter 2, Dr. Michael Grossman of the City University of New York and NBER, Dr. Sara Markowitz of Emory University and NBER, and Dr. Ryan Conrad of the City University of New York address alcohol policies and their effect on child mistreatment. The purpose of this chapter is to empirically estimate the propensity for alcohol-related policies to influence rates of child abuse and neglect. The alcohol regulations of interest include beer, wine, and liquor taxes, drunk driving laws, and areas "dry" for beer. Using a national database on incidents of child abuse and neglect, they estimate the effects of alcohol control policies in reducing child abuse measured as the number of children with confirmed or suspected reports of child maltreatment and the number of children who die as a result of abuse or neglect. Results indicate that higher excise taxes on alcohol may be effective in reducing the incidence of child maltreatment.

In Chapter 3, Dr. Resul Cesur of Georgia State University, Dr. Chris M. Herbst of Arizona State University, and Dr. Erdal Tekin of Georgia State University and NBER analyze the impact of child care utilization on school-age children's body mass index (BMI). They state that childhood obesity rates in the United States have increased dramatically over the past three decades. The growing use of non-parental child care has raised awareness among health care professionals and policy makers of the critical role that these settings play in shaping children's eating and activity habits. However, little empirical research focuses on the relationship between child care utilization and children's weight outcomes. Drawing on rich data from the Kindergarten Cohort of the Early Childhood Longitudinal Study (ECLS-K), this chapter makes a number of contributions to existing research in this area. First, we exploit the longitudinal data structure in the ECLS-K to construct a multiperiod panel of children, with information on BMI and child care attendance observed during the fall of kindergarten and the spring of first, third, fifth, and eighth grades. Second, they specify and estimate a fixed effects quantile regression (FEQR) model that both differences out time-invariant unobserved heterogeneity and allows them to address the possibility that non-parental care has heterogeneous effects on children's weight at different points in the BMI distribution. Finally, they consider different parameterizations of child care utilization, including participation in various modes of child care as well as measures of the intensity of participation (e.g., hours).

In Chapter 4, Dr. W. David Bradford of the University of Georgia observes that time preferences are considered a fundamental characteristic of economic behavior. Dynamic models of utility maximization have strong predictions about the effects of different rates of discounting on individual behavior. In general, we expect that higher rates of discounting lead an individual to more strongly shift consumption of economic goods to the present and economic bads to the future, relative to a person with lower rates of preference for the present. While time preferences are clearly a fundamental of economic behavior, economists devote surprisingly little attention to understanding their origins. Some of the earliest modern theoretical work on the subject was conducted by Paul Samuelson. He proposed a discount factor that indicates a strength of preference for the present over the future. For several decades after Samuelson's work, his model of discounted utility was the standard conceptual basis for economists' understanding of intertemporal choice. Since this time, some – though by no means a great deal of – additional research has been conducted to explore what factors might contribute to the individual's level of discounting. Becker and Mulligan propose a theoretical model of how individuals' time preferences change. This research has direct implications for the expected relationships between (1) important choices a person makes/constraints a person faces and (2) the strength of their discounting of the future.

While some progress has been made in understanding how time preferences might be endogenized, and substantial effort has been devoted to exploring the impact of time preferences on many aspects of economic life, surprisingly little attention has been paid to the effect of time preferences on health and health care – despite the fact that many aspects of health care reflect strongly time-dependent choices. Individual rates of discounting may affect many aspects of health choice. Conceptual models of optimal insurance design often explicitly incorporate individual time preferences (through the introduction of a discount rate) and implicitly incorporate risk preferences (through the shape of the instantaneous utility function being maximized). Empirically, however, relatively little is known about how individual-level time and risk preferences affect selection of insurance types with varying degrees of riskiness and expected future net medical costs. This chapter presents a survey of what is known about the role of time preferences in health-related choices, ranging from risky behaviors (smoking and illicit drug use), to preventative health care, to insurance choice. In addition, original research is presented on health care and health insurance effects of discounting. Finally, the chapter highlights promising areas for future research.

In Chapter 5, Dr. James Marton of Georgia State University, Dr. Cynthia S. Searcy of Georgia State University, and Dr. Jennifer Ghandhi of the University of Alabama question if certain types of children are differentially affected by children's health insurance premiums. Concern over the presence of inequity within the State Children's Health Insurance Program (SCHIP) has motivated studies involving demographic characteristics of SCHIP enrollees, particularly racial disparities among children enrolled in the program. Minority children are more likely to disenroll from SCHIP than their white counterparts, but it is unclear whether these children leave public coverage altogether or whether they simply move into other categories of public coverage. Some worry that increases in cost sharing might worsen racial inequity within SCHIP. Our purpose is to examine the differential short-run effects on children based on sociodemographic characteristics after the introduction of a $20 monthly family premium in Kentucky's SCHIP (KCHIP 3) in late 2003. Drs. Marton and Ghandhi employ a competing risks model (Marton *et al.*, 2009) in order to differentiate between exits to other forms of public coverage and exits to no public coverage. The original model shows that non-white children were 32% more likely to exit within each of the first three months after the premium increase than white children ($p<0.01$). The competing hazard model allows them to see that non-white children were 52% more likely to exit public coverage than their white counterparts ($p<0.01$). The implication is that minority children are more likely to become uninsured than white children, suggesting that the policy change adversely affects non-whites.

In Chapter 6, Carolina C. Felix and Dr. David E. Frisvold of Emory University looks at early childhood education as an investment in health. He states that there is a growing body of evidence that suggests that early childhood socioeconomic conditions have lasting economic consequences, reinforcing and sustaining disparities in health and education. Head Start is the principal federally funded program through which the United States invests directly in the human capital of disadvantaged preschool children. This chapter focuses on whether participation in the Head Start program influences health behaviors, including smoking and drug use, in adolescence. To address this question, Dr. Frisvold begins by reviewing the literature on the relationship between early childhood circumstances and long-run health outcomes. Although there is an extensive body of research on the impact of Head Start participation, there has been little research on the impact on risky behaviors in adolescence.

The difficulty that arises in examining the effect of Head Start participation is that selection into Head Start is the result of choices made by parents and administrators. To examine the potential influence of selection due to observed characteristics and selection due to unobserved characteristics, Dr. Frisvold follows the methodology developed by Altonji *et al.* (2005) to estimate the effect of Head Start participation. Their strategy is to use the amount of observed selection as a guide for the extent of unobserved selection. Dr. Frisvold uses this strategy to examine the impact of Head Start participation on smoking and drug use throughout adolescence and the extent to which varying degrees of selection on unobservables influence this relationship. To further understand the sources of any selection on unobservables, Dr. Frisvold gathers information on the required admissions criteria that Head Start centers use to determine which of the eligible children are offered admission in the center. Head Start centers are required to admit the most disadvantaged children using an established ranking, although the criteria used to determine who are the most disadvantaged can vary across centers. Dr. Frisvold uses data from Fragile Families and the Early Childhood Longitudinal Study-Birth Cohort (ECLS-B) to attempt to narrow the bounds on the estimate of the impact of Head Start participation.

In Chapter 7, Dr. Gulcin Gumus of Florida International University and IZA, Dr. Jenny F. Homer of the University of Miami, and Dr. Michael T. French discuss the impact of universal helmet laws on motorcycle riding and safety. They observe that in 2007, 5,154 motorcyclists were killed and approximately 103,000 were injured in the United States. Although motorcycles accounted for only 3 percent of registered vehicles at that time, motorcyclists were involved in 13 percent of all traffic fatalities. Studies clearly demonstrate that universal helmet laws can reduce the likelihood of being killed or severely injured in a crash. Nevertheless, helmet policies vary across states. As of February 2009, 20 states had universal helmet laws requiring all riders to wear a helmet, 27 had partial helmet laws for some riders, and 3 did not have a helmet law.

Drs. Gumus, Homer, and French further investigate the effectiveness of such policies by focusing on their long-term impact and their effect on motorcycle use. Using state-level longitudinal data for 1975–2005, they estimate how the adoption and repeal of universal helmet laws influence motorcycle safety. In an effort to address the potential endogeneity of adoption or repeal of helmet laws, they use a dynamic specification that includes leads and lags of the helmet law adoptions and repeals. Their results confirm earlier findings that adoption of universal helmet laws prevents fatalities, whereas repeals lead to increases in fatality rates. They also show that the effects of both adoption and repeal persist much past the year the states enact or repeal such laws. In addition, they provide evidence that helmet laws operate in the intended manner such that they reduce fatalities mainly by improving safety rather than by reducing motorcycle riding. These findings have key public health implications for states that may be considering changes to their existing motorcycle helmet policies.

In Chapter 8, Dr. Jason M. Fletcher of Yale University attempts to account for racial and ethnic disparities in children's overweight status at two years of age. Dr. Fletcher observes that recent research has suggested the presence of large racial/ethnic differences in young children. This chapter examines whether family factors other than race/ethnicity explain these large racial/ethnic differences in overweight status of young children. Additionally, this chapter examines previously undocumented determinants of early childhood overweight status. Dr. Fletcher uses longitudinal nationally representative sample of children born in 2001 (ECLS-B). Participants come from diverse socioeconomic and racial/ethnic backgrounds with over-samples of twins, low and very low birth weight children, and minority groups. Multivariate logistic regression analyses are used, and data are weighted to account for the survey design of the data set.

Dr. Fletcher finds evidence that although there are large racial/ethnic differences in the prevalence of being overweight as early as two years of age, these differences can be accounted for by controlling for a small set of family characteristics, including marital status and whether English is the primary language spoken at home. This chapter also presents new findings on the determinants of early childhood overweight status. For example, evidence suggests that parental activities with their young children, such as playing chasing games and walking/playing outside, are associated with lower odds of early overweight status. Dr. Fletcher concludes that family factors other than race/ethnicity may account for the large racial/ethnic differences in early childhood overweight status that have been found in previous research. Health investments in young children targeted to children from single-parent households and from households with low English language skills may be efficient. He also states that additional research is required to examine the mechanisms that confer high overweight rates on children from single-family and non-native households.

In Chapter 9, Dr. Jasmina Spasojevic discusses the results of a natural experiment on the effects of education on adult health in Sweden. Dr. Spasojevic states that understanding health determinants and their mechanisms affecting health is an important social policy issue. Empirical tests in the health literature abound with the undisputed finding that the number of years of formal schooling completed is the most important correlate of good health. There is less consensus as to whether this correlation reflects a causal relationship of more schooling to better health. This chapter capitalizes on a unique social experiment – the 1950 Swedish comprehensive school reform that was implemented in stages and by municipal areas. Consequently, people born between 1945 and 1955 went through two different school systems (one of which required at least one more year of schooling). This chapter uses the instrumental variables (IV) technique to estimate formal schooling's causal effect on adult health in Sweden. The instrumental variable for degree of education (schooling) generated from compulsory school reform yields a consistent estimate of education's causal impact on health as measured by an index of bad health and of BMI in the healthy range. Dr. Spasojevic finds that the additional schooling generated by Sweden's compulsory school reform produces improved adult health (controlling for cohort and county effects, family background characteristics, and individual income).

In Chapter 10, Dr. McCarthy presents a survey of the economics of the pharmaceutical industry. With expenditures totaling $227 billion in 2007, prescription drug purchases are a growing portion of the total medical expenditure, and as this industry continues to grow, prescription drugs will continue to be a critical part of the larger health care industry. In this chapter, Dr. McCarthy focuses on the role of R&D and marketing, the determinants (and complications) of prescription drug pricing, and various aspects of consumer behavior specific to the pharmaceutical industry, such as prescription drug regulation, the patient's interaction with the physician, and insurance coverage. This chapter also provides background in areas not often considered in the economics literature, such as the role of pharmacy benefit managers in prescription drug prices and the differentiation between alternative measures of prescription drug prices. As is evident from this chapter, the prescription drug industry is complex and much of the research in this industry remains inconclusive.

In Chapter 11, the final chapter of this volume, Drs. Joe Hirschberg and Jenny Lye of University of Melbourne discuss effects of the smoking bans in gaming venues. The authors show that, while the effects of smoking bans on smoking might seem obvious, other effects could be less intuitive if smokers are more likely than non-smokers to frequent gaming venues. The authors use data from gaming venues in Victoria, Australia, and examine the consequences of the smoking ban on gaming expenditures and tax revenues.

CHAPTER 1

School Policies and Children's Obesity

Patricia M. Anderson*, Kristin F. Butcher and Diane Whitmore Schanzenbach

Abstract

Questions have arisen as to whether the school environment is currently a contributing factor to the increase in childhood obesity, and whether changes in school policies could help curb the increase. In this chapter, we discuss key aspects of the literature on the role of the school food environment, and the role of the school activity environment in effecting the caloric intake and expenditure of children. We also simulate the effect of a range of reasonable changes in weekly minutes spent being active in school, and changes in weekly calories consumed in school.

Keywords: childhood obesity, school environment, school policies

JEL classifications: I10, I20

1. Introduction

Given the large amount of time that children spend in school, public health policymakers have tended to focus on schools as an important battleground in the fight against childhood obesity. The question of interest is whether the school environment is currently a contributing factor to the increase in

---

* Corresponding author.

CONTRIBUTIONS TO ECONOMIC ANALYSIS
VOLUME 290 ISSN: 0573-8555
DOI:10.1108/S0573-8555(2010)0000290004

childhood obesity, and whether changes in school policies could help curb the increase. It is important to realize, though, that fundamentally obesity is the result of an energy imbalance – more calories are consumed than are burned. For school policies to have an impact on children's obesity, it must be the case that the school environment has an effect on either side of this equation. Thus, this chapter focuses on reviewing what we know about the role of the school food environment as well as the school activity environment. Additionally, there may be school policies not directly meant to impact the food or activity environment, which nonetheless do just that.

In considering the school food environment, we first review the literature on school meals, in particular, participation in the National School Lunch Program (NSLP) and the School Breakfast Program (SBP). We then turn to an aspect of the food environment that has received a large amount of attention, the availability of competitive foods, where by competitive foods we mean foods sold outside of the school meals programs. While the meals programs are required to meet federal nutrition standards, competitive foods are often of the high calorie–low nutrient type. Thus, there is much concern over the impact the availability of these types of foods in schools may have on children's weight.

On the other hand, schools generally provide children with opportunities for activity, via physical education (PE) classes. Additionally, for the younger children, periods of active play are often available via recess. Next, we review the literature on the school activity environment. Following this, we look at school policies that may inadvertently affect either the food or activity environment. In particular, we focus on school accountability measures. The need to increase scores in subjects tested under federal mandates, such as mathematics and English, may result in time reallocation away from physical activity and recess. Similarly the desire to spend more preparing students for tests in these subjects may imply raising funds through competitive food sales.

Finally, having reviewed the literature on school policies and obesity, we carry out a series of policy simulations. By making straightforward assumptions about the changes in activity levels or caloric intake implied by a given policy, we can implement a model of basal metabolic rate (BMR) and metabolic equivalent (MET) intensities of activity. Using the fact that an excess of 7,500 calories adds a kilogram of weight, we can simulate the potential effect of a range of policies on the weight distribution of children.

2. *The food environment*

The NSLP serves over 30 million students every school day (USDA, 2010a). While local schools make their own decisions about exactly what foods to serve for each meal, the meals must meet federal nutrition requirements. Of particular note is that the lunches are expected to provide one-third of the Recommended Dietary Allowance of calories, while following the 1995 Dietary Guidelines for Americans (USDA, 2010a). The SBP is about a third of the size of NSLP, and must also follow these dietary guidelines, while providing one quarter of the Recommended Dietary Allowance of calories (USDA, 2010b).

While these school meals programs do have a focus on nutrition, Schanzenbach (2009) finds that children partaking of the school lunch consume about 46 more calories compared to those bringing lunch from home. It is perhaps not surprising then that she estimates that NSLP participation increases the probability that a student is overweight. Important to note is that she is controlling for weight at the start of kindergarten, so the findings are not simply due to inherent differences in participants and non-participants. Rather, the implication is that weight gain while in school is larger for participants. Both of the very different empirical approaches come to this conclusion. One takes advantage of the fact that NSLP is heavily subsidized for students with family income less than 185 percent of the poverty line. Thus, the incentive to be a participant is much larger for a student at 184 percent of the poverty line versus one at 186 percent of that line, resulting in a noticeable increase in participation. Students who are very similar in terms of family income (i.e. 186 percent versus 184 percent), with no difference in the probability of being overweight at the start of kindergarten, are then seen to have different probabilities of being overweight by the end of first grade, which can logically be attributed to the higher rate of NSLP participation. The alternative approach focuses on only those paying full price for lunch. For this sample, conditional on weight at the start of kindergarten and a full range of background characteristics, NSLP participants are more likely to be overweight by the end of first grade.

While the work of Schanzenbach is quite convincing, other studies are less certain of the impact of NSLP on children's obesity. For example, Gleason and Dodd (2009) find no relationship between usual participation and weight status when using data from the third School Nutrition Dietary Assessment Study (SNDA-III). It is important to note, however, that the point estimates in Gleason and Dodd are positive, although for the model estimating the probability of being overweight only logit coefficients are reported, so it is not possible to make a direct comparison with the point estimates in Schanzenbach. One key difference in the Gleason and Dodd study is that the data are for students in all grades from 1 to 12 in school year 2004–2005, while the Schanzenbach study focused only on one cohort of students who started kindergarten in the fall of 1998 (Early Childhood Longitudinal Study – Kindergarten Class of 1998–1999, or ECLS-K). The SNDA-III sample is much smaller than the ECLS-K sample, though, which may partially be the cause of the relatively imprecise estimates. It is also worth pointing out that when comparing 2004–2005 to 1998–1999, fewer schools exceeded the standards for saturated fat (Gordon *et al.*,

2009). Thus, changes in the content of school lunches across the samples may also play a role in the different estimates.

Gleason and Dodd (2009) also investigate the role of the SBP using the SNDA-III data. For this program, the point estimate implies a negative effect on the probability of being obese (although again the coefficient is not significant), but they do estimate a significantly negative impact on body mass index (BMI). Millimet *et al.* (2010) also study both NSLP and SBP simulataneously, but using the same ECLS-K data used by Schanzenbach. They conclude that SBP participation is likely to reduce the likelihood that a student is overweight, but that NSLP participation is likely to increase that likelihood. Overall, the finding that SBP is beneficial is consistent with studies focused on the nutritional content of the meals. For example, Bhattacharya *et al.* (2006) find that SBP participants have higher blood serum levels of most key nutrients than do non-participants.

Much of the concern about the school food environment revolves not around the meal programs, but around the availability of competitive foods. According to Fox *et al.* (2009b), 40 percent of children consumed competitive foods on an average school day in 2004–2005. Competitive foods, i.e. foods sold outside of the school meals programs, are often thought of as "junk" food, as they include vending machine items such as sodas, candy, and chips, as well as other snack items sold in school stores or in a la carte lines in school cafeterias. Assumptions about the deleterious effects of competitive foods have resulted in many school districts banning soft drinks and vending machine items. However, it is not clear that such bans will have the desired impact. For example, Blum *et al.* (2008) studied soda consumption among Maine students after a reduction in the availability of sodas in their schools, and found no significant reduction compared to students whose schools did not reduce availability.

Results from studies focused directly on the effect of competitive foods on students' obesity are somewhat mixed. Anderson and Butcher (2006) look at overweight rates for public school students of age 14 and over in the National Longitudinal Study of Youth 1997 Cohort (NLSY97), combined with competitive food availability from the School Health Policies and Programs Survey (SHPPS). The probability that a student is exposed to sodas or snack foods in their school is predicted based on state and local characteristics available in both the SHPPS and NLSY97 data. They find that for every 10 percentage point increase in the probability of being exposed to junk food, a student's BMI is about 1 percent higher. Interestingly, this effect is driven entirely by students with an overweight parent, for whom a 10 percentage point increase in exposure increases BMI by just over 2 percent. One interpretation of this finding is that individuals have a genetic predisposition toward weight gain when the environment is conducive, and the availability of competitive foods in schools creates just such an environment.

Larson and Story (2010) review the literature on competitive foods, concluding that the general finding is one of students having better diet quality when they are not exposed to competitive foods. At the same time, not all studies find a consistent impact on students' weights. For example, Fox *et al.* (2009a) find that while competitive foods sold in vending machines are associated with higher BMI, when sold in an a la carte line they are associated with lower BMI. Also, Datar and Nicosia (2009) conclude that there is no effect of competitive food sales on BMI. They base their study on the fact that competitive foods become more common at schools serving higher grade levels. Thus, a fifth grade student in a K-5 or K-6 school is less likely to be exposed than if they attended a K-8, K-12, or 5–8 school. The grade span of the school predicts availability of competitive foods, and higher availability increases consumption, but they find no significant effect on BMI.

Ultimately, then, what can we say about the role of the school food environment in children's overweight? While the results are not unanimous, there are several studies with credible research designs that find a positive effect of NSLP participation on the probability of being overweight. At the same time, the consensus on SBP is that it does not contribute to overweight, and may actually be protective. As with the NSLP studies, there is no unanimity on the effect of competitive foods, but again there are a range of convincing studies finding a positive effect on student weight. Thus, while there remains the possibility that the school food environment does not have any impact on children's overweight, the bulk of the evidence implies that there is likely to be an effect. In Section 6, we will simulate the impact of increased caloric intake via NSLP participation or competitive foods availability. To the extent that these simulations predict weight effects that are in line with the estimates of the papers finding an effect, we can consider it additional evidence for the role of the school food environment.

3. The activity environment

There are no federal requirements for recess or PE in schools, although many states do implement recess or PE requirements. Typically, the exact amount of physical activity offered by a school is a local decision. The American Heart Association (2009) reports that 3.8 percent of elementary schools, 7.1 percent of middle schools, and just 2.1 percent of high schools provide daily PE, with 22 percent of schools not requiring any PE. According to Robert Wood Johnson Foundation (2009), 40 percent of school districts have reduced or even eliminated recess, with a quarter of elementary schools no longer having recess for all grades. While there is good evidence of a reduction in opportunities for activity in schools, the effect of PE and recess on student weight is less clear.

In terms of younger students, there is reasonable evidence that more time in active play at school is associated with a lower BMI. Datar and Sturm (2004) find that when PE and recess time increases between kindergarten and first grade, girls who were overweight in kindergarten had a reduction in BMI. Using the same ECLS-K data, Miras-Wilson (2007) updates this study through the fifth grade, and finds that higher frequency PE is associated with a lower probability of obesity for all students. While the role of PE and recess in reducing overweight for elementary-age children is observed in multiple studies, evidence is more mixed for older students.

Cawley *et al.* (2007) approach the issue by focusing on states with a PE requirement for high school students. While students in such states are physically active for an additional 31 min per week, there does not appear to be a significant impact on BMI or the probability of being overweight. Interestingly, for boys, the requirement does not increase the number of days with vigorous activity, but it does for girls. It may be that PE requirements have a bigger effect on more sedentary students, so that if boys are more likely to be active in any case, we only observe an impact on girls. The lack of an effect on weight outcomes for either gender, though, may be harder to explain. One possibility is that the additional PE time did make students more fit, but since muscle weighs more than fat, an effect on BMI was not detected. If more precise body fat measurements could be taken, perhaps a positive effect on student health could be observed. Another study focusing on older students (age 12–18) is Durant *et al.* (2009), which finds that more days of PE per week is positively associated with overall physical activity. However, like the Cawley *et al.* study, a significant relationship with BMI is not detected.

While in theory it is clear that burning more calories than one consumes should result in weight loss, the evidence on the role of the school activity environment on student body weight is less clear. It may be that for younger students recess and PE provide a true increase in activity. That is, without the time spent in recess and PE, these students would be taking part in sedentary classroom activities, and that the amount of school activity has no impact on the amount of afterschool activity. In contrast, for older students it may be the case that while PE does directly replace sedentary classroom activities, it is also a substitute for afterschool activity, resulting in very little net increase in activity.

4. Other school policies with possible effects on student weight

Having looked specifically at the school food and activity environments, we now turn to school policies that do not focus on these environments, but may nonetheless have unintended impacts on them. Foremost among these is accountability, as seen with the federal No Child Left Behind

(NCLB) legislation, as well as some state systems. Typically, the only outcomes that schools are required to improve upon are academic, with no accountability for health outcomes. Given the pressures to do well on standardized tests, schools are likely to reallocate time away from recess and PE, and toward tested academic subjects.[1] Similarly, accountability rules may lead to financial pressures, as schools wish to spend more on test preparation (e.g. hiring more aides, purchasing worksheets, etc.). Administrators who still hope to spend the same amounts on other budget items as previously may now have a larger motivation to raise new funds through outside food and beverage contracts.[2] Finally, schools may use food rewards to incentivize their students to work hard toward passing the standardized tests. These rewards could take the form of parties with cupcakes or other high-calorie snacks, or coupons for fast food restaurants for exemplary performance.

Anderson *et al.* (2010) investigate this possibility, using data from schools in Arkansas. They categorize a school as marginal, i.e. most likely to respond to NCLB pressures in the manners described above, if they came within 5 points of meeting Annual Yearly Progress (AYP) on their NCLB tests the previous year. Schools that made AYP by more than 5 points are assumed not to feel much pressure, while those missing AYP by more than 5 points are likely to feel that their problems are too large to be solved by simple resource reallocations and reward schemes. Anderson *et al.* (2010) find that these middle-achieving marginal schools have a significantly higher rate of student obesity. A survey of Arkansas principals indicates that since the passage of NCLB, schools are indeed undertaking the types of behaviors described above that may have unintended impacts on student weight.

Yin (2009) takes a different approach to the same question, taking advantage of the fact that state accountability systems were implemented at different times. Differences in exposure to state accountability can then be used to estimate the causal impact of accountability. Using nationally representative data from the Youth Risk Behavioral Surveillance System (YRBSS), she finds that, in fact, exposure to accountability does increase student BMI, and increases the probability of being obese. The approach here is very different from the one taken by Anderson *et al.* (2010), and focuses on state accountability systems, not the federal NCLB, but both papers still find that accountability has a significant impact on body weight.

---

[1] Center on Education Policy (2007) finds 20% of school districts have decreased recess time since NCLB was enacted, with an average decrease of 50 min per week.

[2] Anderson and Butcher (2006) find evidence that schools that are under more financial pressure are more likely to give students access to junk food and that students in these schools have higher BMI.

Accountability is the only school policy with unintended effects on student weight that has been closely studied. However, it is possible that other school policies that have yet to be studied may have similar unintended effects. Because the effects are completely unintended, it may not currently be clear what policies might be of concern. Overall, though, we have seen that there are a range of policies that do affect student weight, from the food environment, to the activity environment, to accountability, to perhaps other policies. While it thus seems clear that some school policies are worse for students than other school policies, what is not clear is whether school itself is bad for student weight. We explore this issue in the next section.

5. Being in school versus not being in school

While a range of school policies have been found to be associated with higher levels of student obesity, being in school may still be better than not being in school. One approach to exploring this question is to compare student outcomes during the summer with those over the school year. For example, using the ECLS-K, von Hippel *et al.* (2007) find faster growth in BMI during the summer between kindergarten and first grade than during the kindergarten and first grade school years. The growth rates were especially large for Black and Hispanic children, the same groups who were most likely to be overweight at the start of kindergarten. The possibility that a more structured environment is helpful in preventing weight gain is hinted at in Tovar *et al.* (2010). This study surveys families in Somerville, MA, during the summer months about their children's diet and activity levels. They find that students spending more time in parental care are more sedentary, while those spending more time in structured day camp settings are more active. Diet over the summer did not appear significantly different from nationally reported school year averages, but it was true that children spending more time in camps were less likely to eat in front of the television.

An alternative approach to answering the question of whether it is better to be in school or not is taken by Anderson *et al.* (2008). They take advantage of the fact that most states have a date by which a child is required to be 5 years old before starting kindergarten. Consider a cutoff date of September 1. A student who turns 5 on August 31 will start kindergarten right after turning 5. This student will be observed at the end of first grade as an almost 7-year-old who has been exposed to 2 years of school. At the same time, a student who turns 5 on September 2 will not start kindergarten that fall. This student will be observed at the end of kindergarten as an almost 7 year-old who has been exposed to only 1 year of school. Given that these children were born just 2 days apart, the only real difference in any observed outcomes can reasonably be attributed to the difference in their school exposure.

Based on this approach, there is little evidence that being exposed to school for an additional year is either good or bad for student weight outcomes. Interestingly, if one had simply compared students with more actual exposure to those with less, it would appear that more exposure was positively related with BMI. The implication is that when families choose to ignore the state cutoff dates, it is to hold back a smaller child or send a larger child. This spurious effect of school on BMI disappears when using only the variation in school exposure that comes from following the cutoff rules. In this case, the overall point estimates are negative, but economically small. All estimates are very imprecise, though, such that none are significantly different than zero.

The impact of school, per se, on children's obesity remains unclear. There is some evidence that the structured setting is preferable to the unstructured days of summer, but at the same time there is no evidence that a 7-year-old who has been exposed to 2 years of schooling has a significantly lower BMI or a significantly lower probability of being overweight than one exposed to just 1 year.

6. Policy simulations

While school exposure may not be clearly good or bad for student weight outcomes, changes to specific policies may have an impact. In this section, we simulate the effect of some basic policies that impact either calories burned or calories consumed. Over the course of a school year, seemingly small changes can have noticeable impacts. Recognizing that the only way to affect a child's weight is to have an imbalance between calories taken in and calories burned, we start with a model of the BMR, the resting energy expenditure. We chose to use equations from Schofield (1995), which were found by Wong *et al.* (1996) to be similar on average to measuring BMR by indirect calorimetry. The Schofield equations are based solely on observed height and weight, but with separate equations for younger and older children:

$$\text{BMR} = 17.0^{*}(\text{weight in kg}) + 1.6^{*}(\text{height in cm}) + 371 \quad (1)$$

(for ages 3–10 years) and

$$\text{BMR} = 8.4^{*}(\text{weight in kg}) + 4.7^{*}(\text{height in cm}) + 200 \quad (2)$$

(for ages 10–18 years).

These equations (taken from Wong *et al.*, 1996) represent the number of calories burned by a child of a given age, height, and weight if they did nothing but exist.

Activity also burns calories, though, at a rate that depends on the amount of time spent in the activity, the level of intensity, and current weight. Activity levels can be measured as MET intensities, which can be thought of as calories burned per kilogram per hour (Ainsworth, 2002). Thus, given the MET for the activity, we can define calories burned (CB) in activities quite simply as

$$\text{CB} = (\text{hours spent in activity})^{*}(\text{weight in kg})^{*}\text{MET} \quad (3)$$

A small number of calories are also burned via the thermic effect of food, which is estimated to be about 10 percent of the calories contained in that food. Thus, if we assume an individual is currently in balance, the amount of calories taken in should be equal to 1.1^{*} (BMR + CB). All calculations are adjusted to represent calories per week.

To carry out our simulations, we take a sample of children of age 6–16 years from the 1999–2004 panels of the National Health and Nutrition Examination Survey (NHANES). Using the measured age, height, and weight, we can calculate BMR for each child. According to CEP (2007), elementary schools devoted about 5 h per week to PE and recess.[3] We also assume that children are active outside of school for about 1.5 h per day on a weekday and 3 h per day on a weekend, resulting in a baseline level of activity of 18.5 h per week. We calculate CB from these activities by assigning a MET of 2.8, equivalent to a light level of activity.[4] Assuming all else equal and that the children are currently in balance, we can calculate current caloric intake for each child. Starting with this baseline balance of calories consumed and expended, we can then simulate a change in the school food environment or activity environment as a change in either weekly calories consumed or weekly calories expended via activity, creating an imbalance. Using the fact that an excess of 7,500 calories will result in a weight gain of 1 kg, we adjust each sample member's weight after each week of imbalance, recalculate the BMR, then calculate the next week's imbalance, etc. for 36 weeks (the standard school year). We then compute the simulated rate of overweight and average BMI after a full school year of exposure to the policy change.

Because it is not entirely clear how much the activity levels (or caloric intake) of the average student are impacted by school policies, we start with a simple table that simulates a range of possibilities. The top panel considers policy changes in the weekly amount of activity at school. We simulate policies that range from adding 1 h to subtracting 1 h, in increments of 12 min. Note that zero change represents the baseline rate of overweight and the baseline average BMI, of 0.364 and 21.24, respectively. The bottom panel considers policies that imply changes in weekly caloric intake, ranging

---

3 The survey of Arkansas principals in Anderson *et al.* (2010) also implies about 5 h of in-school activity.

4 This is the MET assigned to such activities as "standing – playing with children – light." We also investigate "walk/run – playing with children – moderate," which has an MET of 4.0. See Ainsworth (2002).

from a decrease of 750 to an increase of 750. All calculations are carried out first assuming that the children's activity levels are on average light, but we also repeat the exercise assuming activity levels are moderate. Note that while it is obvious why the assumption about activity level will matter for policies changing the amount of activity, it will also matter for calorie changes. The reason is twofold. First, the initial caloric intake is based on equilibrating with caloric expenditure, which is higher when a higher level of activity is assumed. Second, a given increase in caloric intake will imply a larger excess when the fixed level of activity is lower.

Looking first at the top panel of Table 1, we see that changing the amount of activity provided in schools can alter the overweight rate by between about 1 and 2 percentage points, depending on the level of intensity. The equivalent change in average BMI is between about 0.23 and 0.31, again depending on the assumed level of intensity. While there are clear impacts from changing the amount of activity available in school, it is clear that

Table 1. Simulating the impact of changes in weekly in-school activity and calories consumed on children's weight

	Assuming light activity				Assuming moderate activity			
	Overweight	Change	BMI	Change	Overweight	Change	BMI	Change
Minutes								
+60	0.350	−0.014	21.01	−0.226	0.344	−0.019	20.93	−0.306
+48	0.353	−0.011	21.06	−0.181	0.349	−0.015	21.00	−0.245
+36	0.357	−0.007	21.10	−0.136	0.353	−0.011	21.06	−0.184
+24	0.359	−0.005	21.15	−0.091	0.357	−0.006	21.12	−0.123
+12	0.361	−0.003	21.20	−0.045	0.360	−0.004	21.18	−0.062
0	0.364	0.000	21.24	0.000	0.364	0.000	21.24	0.000
−12	0.367	0.003	21.29	0.046	0.368	0.004	21.30	0.062
−24	0.371	0.007	21.33	0.091	0.373	0.010	21.36	0.124
−36	0.374	0.011	21.38	0.137	0.377	0.014	21.43	0.186
−48	0.377	0.014	21.42	0.183	0.383	0.019	21.49	0.249
−60	0.381	0.018	21.47	0.229	0.387	0.023	21.55	0.312
Calories								
−750	0.289	−0.074	20.07	−1.171	0.292	−0.072	20.13	−1.115
−600	0.303	−0.061	20.30	−0.937	0.305	−0.058	20.35	−0.892
−450	0.317	−0.047	20.54	−0.703	0.319	−0.045	20.57	−0.669
−300	0.333	−0.031	20.77	−0.468	0.334	−0.029	20.79	−0.446
−150	0.348	−0.015	21.01	−0.234	0.350	−0.014	21.02	−0.223
0	0.364	0.000	21.24	0.000	0.364	0.000	21.24	0.000
+150	0.382	0.018	21.47	0.234	0.381	0.017	21.46	0.223
+300	0.404	0.040	21.71	0.468	0.401	0.037	21.69	0.446
+450	0.426	0.062	21.94	0.703	0.423	0.060	21.91	0.669
+600	0.450	0.086	22.18	0.937	0.446	0.083	22.13	0.892
+750	0.473	0.109	22.41	1.171	0.465	0.102	22.36	1.115

Note: See text for description of simulations, based on 7,562 children aged 6–16 in NHANES 1999–2004.

changes of the type implied by NCLB cannot have large impacts. According to Anderson *et al.* (2010), among the schools that reported a decrease in recess and/or PE, the total reduction in activity was just under an hour. As can be seen in the table, a full 1 h reduction would only increase the rate of overweight by at most 2.3 percentage points, if the displaced activity was of a moderate level. While not shown in the table, we also simulated an extreme change, in which all activity is vigorous, and an additional hour per day of vigorous activity is added. In this case, the rate of overweight would be reduced to 0.25 and the average BMI would fall to 19.5.[5] Thus, with major changes in policy, significant changes in weight outcomes could be obtained.

Turning now to the bottom panel of Table 1, we see that changing the amount of calories provided in school can have fairly large impacts. Considering a weekly change of up to 750 calories could change the overweight rate by 0.07 to 0.11 percentage points, depending on the activity level assumed.[6] While these results may seem extreme, the caloric changes are within the realm of possibility. For example, Schanzenbach (2009) find that NSLP participants consume between 40 and 60 additional calories at lunch each day. This would imply an increase in overweight of between 2 and 3 percentage points. At the same time, Gleason and Suitor (2001) estimated that school lunch may result in up to 120 extra calories per day, or 600 per week. Such an increase would imply an 8 or 9 percentage point increase in overweight.

In thinking about competitive foods, Larson and Story (2010) report that recent studies have found that lack of access to a school store or snack bar reduces consumption of sodas by 22 to 28 calories per day. Rounding up to 30 per day implies a reduction of 150 calories per week, which would reduce rates of overweight by about 1.5 percentage points. More broadly speaking, a can of non-diet soda contains about 150 calories, so the simulation in Table 1 can be interpreted as adding or subtracting between one and five sodas per week. If the recent announcement of leading soda companies that they will remove all non-diet sodas from schools results in a net reduction in soda consumption, real results may be achieved.[7] Given that the extremes shown in Table 1 are generally outside the range of typical estimates of the effect of school policies on children's obesity, it seems unlikely that the average child is adding the equivalent of a soda per day at school to their diet. Nonetheless, it is clear that this seemingly small change can have large effects over the course of a school year.

[5] Note that if all activity is only moderate (light), the overweight rate is 0.27 (0.29) and the average BMI is 19.8 (20.1).

[6] Note that the changes are not symmetric with respect to calories added and subtracted, because BMR changes with weight gain/loss, altering the size of the imbalance differentially.

[7] See http://www.ameribev.org/news–media/news-releases–statements/more/183/ for a discussion of the soda companies' pledge.

7. Conclusions

Children spend about 6.5 h per day in school, for about 9 months of the year. Thus, it is not surprising that questions have arisen as to the role of school policies on children's obesity. In this chapter, we have discussed key aspects of the literature on the role of the school food environment and the role of the school activity environment in affecting the caloric intake and expenditure of children. The bulk of the evidence points to the strong possibility that the school lunch program adds to student's net daily calories, increasing the probability of overweight. School breakfast does not seem to have the same deleterious effect. At the same time, there is also evidence that exposure to competitive foods (often sweet or salty snacks or high-calorie beverages) may contribute to students' weight gain.

While there is strong support for the idea that schools have reduced the level of activity required, and even available, there is less evidence on the impact this change has had on student outcomes. For younger children, it does appear that cutting back on recess and PE results in a reduction in overall activity and thus to weight gain. For older students, effects on weight are not detectable. One source of changes in both the school activity environment and food environment may be the increased pressures of accountability. Schools have reallocated time toward academic subjects, reducing the time available for PE and recess. At the same time, monetary resources have been reallocated toward test preparation, increasing the incentive to raise funds through the sale of competitive foods. These types of behavioral changes appear to be clearly taking place, and there are indications that the unintended effect of stricter accountability laws is an increase in children's obesity.

In light of the literature on the potential role for school policies on children's obesity, we simulated the effect of a range of reasonable changes in weekly minutes spent being active in school and changes in weekly calories consumed in school. Similar to the findings in the literature, larger impacts on weight were seen for seemingly small changes in consumption than for realistic changes in activity levels. That said, larger changes in activity, such as adding an hour a day of vigorous exercise, could have effects slightly larger than cutting out a soda per day. Thus, while increases in activity can be helpful, it is the small changes in consumption that can really add up.

References

Ainsworth, B.E. (2002), "The compendium of physical activities tracking guide", Prevention Research Center, Norman J. Arnold School of Public Health, University of South Carolina (http://prevention.sph.sc.edu/tools/docs/documents_compendium.pdf).

American Heart Association (2009), "Facts-learning for life: physical education in public schools" (http://www.americanheart.org/downloadable/heart/1267456431689Edited%20FINAL%20Learning%20for%20Life%20-%20PE%20Fact%20sheet.pdf).

Anderson, P.M. and K.F. Butcher (2006), "Reading, writing, and refreshments: do school finances contribute to childhood obesity?", *Journal of Human Resources*, Vol. 41, pp. 467–494.

Anderson, P.M., K.F. Butcher, E. Cascio and D.W. Schanzenbach (2008), "Is being in school better? Using school starting age to identify the impact of schools on children's obesity" (http://www.dartmouth.edu/~pmaweb/Kindergarten.pdf).

Anderson, P.M., K.F. Butcher and D.W. Schanzenbach (2010), "The effect of school accountability policies on children's health" (http://www.dartmouth.edu/~pmaweb/ABSforLSU.pdf).

Bhattacharya, J., J. Currie and S.J. Haider (2006), "Breakfast of champions? The School Breakfast Program and the nutrition of children and families", *Journal of Human Resources*, Vol. 41, pp. 445–466.

Blum, J.E.W., A.-M. Davee, C.M. Beaudoin, P.L. Jenkins, L.A. Kaley and D.A. Wigand (2008), "Reduced availability of sugar-sweetened beverages and diet soda has limited impact on beverage consumption patterns in Maine High School Youth", *Journal of Nutrition and Behavior*, Vol. 40, pp. 341–346.

Cawley, J., C.D. Meyerhoefer and D. Newhouse (2007), "The impact of state physical education requirements on youth physical activity and overweight", *Health Economics*, Vol. 16, pp. 1287–1301.

Center on Education Policy (2007), "Choices, changes, and challenges: curriculum and instruction in the NCLB era", Washington, DC.

Datar, A. and N. Nicosia (2009), "Junk food in schools and childhood obesity: much ado about nothing?", RAND Working Paper WR-672.

Datar, A. and R. Sturm (2004), "Physical education in elementary school and body mass index: evidence from the Early Childhood Longitudinal Study", *American Journal of Public Health*, Vol. 94, pp. 1501–1506.

Durant, N., S.K. Harris, S. Doyle, S. Person, B.E. Saelens, J. Kerr, G.J. Norman and J.F. Sallis (2009), "Relation of school environment and policy to adolescent physical activity", *Journal of School Health*, Vol. 79, pp. 153–159.

Fox, M.K., A.H. Dodd, A. Wilson and P. Gleason (2009a), "Association between school food environment and practices and body mass index of US public school children", *Journal of the American Dietetic Association*, Vol. 109, pp. S108–S117.

Fox, M.K., A. Gordon, R. Nogales and A. Wilson (2009b), "Availability and consumption of competitive foods in US public schools", *Journal of the American Dietetic Association*, Vol. 109, pp. S57–S66.

Gleason, P.M. and A.H. Dodd (2009), "School Breakfast Program but not School Lunch Program participation is associated with lower body mass index", *Journal of the American Dietetic Association*, Vol. 109, pp. S118–S128.

Gleason, P.M. and C.W. Suitor (2001), "Children's diets in the mid-1990s: dietary intake and its relationship with school meal participation", U.S. Department of Agriculture Report CN-01-CD1, Washington, DC.

Gordon, A.R., M.K. Crepinsek, R.R. Briefel, M.A. Clark and M.K. Fox (2009), "The third school nutrition dietary assessment study: summary and implications", *Journal of the American Dietetic Association*, Vol. 109, pp. S129–S135.

Larson, N. and M. Story (2010), "Are 'competitive foods' sold at school making our children fat?", *Health Affairs*, Vol. 29, pp. 430–435.

Millimet, D., R. Tchernis and M. Husain (2010), "School nutrition programs and the incidence of childhood obesity", *Journal of Human Resources*, Vol. 45, pp. 640–654.

Miras-Wilson, R (2007), "The impact of physical education on childhood obesity: a tradeoff between health and academics?", Georgetown University M.P.P Thesis, Washington, DC.

Robert Wood Johnson Foundation (2009), "The state of play: Gallup survey of school principals on school recess" (http://www.playworksusa.org/files/StateOfPlayFeb2010.pdf).

Schanzenbach, D.W. (2009), "Do school lunches contribute to childhood obesity?", *Journal of Human Resources*, Vol. 44, pp. 684–709.

Schofield, W.N. (1995), "Predicting basal metabolic rate, new standards and review of previous work", *Human Nutrition–Clinical Nutrition*, Vol. 39C, pp. 5–41.

Tovar, A., K. Lividni, C.D. Economos, S. Folta, J. Goldberg and A. Must (2010), "School's out: what are urban children doing? The Summer Activity Study of Somerville Youth (SASSY)", *BMC Pediatrics*, Vol. 10(16), pp. 1–9.

U.S. Department of Agriculture, Food and Nutrition Service (2010a), "National School Lunch Program" (http://www.fns.usda.gov/cnd/lunch/AboutLunch/NSLPFactSheet.pdf).

U.S. Department of Agriculture, Food and Nutrition Service (2010b), "The School Breakfast Program" (http://www.fns.usda.gov/cnd/breakfast/AboutBfast/SBPFactSheet.pdf).

von Hippel, P.T., B. Powell, D.B. Downey and N.J. Rowland (Powell, Downey, & Rowland (2007)), "The effect of school on overweight in childhood: gain in body mass index during the school year and during summer vacation", *American Journal of Public Health*, Vol. 97, pp. 696–702.

Wong, W.W., N.F. Butte, A.C. Hergenroeder, R.B. Hill, J.E. Stuff and E. O'Brian Smith (1996), "Are basal metabolic rate prediction equations appropriate for female children and adolescents", *Journal of Applied Physiology*, Vol. 81, pp. 2407–2414.

Yin, L. (2009), "Are school accountability systems contributing to adolescent obesity?" (http://bear.warrington.ufl.edu/yin/Are%20School%20Accountability%20Systems%20Contributing%20to%20Adolescent%20Obesity.pdf).

CHAPTER 2

Alcohol Policies and Child Maltreatment

Sara Markowitz*, Michael Grossman and Ryan Conrad

Abstract

The purpose of this chapter is to empirically estimate the propensity for alcohol-related policies to influence rates of child abuse. Child maltreatment is measured by the number of abused children and the number of child fatalities due to abuse. The alcohol regulations of interest include beer, wine, and liquor taxes and prices, drunk driving laws, and measures of alcohol availability. Results indicate that higher excise taxes on alcohol and reductions in availability may be effective in reducing the incidence of child maltreatment.

Keywords: alcohol, taxes, child abuse

JEL classifications: I0, J12

1. Introduction

Parental substance abuse problems can be extremely detrimental to the health and well being of children. Children of substance abusers are at a much greater risk of physical, mental, and sexual abuse, and suffer more physical and mental health problems than children in the general population (Puttler *et al.*, 1998; Center on Addiction and Substance Abuse (CASA), 2001). The Substance Abuse and Mental Health Services Administration

---

* Corresponding author.

CONTRIBUTIONS TO ECONOMIC ANALYSIS
VOLUME 290 ISSN: 0573-8555
DOI:10.1108/S0573-8555(2010)0000290005

estimates that approximately 5.156 million children live with parents who abuse or are dependent on alcohol (Office of Applied Studies, 2003).

Nearly 1 million children annually are victims of child abuse and neglect. Estimates of alcohol involvement in cases of maltreatment range from 40 percent to 70 percent of all cases (Famularo *et al.*, 1986; Children of Alcoholics Foundation, 1996; CASA, 2001). Some of the children of substance-abusing parents will have encounters with state child protective services, and these children may be temporarily or permanently separated from their parents in order to provide a safe and stable environment. The problems related to parental substance abuse places a tremendous burden on the child welfare system. The U.S. Department of Health and Human Services (USDHHS, 1999) states, "... it is clear that throughout the child welfare system, but especially with respect to children in foster care, alcohol and other drug abuse are recognized as major contributing factors to child neglect and abuse and are two of the key barriers to family reunification." The burden of substance abuse problems translates into an estimated annual \$5.3 billion of state spending for child welfare and over \$10 billion in combined federal, state, and local government spending (CASA, 1999, 2001).

The close association of parental alcohol abuse and the maltreatment of children suggests that alcohol control policies can play a tremendous role in improving the lives of abused children. This has implications for not only the current situation of these children, but also for their future success. Research has linked abuse during childhood to adverse outcomes such as delinquency and poor mental and physical health, which in turn have implications for labor market outcomes later in life (Widom, 1989; Felitti *et al.*, 1998; Smith *et al.*, 2005; Tekin and Markowitz, 2008).

The link between excessive alcohol consumption or alcohol abuse and child abuse, which has been found in many studies, does not necessarily imply causality from the former behavior to the latter. It is possible that variations in one or more unobserved "third variables" may cause these behaviors to vary in the same direction (see Markowitz, 2000 for a discussion of the causality issue as it relates to domestic violence). Nevertheless, the studies showing a high prevalence of alcohol abuse and dependency among parents of abused children provide the motivating context for this study. Estimates of alcoholism among parents of abused children range from 38 percent to 69 percent (Behling 1979; Famularo *et al.*, 1986). Studies find that parents of abused or neglected children have much higher reported substance use than non-abusive parents. For example, Kelleher *et al.* (1994) control for some possibly confounding variables and find that parents of abused (neglected) children are 2.7 (4.1) times more likely to have a substance abuse problem than other parents. DeBellis *et al.* (2001) also show a higher incidence of alcohol and/or substance abuse or dependence disorders among parents of maltreated children as compared to sociodemographically similar parents of non-maltreated children.

In substantiated cases of child abuse and neglect, one-third to two-thirds are believed to involve parental alcohol abuse or abuse of other drugs, although estimates go as high as 97 percent (CASA, 1999; USDHHS, 1999). Alcohol is the primary culprit in these reports. One report found that alcohol was involved in 77 percent of cases and was more harmful than drugs (cocaine, primarily) in 64 percent of the cases (USDHHS, 1999).

The effectiveness of alcohol control policies in improving the lives of children is an understudied area in the disciplines of economics and public policy. Previous research approaches the study of the alcohol–violence relationship using the large body of economic literature on the demand for alcohol (see Grossman, 2005 for a survey of this literature). This literature demonstrates that alcohol consumption and excessive alcohol consumption are inversely related to the price of alcohol and to measures of its availability. The measures of availability include the minimum legal drinking age, the number and types of outlets that are permitted to sell alcohol, and statutes pertaining to alcohol advertising and server liability. Based on this literature and on the well-documented relationship between alcohol and domestic violence, Markowitz and Grossman (1998, 2000) estimate the effects of higher alcohol prices and restricted availability on reducing the incidence of child abuse. In a technique similar to that of this current project, we capitalize on substantial differences in alcoholic beverage prices among states that arise primarily from variations in state excise tax rates on these beverages.

In the first paper by Markowitz and Grossman (1998), we examine the effect of alcohol regulations on the incidence of child abuse. Using data from the 1976 National Family Violence Survey, we estimate models in which the incidence of child abuse is affected by the state excise tax rate on beer, illegal drug prices, marijuana decriminalization, laws restricting alcohol advertising, the per capita number of outlets licensed to sell alcohol, and demographic and socioeconomic characteristics of parents. Violence measures are collected in the survey by use of the Conflict Tactic Scale (CTS). The CTS gathers information on the number of times in the past year a parent has committed a violent act by first asking questions about verbal solutions to disagreements and building up to questions on the occurrence of violent acts. Results from this study show that increasing the tax on beer can be an effective policy tool in reducing violence. The findings imply that a 10 percent increase in the tax on beer would reduce the probability of severe violence by 2.3 percent and the probability of any degree of violence by 1.2 percent. Our estimates suggest that a 10 percent hike in the beer tax would have lowered the number of severely abused children by about 132,000 in 1975. We also find that laws designed to make obtaining beer more difficult also may be effective in reducing violence. These laws include "dry" county laws, laws prohibiting beer sales in grocery stores, and liquor outlet densities. However, restrictions in advertising and increases in illegal drug prices have no effects on child abuse.

In a follow-up study on child abuse (Markowitz and Grossman, 2000), we pool data from the 1985 and 1976 National Family Violence Surveys to establish two important results. First, violent acts against children committed by females are much more responsive to beer taxes than similar acts committed by males. One explanation of this finding is that alcohol consumption by females is more sensitive to the price of alcohol than alcohol consumption by males. Second, by pooling the two surveys with a set of state dummies, we establish that the negative tax effects for females are not due to unobserved state factors. In particular, the magnitude of these effects are largely unaffected by the inclusion of the state dummies.

Freisthler (2004) and Freisthler *et al.* (2005) examine the relationship between alcohol outlet densities and rates of child abuse. These papers both find that areas in California with higher densities of alcohol outlets also have higher rates of child maltreatment. The results of these studies must be interpreted with caution as it is impossible to know whether the abusers are choosing to locate in areas with high-density outlets or whether the availability of alcohol contributes to the abuse.

Economists have also examined other determinants of child abuse using the state-level panel data used in this chapter. For example, Paxson and Waldfogel (2002) examine the ways in which children are affected by the economic circumstances of the parents. Bitler and Zavodny (2004) and Seiglie (2004) also examine state-level panels of child abuse and neglect, with a focus on the effects of abortion restrictions in reducing child maltreatment.

We want to emphasize the key difference between our previous research on child abuse just described and this current work. Our new research is based on objective measures of child maltreatment as opposed to parental reports of this behavior. Our measures represent the most severe cases – cases that are serious enough to warrant investigation by child protection services. This new research also employs much more recent data.

2. *Analytical framework*

The framework for this project involves two well-established relationships: the relationship between alcohol consumption and the maltreatment of children, and the negative relationship between alcohol consumption and the full price of alcohol. If a parent's alcohol consumption leads to an increased risk for child maltreatment, then following the law of demand, an increase in the price of alcohol should reduce consumption and thereby reduce the risk of maltreatment. The "reduced form" equation directly relates alcohol prices and policies to the outcome of interest, measures of child maltreatment. This strategy has been used extensively in the economics literature to study the role of alcohol policies in reducing the negative outcomes associated with consumption (Cook and Moore, 1993; Markowitz and Grossman, 1998, 2000; Chesson *et al.*, 2000; Dee, 2001; Markowitz *et al.*, 2003).

The empirical equation for child maltreatment takes the following general form:

$$M_{jt} = f(P_{jt},\ X_{jt},\ \lambda_j, \tau_t) \tag{1}$$

Eq. (1) shows the determinants of child maltreatment (*M*) for state *j* in time *t*. The vector *P* represents components of the full price of alcohol, which will be measured with variables such as alcohol prices and taxes, alcohol availability, and drunk driving laws. These variables are described in more detail below. The coefficients on the price and policy variables will show the effectiveness of higher prices/taxes and strict alcohol regulations in decreasing child maltreatment. The model includes variables designed to capture observed characteristics of the state (*X*) as described below. In addition, state dummies (λ) will capture unobserved time-invariant state-level effects that may influence maltreatment rates. Time dummies (τ) will capture secular trends.

There is some question in the existing literature as to the nature of the causal relationship between alcohol consumption and child maltreatment. Some researchers have identified a direct causal relationship from use to maltreatment (Pernanen, 1981; Fagan, 1993), while others show that the link may be primarily through confounding factors, such as psychiatric disorders, which are often correlated with substance use (Bland and Orn, 1986; Kelleher *et al.*, 1994; Walsh *et al.*, 2002). One advantage of using the reduced form model is that the conclusions will hold without regard to the nature of the causal relationship between alcohol use and child maltreatment because consumption is substituted out of the equation. So long as the prices and policies are uncorrelated with the error term in the violence equation and there is no reason to believe that state-level substance use policies will affect violence other than through consumption, the reduced form coefficients are unbiased estimates. If alcohol consumption is not directly related to child maltreatment, the reduced form coefficients will reflect this with values that are not statistically different from zero.

3. Data

State-level counts of reported child abuse and neglect come from the National Child Abuse and Neglect Data System (NCANDS). NCANDS provides information on all cases of child maltreatment that are investigated by state child protection service agencies. The series begins in 1990, and our data run through 2004. These data represent the best available national counts of children suffering from abuse and neglect. From these data, we create annual state-level counts of two measures of severe child abuse: (1) the number of children with confirmed or suspected reports of maltreatment and (2) the number of child fatalities resulting from maltreatment.

We use the number of substantiated or indicated investigations from the NCANDS to represent child maltreatment. Substantiated cases are those "in which the allegation of maltreatment or risk of maltreatment was supported or founded according to State law or State policy" (USDHHS, 2000). Indicated cases are those "for which the allegation of maltreatment was indicated, or there was reason to suspect maltreatment, but it was unable to be founded, under State law or State policy" (USDHHS, 2000). Because some states do not distinguish between substantiated cases or indicated cases, and because both represent some degree of child maltreatment, we will use the combined number of substantiated and indicated cases as a measure of child maltreatment.

The numbers of substantiated and indicated cases are provided on the incident level and child level. Since children can have multiple incidents, child-level data are the focus of this chapter. Ideally, we would like to investigate the number of cases at the family level since this would more closely represent the number of adults whose behaviors are susceptible to changes in alcohol policies; however, this information is not available from the NCANDS state-level data. Instead, we use the number of child-level cases and answer the question of how many children possibly can be helped with changes in the full price of alcohol.

Child maltreatment includes a variety of different types of abuse and neglect including physical abuse, neglect or deprivation of necessities, sexual abuse, and psychological or emotional abuse or neglect. The alternative measure of child abuse from NCANDS is the number of children who died as a result of maltreatment. The death may have occurred while in foster care, day care, or in the care of their parents.

There are some drawbacks to these measures of child abuse. First, the definition of child abuse differs across states, so that what is considered abuse in one state may not be in another. For physical and sexual abuse, although there are differences in the severity of the abuse or in the definition of who is a caregiver, the state definitions have many common elements (Paxson and Waldfogel, 2002). There are also differences in the requirements for who is considered a mandatory reporter and the amount of evidence required to substantiate a report of abuse. Because of these differences in state reporting practices, it is important to control for state fixed effects. Nevertheless, there may exist reporting error in the data. Underreporting may be a second issue since only the cases of child mistreatment that are reported to authorities are included in the data. Furthermore, some investigations are closed without a finding because the family moved or the investigation time exceeded that allowed. Such reporting error or underreporting is not problematic for our analysis. So long as it is random, the reporting problems will raise the standard errors but will not bias the coefficients.

3.1. Alcohol regulations

Several variables are used to measure state-level alcohol regulations. First, four different measures of the tax on alcohol are examined and compared. First, we use the sum of the real (1982–1984 = 1) state and federal excise taxes on beer. Beer taxes come from the Beer Institute's *Brewers Almanac*. As wine rivals beer in popularity (Bloomberg, 2005), the sum of the real state and federal excise taxes on wine is the second measure of the tax on alcohol. Wine taxes come from the Distilled Spirits Council of the United States (DISCUS), *History of Beverage Alcohol Tax Change, 1996*, and the National Conference of State Legislatures, *State Tax Actions, 1995–2003*.

Liquor taxes are the third measure of the tax on alcohol. These taxes, which come from the same sources as the wine taxes, are employed because of the widespread opinion that consumption of spirits is potentially more dangerous than beer or wine consumption (for example, Saffer, 1991) and because of Cook and Tauchen's (1982) seminal study that reports a strong inverse relationship between spirits taxes and cirrhosis mortality. State excise tax rates on liquor are only available for the 33 "license" states (including the District of Columbia) where the state government does not have monopoly control of the retail sale of liquor. The 18 monopoly states derive their revenue from the sale of liquor from markups rather than from excise taxes. (A complete listing of the liquor sales control method for all states can be seen in Appendix A.) Implicit tax rates for these states can be imputed along the lines suggested by Cook *et al.* (2005). Let $\mathrm{LP}_{\mathrm{l}t}$ be the average price of liquor in the 33 license states in year t and let $\mathrm{LT}_{\mathrm{l}t}$ be the average excise tax (including the federal tax) in these states in year t. Define $Q_{\mathrm{l}t}$ as price exclusive of tax ($Q_{\mathrm{l}t} \equiv \mathrm{LP}_{\mathrm{l}t} - \mathrm{LT}_{\mathrm{l}t}$). Then the implicit tax in the jth monopoly state in year t ($\mathrm{LT}_{\mathrm{m}jt}$) is

$$\mathrm{LT}_{\mathrm{m}jt} = \mathrm{LP}_{\mathrm{m}jt} - Q_{\mathrm{l}t} \tag{2}$$

This assumes that the average cost incurred by state-owned stores in selling liquor is approximately equal to the mean of this cost in license states. Unlike Cook *et al.* (2005), we allow $Q_{\mathrm{l}t}$ to vary by year. The liquor price is taken from ACCRA's *Cost of Living Index*, but is missing for Maine (all years), Vermont (2002), and New Hampshire (2002–2004). Therefore, the imputed liquor tax is missing for these states and years as well.

Note that beer is sold privately in all monopoly states and wine is sold privately in all these states except for Pennsylvania, New Hampshire, and Utah. Hence, beer excise taxes are available for all states, and wine excise taxes are available for all states except for Pennsylvania, New Hampshire, and Utah. For those three states, we will employ an imputation procedure similar to the one described above for liquor. A dichotomous indicator for the imputation (i.e. monopoly states) is included in the models with liquor taxes and wine taxes.

Beer, wine, and liquor tax rates are too highly correlated to include in the same regression. A specification can be obtained, however, that contains a summary measure of the three tax rates, namely the tax rate on an ounce of pure ethanol. This tax is computed by first computing the tax on an ounce of ethanol in each beverage and then averaging, using the fractions of total ethanol consumption accounted for by beer, wine, liquor, respectively, as weights. These weights are fixed over time and are averages for the United States as a whole during our sample period.[1] Indicators for observations with imputed liquor and wine taxes are included in these models as well.

Alcohol taxes have been shown to be excellent predictors of alcohol consumption (for example, Cook and Tauchen, 1982; Cook and Moore, 1993; Grossman *et al.*, 1998), but successful estimation of effects in a panel of states relies on variation in the nominal taxes over the sample period. From 1990 through 2004, state nominal beer taxes changed 40 times in 15 states, wine taxes changed 28 times in 14 states, and liquor taxes in license states changed 23 times in 11 states. Additional variation arises due to changes in markups on liquor in monopoly states.

Retail prices that are inclusive of state and federal taxes for beer, wine, and liquor are published quarterly by ACCRA in the *Inter-City Cost of Living Index* for between 250 and 300 cities across the United States. State average annual prices are generated by using a population weighted average of the city prices present in each state. All prices are deflated by the consumer price index (CPI) and the ACCRA cost of living index. We have also adjusted the price data for brand changes in beer over time. In the models below, we include each alcohol price separately and as a composite price of ethanol computed in the same manner as the ethanol tax.

The availability of alcohol is an important component of the full price. Two variables will be used to represent availability. The first is the percentage of each state's population living in counties "dry" for beer. These data come from the *Brewers Almanac*. The second is the number of retail outlets per 100,000 population that are licensed to sell liquor for on-premise or off-premise consumption. These data come from *Jobson's Liquor Handbook*. With larger percentages of populations living in dry counties or with fewer outlets available, travel time to obtain alcohol increases, adding to the full price of alcohol. If alcohol consumption contributes to child maltreatment, then it is expected that policies that make obtaining alcohol more costly will reduce the incidence of maltreatment.

---

[1] We use ethanol contents of 4.5 percent for beer, 12.9 percent for wine, and 41.1 percent for spirits. Based on the average consumption over the sample period, we assign beer 56 percent of total consumption, wine 14 percent, and liquor 30 percent.

Blood alcohol concentration (BAC) laws make it illegal per se to drive with a BAC greater than a certain level. Adults living in states with more stringent BAC laws face a higher full price of alcohol relative to those living in less stringent states because the probability of being charged with drunk driving increases. Thus, it is expected that the stricter BAC laws will reduce alcohol consumption and possibly reduce child maltreatment. The 1990s and early 2000s is a time period in which many states enacted the 0.08 laws, so our models include a dichotomous indicator for whether the state had a 0.08 BAC law in effect or whether a higher limit was applicable.[2]

Eq. (1) also includes state characteristics that may help determine child abuse rates. In all models we will include the female labor force participation rate, the unemployment rate, real income per capita, the percentage of the population living in rural areas, and the percentage of the population 25 years and over that has obtained a bachelor's degree. The percentages of each state's population identifying with certain religions (Catholic, Protestant, Southern Baptist, and Mormon) are included as well. All models also include state dummies to help capture any unobserved time-invariant state effects that may influence child maltreatment and may be correlated with the alcohol control policies. Time dummies are included to capture secular trends in child maltreatment and foster care entries.

4. Empirical estimation

We examine the determinants of the number of child fatalities and child maltreatment rates from the NCANDS child abuse data in the tables below. The means of all variables are shown in Table 1. As can be seen from this table, child fatalities are a relatively rare event while maltreatment is much more common. The mean annual fatality count for states during the period 1990–2004 is approximately 25 deaths, with a minimum of 0 (which occurs 18 times) and a maximum of 212. Because of the discrete count nature of fatalities and the presence of observations with a value of zero, we use a fixed effects Poisson (FEP) method as the estimation technique for this dependent variable (Cameron and Trivedi, 1998; Wooldridge, 2002). This estimator is a quasi-maximum likelihood estimator that includes parameters or "fixed effects" to account for unobserved heterogeneity across the units of observation (states). Estimates are consistent regardless of whether the counts actually have a

---

[2] In the same period many states enacted "zero tolerance" drunk driving laws that set the BAC level for under-age drinkers at 0.02 or less. Since young unmarried mothers under the age of 21 are subject to zero tolerance laws, a dichotomous indicator for states with zero tolerance laws was tested in the models. However, the coefficient on zero tolerance laws was statistically insignificant in all models, so it is excluded from the results shown.

Table 1. Summary statistics

	Years 1990–2004 ($N = 717$)			
	Mean	Std. dev.	Min	Max
Fatality count	24.84	29.32	0	212
Child maltreatment count	18,527	25,301	270	182,160
Child maltreatment rate per 1,000 children	13.98	8.25	1.61	83.92
Beer tax	0.50	0.13	0.24	1.08
Liquor tax	9.69	1.59	6.51	15.32
Ethanol tax	0.11	0.02	0.08	0.19
Liquor monopoly	0.34		0	1
Wine monopoly	0.05		0	1
Beer price	2.65	0.28	1.72	3.41
Liquor price	11.49	1.49	7.07	16.30
Ethanol price	0.86	0.10	0.52	1.10
Percent dry	4.11	9.55	0	45.97
Liquor outlets per 100,000 state residents	125.99	64.47	13.27	398.14
0.08 BAC law	0.36		0	1
College education	23.83	5.20	12.40	46.40
Female labor force participation rate	60.62	4.19	47.70	71.20
Real income (in $1,000s)	15.53	2.64	10.01	27.58
Unemployment	5.25	1.40	2.20	9.20
Percent rural	28.42	14.95	0	67.80
Mormon	3.09	10.20	0.06	71.41
Southern Baptist	7.28	9.86	0.11	33.73
Catholic	19.74	12.69	2.24	62.97
Protestant	19.90	9.34	2.82	47.63

Poisson distribution (Wooldridge, 2002). To permit overdispersion, a common feature of count data that is not accommodated by the Poisson maximum likelihood estimator, standard errors are adjusted for heteroskedasticity of unknown form that includes a within-state cluster correlation (Bertrand *et al.*, 2004; Cameron and Trivedi, 2005). Each model includes the log of the number of children (under age 18) in each state for each year as a right-hand side variable to normalize for exposure. The coefficient on this log population is constrained to equal one.[3]

Maltreatment is amenable to estimation as a rate. No state has a zero value and the numbers are more continuous in nature. Values for annual maltreatment counts per state range from 270 to 182,160, and no one value is observed in the data more than twice. The mean maltreatment rate is approximately 14 per 1,000 children. Because of skewness in these data, we analyze the log of these rates. Weighted least squares (WLS) are used to

[3] Models estimated using negative binomial yield very similar results.

Table 2. Child fatalities from maltreatment fixed effects Poisson models

	Models with tax included				Models with price included		
	(1)	(2)	(3)	(4)	(5)	(6)	(7)
Beer tax/price	−1.613				−0.341		
	(−2.46)				(−2.12)		
Liquor tax/price		−0.023	−0.047			−0.038	
		(−0.54)	(−1.41)			(−1.02)	
Ethanol tax/price				−6.334			−1.206
				(−2.35)			(−2.05)
Liquor monopoly			3.456	1.344			
			(1.99)	(2.99)			
Wine monopoly				0.367			
				(2.01)			
Percent dry	0.009	−0.018	0.007	0.007	0.012	0.007	0.007
	(0.52)	(−0.48)	(0.49)	(0.41)	(0.79)	(0.46)	(0.49)
Liquor outlets	−0.0004	−0.001	−0.0005	−0.0005	0.0001	−0.0002	0.0001
	(−0.58)	(−0.67)	(−0.55)	(−0.66)	(0.17)	(−0.19)	(0.09)
0.08 BAC law	0.051	0.041	0.041	0.046	0.065	0.044	0.062
	(0.67)	(0.55)	(0.56)	(0.62)	(0.92)	(0.62)	(0.89)
College education	0.008	0.011	0.009	0.009	0.008	0.01	0.008
	(0.57)	(0.78)	(0.67)	(0.62)	(0.59)	(0.71)	(0.63)
Female LFP	0.034	0.038	0.035	0.035	0.04	0.037	0.038
	(2.15)	(2.32)	(2.22)	(2.19)	(2.49)	(2.26)	(2.38)
Real income	0.055	0.039	0.047	0.048	0.033	0.046	0.032
	(0.91)	(0.65)	(0.79)	(0.81)	(0.53)	(0.72)	(0.51)
Unemployment	−0.062	−0.079	−0.073	−0.067	−0.081	−0.088	−0.087
	(−1.60)	(−2.25)	(−2.09)	(−1.86)	(−2.20)	(−2.33)	(−2.39)
Percent rural	−0.005	−0.014	−0.007	−0.006	−0.005	−0.01	−0.009
	(−0.36)	(−0.90)	(−0.53)	(−0.46)	(−0.40)	(−0.69)	(−0.66)
Mormon	0.088	0.218	0.084	0.100	0.051	0.073	0.063
	(1.55)	(1.25)	(1.42)	(1.59)	(0.91)	(1.26)	(1.09)
Southern Baptist	−0.153	−0.163	−0.164	−0.157	−0.172	−0.171	−0.172
	(−2.80)	(−3.14)	(−3.08)	(−2.89)	(−3.38)	(−3.23)	(−3.31)
Catholic	−0.016	−0.011	−0.016	−0.016	−0.024	−0.023	−0.023
	(−0.92)	(−0.67)	(−0.95)	(−0.94)	(−1.54)	(−1.37)	(−1.37)
Protestant	0.015	0.014	0.008	0.012	0.004	0.006	0.006
	(0.92)	(0.93)	(0.52)	(0.75)	(0.30)	(0.43)	(0.43)
N	686	637	667	664	636	636	636
Tax/price elasticity	−0.814	−0.223	−0.456	−0.719	−0.903	−0.437	−1.033

Note: *t*-statistics in parentheses and intercept not shown. All models include year and state fixed effects. The sample in Column 2 includes only the license liquor states. The sample in Column 3 includes all states and imputed values for the states with government run liquor stores.

account for the heteroskedasticity in the error term of a known form (Johnston and Dinardo, 1996). Standard errors are also corrected for within-state cluster correlation (Bertrand *et al.*, 2004).

Table 2 shows the results for the FEP estimation of the child fatality count, and Table 3 shows results for the WLS estimation of the log child

Table 3. Child maltreatment rates log-linear models

	Models with tax included				Models with price included		
	(1)	(2)	(3)	(4)	(5)	(6)	(7)
Beer tax/price	−1.797				−0.382		
	(−1.53)				(−2.21)		
Liquor tax/price		−0.112	−0.116			0.011	
		(−1.42)	(−3.44)			(0.24)	
Ethanol tax/price				−10.194			−0.906
				(−2.10)			(−1.30)
Liquor monopoly			0.005	0.792			
			(0.01)	(0.42)			
Wine monopoly				0.100			
				(0.64)			
Percent dry	−0.007	−0.067	−0.003	−0.007	−0.009	−0.003	−0.006
	(−0.28)	(−1.38)	(−0.11)	(−0.27)	(−0.31)	(−0.10)	(−0.21)
Liquor outlets	0.0015	0.001	0.0014	0.0014	0.002	0.001	0.002
	(1.67)	(0.72)	(1.41)	(1.49)	(1.77)	(1.45)	(1.71)
0.08 BAC law	−0.089	−0.111	−0.082	−0.084	−0.073	−0.116	−0.084
	(−1.36)	(−1.19)	(−1.20)	(−1.21)	(−1.23)	(−1.65)	(−1.32)
College education	0.012	0.010	0.015	0.013	0.012	0.015	0.013
	(0.80)	(0.63)	(0.99)	(0.86)	(0.79)	(0.98)	(0.83)
Female LFP	−0.003	−0.013	−0.004	−0.004	0.000	−0.004	−0.003
	(−0.23)	(−0.73)	(−0.29)	(−0.24)	(−0.01)	(−0.24)	(−0.21)
Real income	−0.069	−0.114	−0.077	−0.069	−0.111	−0.080	−0.098
	(−0.90)	(−1.63)	(−1.05)	(−0.92)	(−1.79)	(−1.03)	(−1.34)
Unemployment	0.037	0.040	0.028	0.037	0.019	0.021	0.014
	(1.39)	(0.98)	(0.91)	(1.28)	(0.72)	(0.73)	(0.52)
Percent rural	−0.017	−0.032	−0.019	−0.017	−0.021	−0.022	−0.023
	(−0.88)	(−0.90)	(−0.94)	(−0.84)	(−0.98)	(−1.10)	(−1.11)
Mormon	0.093	1.028	0.093	0.094	0.053	0.077	0.069
	(1.21)	(2.20)	(1.18)	(1.20)	(0.70)	(0.95)	(0.86)
Southern Baptist	0.013	0.013	0.002	0.010	0.014	0.008	0.010
	(0.24)	(0.25)	(0.04)	(0.18)	(0.24)	(0.15)	(0.17)
Catholic	0.023	0.062	0.025	0.024	0.017	0.019	0.021
	(1.62)	(3.23)	(1.83)	(1.71)	(0.93)	(1.15)	(1.18)
Protestant	0.041	0.059	0.033	0.039	0.026	0.029	0.029
	(2.12)	(2.76)	(1.74)	(2.02)	(1.38)	(1.51)	(1.50)
N	717	472	698	695	666	666	666
Tax/price elasticity	−0.906	−1.084	−1.123	−1.157	−1.012	0.124	−0.776

Note: *t*-statistics in parentheses and intercept not shown. All models include year and state fixed effects. The sample in Column 2 includes only the license liquor states. The sample in Column 3 includes all states and imputed values for the states with government run liquor stores.

maltreatment rate. Seven models are shown within each table: Column 1 includes the excise tax on beer. Column 2 includes the liquor tax among license states only so that no imputed values are included. Column 3 shows the liquor tax for all states with the imputed values and the indicator variable for the monopoly states. Column 4 has the tax on pure ethanol and includes the imputed liquor and wine tax values. Columns 5, 6, and 7 include the ACCRA real beer, liquor, and ethanol prices, respectively. Models that include the wine tax and wine prices were run but are not shown in the tables for brevity, since the coefficients on the wine tax are always statistically insignificant.

All models in the tables also include the 0.08 BAC indicator, the percent of the state's population living in counties that are "dry" for beer, the number of liquor outlets per capita, the state characteristics, year indicators, and state fixed effects.

5. *Results*

Table 2 shows that all types of alcohol taxes and prices are negatively related to child fatalities. It can be argued that a one-tailed test is relevant for assessing statistical significance given that our interest is testing whether or not the tax coefficients are negative, and not simply different from zero. Using this criterion, statistical significance is achieved at the 1 percent level when beer taxes and ethanol taxes are considered, at the 2.5 percent level when beer and ethanol prices are considered, and at the 10 percent level when liquor taxes are included in the full sample (Column 3).

The price and tax coefficients in the FEP can be interpreted as semi-elasticities, that is, the percentage change in the fatality count from a $1 change in the price/tax. Given the sample means, a $1 change is an extremely large change. The elasticities presented at the bottom of Table 2 provide more reasonable estimates and show that a 1 percent increase in the tax on beer is associated with a 0.81 percent decrease in the number of child fatalities. The liquor tax elasticities are −0.22 and −0.46 and the ethanol elasticity is −0.72. The price elasticities are slightly higher at −0.90, −0.44, and −1.03 for beer, liquor, and ethanol, respectively.

None of the other alcohol control variables are associated with child fatalities, although the indicator for monopoly states for liquor is positive and statistically significant, and the indicator for monopoly states for wine is negative and statistically significant. It is difficult to interpret these results since monopoly status might reflect a variety of factors, including measurement error in the imputation, alcohol availability, or unmeasured attitudes toward alcohol control and consumption common to the monopoly states.

Results from the labor market variables are interesting in that higher female labor force participation rates are associated with more child fatalities and higher unemployment rates are associated with fewer deaths. These results point to the importance of time spent caring for and supervising children.

Table 3 contains results for child maltreatment rates. As in Table 2, the coefficients on the alcohol taxes and prices are negative in all but one case, with statistical significance achieved at various levels for the beer tax, liquor tax, and ethanol tax. The tax elasticities are larger for child maltreatment than that for fatalities. Here, a 1 percent increase in the tax on beer is associated with a 0.91 percent decrease in the child maltreatment rate. The liquor tax elasticities are −1.08 and −1.12, and the ethanol elasticity is −1.16. The beer price elasticity is slightly higher at −1.01, while the ethanol price elasticity is lower at −0.78.

The coefficients on the 0.08 BAC law and the percent dry are also negative, but these coefficients are generally not statistically significant. However, the coefficients on per capita liquor outlets are positive, and in six of the models, statistically significant at the 5 percent or 10 percent levels in a one-tailed test. This finding indicates that more liquor outlets are associated with higher rates of child abuse, but this does not necessarily mean that it is a causal relationship. While we do control for unobserved, time-invariant state fixed effects, it is possible that time-varying factors may influence this relationship. It is also possible that abusive parents locate near outlets to have easy access to alcohol. This might be particularly important if parents wish to "self-medicate" after being abusive, or if they wish to use alcohol as an excuse for their behavior (see Gelles and Cornell, 1990 or Fagan, 1990 for details).

6. *Conclusions*

This chapter seeks to evaluate whether policies that increase the full price of alcohol can be effective in reducing the maltreatment of children. The evidence presented here points to the conclusion that it can. We use data from state child protection agencies on the number of child fatalities due to abuse and the number of abused children. Abuse includes physical abuse, sexual abuse, neglect, deprivation, and emotional abuse.

We measure the full price of alcohol with taxes, prices, the availability of alcohol, and regulations. Alcohol regulations are measured with taxes and prices of beer, wine, and liquor. A composite price and tax for pure ethanol are also used. To represent the availability of alcohol, we use the percent of each state's population living in counties that are "dry" for beer and the per capita number of outlets licensed to sell liquor. Models also include an indicator for whether or not the state has a blood alcohol content limit of 0.08 or less for operating a motor vehicle.

In general, the results show that higher taxes and prices of beer, liquor, and ethanol are negatively related to the measures of child abuse, and therefore increases in these prices can lead to decreases in the incidence of child maltreatment. Restrictions on alcohol in the form of fewer licensed outlets per capita are also associated with improvements in child welfare. We caution that possible endogeneity may bias the coefficients on alcohol availability, particularly if reverse causality is present.

The efficacy of alcohol control policies to improve child well-being can be seen by examining the results in terms of the number of lives affected in a given year. For example, in 2004, the last year of data in our sample, there were 1,387 child fatalities nationally and 869,028 cases of child abuse. In the same year, the nominal average state tax plus federal tax on an ounce of pure ethanol was about $0.20. This value is a consumption-weighted average where the nominal taxes are $0.14 for the ethanol in beer, $0.11 for the ethanol in wine, and $0.34 for the ethanol in liquor. Using the elasticity for the ethanol tax in Table 2, a 10 percent increase in the ethanol tax would reduce the total number of fatalities in the United States by 100, or 2 per state in 2004. The reductions in abuse would be much larger. Using the relevant elasticity in Table 3, a 10 percent ethanol tax increase would reduce the total number of abused children across the United States by 100,547.

Acknowledgments

Funding for this project was provided by grant #R03AA016836 from the National Institute on Alcohol Abuse and Alcoholism. The content is solely the responsibility of the authors and does not necessarily represent the official views of the National Institute on Alcohol Abuse and Alcoholism or the National Institutes of Health. We would like to thank Edward Norton for very helpful comments on an early draft.

References

Behling, D. (1979), "Alcohol abuse encountered in 51 instances of reported child abuse", *Clinical Pediatrics*, Vol. 18(1), pp. 87–91.

Bertrand, M., E. Duflo and S. Mullainathan (2004), "How much should we trust differences-in-differences estimates?", *Quarterly Journal of Economics*, Vol. 119(1), pp. 249–275.

Bitler, M.P. and M. Zavodny (2004), "Child maltreatment, abortion availability, and economic conditions", *Review of Economics of the Household*, Vol. 2(2), pp. 119–141.

Bland, R.C. and H. Orn (1986), "Psychiatric disorders, spouse abuse and child abuse", *Acta Psychiatrica Belgica*, Vol. 86(4), pp. 444–449.

Bloomberg, C.D. (2005), "Drinkers vote wine gains over beer in U.S.; beer still leads in state Pittsburgh post-gazette", September 8, 2005, F-2.

Cameron, C.A. and P.K. Trivedi (1998), "Regression analysis of count data", Econometric Society Monograph No. 30, Cambridge University Press.

Cameron, C.A. and P.K. Trivedi (2005), *Microeconomic Methods and Applications*, New York: Cambridge University Press.

Center on Addiction and Substance Abuse (1999), *No Safe Haven: Children of Substance-Abusing Parents*, New York: Center on Addiction and Substance Abuse.

Center on Addiction and Substance Abuse (2001), *Shoveling Up: The Impact of Substance Abuse on State Budgets*, New York: Center on Addiction and Substance Abuse.

Chesson, H., P. Harrison and W.J. Kassler (2000), "Sex under the influence: the effect of alcohol policy on sexually transmitted disease rates in the U.S.", *Journal of Law and Economics*, Vol. 43(1), pp. 215–238.

Children of Alcoholics Foundation (1996), *Helping Children Affected by Parental Addiction and Family Violence: Collaboration, Coordination, and Cooperation*, New York: Children of Alcoholics Foundation.

Cook, P.J. and M.J. Moore (1993), "Economic perspectives on reducing alcohol-related violence", pp. 193–211 in: S.E. Martin, editor, *Alcohol and Interpersonal Violence: Fostering Multidisciplinary Perspectives*, National Institute on Alcohol Abuse and Alcoholism Research Monograph 24, NIH Publication No. 93-3469, U.S. Government Printing Office, Washington, DC.

Cook, P.J. and G. Tauchen (1982), "The effect of liquor taxes on heavy drinking", *Bell Journal of Economics*, Vol. 13(2), pp. 379–390.

Cook, P.J., J. Ostermann and F. Sloan (2005), "Are alcohol excise taxes good for us? Short and long-term effects on mortality rates", National Bureau of Economic Research Working Paper No. 11138.

DeBellis, M.D., E.R. Broussard, D.J. Herring, S. Wexler, G. Moritz and J.G. Benitez (2001), "Psychiatric co-morbidity in caregivers and children involved in maltreatment: a pilot research study with policy implications", *Child Abuse & Neglect*, Vol. 25(7), pp. 923–944.

Dee, T.D. (2001), "Does setting limits save lives? The case of 0.08 BAC laws", *Journal of Policy Analysis and Management*, Vol. 20(1), pp. 111–128.

Fagan, J. (1990), "Intoxication and aggression", in: M. Tonry and J.Q. Wilson, editors, *Drugs and Crime: Crime and Justice, A Review of Research*, Vol. 13, Chicago, IL: The University of Chicago Press.

Fagan, J. (1993), "Interactions among drugs, alcohol and violence", *Health Affairs*, Vol. 12(4), pp. 65–79.

Famularo, R.K.S., R. Barnum and R. Wharton (1986), "Alcoholism and severe child maltreatment", *American Journal of Orthopsychiatry*, Vol. 56(3), pp. 481–485.

Felitti, V., R. Anda, D. Nordenberg, D. Williamson, A. Spitz, V. Edwards, M. Koss and J. Marks (1998), "Relationship of childhood abuse and household dysfunction to many of the leading causes of death in adults: the Adverse Childhood Experiences (ACE) study", *American Journal of Preventive Medicine*, Vol. 14(2), pp. 245–250.

Freisthler, B. (2004), "A spatial analysis of social disorganization, alcohol access, and rates of child maltreatment in neighborhoods", *Children & Youth Services Review*, Vol. 26(9), pp. 803–819.

Freisthler, B., B. Needell and P.J. Gruenwald (2005), "Is the physical availability of alcohol and illicit drugs related to neighborhood rates of child maltreatment?", *Child Abuse & Neglect*, Vol. 29(9), pp. 1049–1060.

Gelles, R.J. and C.P. Cornell (1990), *Intimate Violence in Families*, Newbury Park, CA: Sage Publications, Inc.

Grossman, M. (2005), "Individual behaviors and substance use: the role of price", pp. 15–39 in: B. Lindgren and M. Grossman, editors, *Substance Use: Individual Behavior, Social Interaction, Markets and Politics. Volume 16 of Advances in Health Economics and Health Services Research*, Amsterdam: JAI, an imprint of Elsevier Ltd.

Grossman, M., F.J. Chaloupka and I. Sirtalan (1998), "An empirical analysis of alcohol addiction: Results from the monitoring the future panels", *Economic Inquiry*, Vol. 36(1), pp. 39–48.

Johnston, J. and J. Dinardo (1996), *Econometric Methods*, New York: McGraw-Hill.

Kelleher, K.M., J. Chaffin, J. Hollenberg and E. Fisher (1994), "Alcohol and drug disorders among physically abusive and neglectful parents in a community-based sample", *American Journal of Public Health*, Vol. 84(10), pp. 1586–1590.

Markowitz, S. (2000), "The price of alcohol, wife abuse and husband abuse", *Southern Economic Journal*, Vol. 67(2), pp. 279–303.

Markowitz, S. and M. Grossman (1998), "Alcohol regulation and domestic violence towards children", *Contemporary Economic Policy*, Vol. 16(3), pp. 309–320.

Markowitz, S. and M. Grossman (2000), "The effects of beer taxes on physical child abuse", *Journal of Health Economics*, Vol. 19(2), pp. 271–282.

Markowitz, S., P. Chatterji and R. Kaestner (2003), "Estimating the impact of alcohol policies on youth suicide", *Journal of Mental Health Policy and Economics*, Vol. 6(1), pp. 37–46.

Office of Applied Studies, Substance Abuse and Mental Health Services Administration (2003), *The NHSDA Report, Children Living with Substance-Abusing or Substance-Dependent Parents*, U.S. Government Printing Office, Washington, DC.

Paxson, C. and J. Waldfogel (2002), "Work, welfare, and child maltreatment", *Journal of Labor Economics*, Vol. 20(3), pp. 435–474.

Pernanen, K. (1981), "Theoretical aspects of the relationship between alcohol use and crime", pp. 1–69 in: J. Collins, Jr., editor, *Drinking and Crime: Perspectives on the Relationship between Alcohol Consumption and Criminal Behavior*, New York: The Guilford Press.

Puttler, L.I., R.A. Zucker, H.E. Fitzgerald and C.R. Bingham (1998), "Behavioral outcomes among COAs during the early and middle childhood years: familial subtype variations", *Alcoholism: Clinical and Experimental Research*, Vol. 22(9), pp. 1962–1972.

Saffer, H. (1991), "Alcohol advertising bans and alcohol abuse: an international perspective", *Journal of Health Economics*, Vol. 10(1), pp. 65–79.

Seiglie, C. (2004), "Understanding child outcomes: an application to child abuse and neglect", *Review of Economics of the Household*, Vol. 2(2), pp. 143–160.

Smith, C.A., T.O. Ireland and T.P. Thornberry (2005), "Adolescent maltreatment and its impact on young adult antisocial behavior", *Child Abuse & Neglect*, Vol. 29(10), pp. 1099–1119.

Tekin, E. and S. Markowitz (2008), "The relationship between suicidal behavior and productive activities of young adults", *Southern Economic Journal*, Vol. 75(2), pp. 300–331.

U.S. Department of Health and Human Services, Administration for Children and Families, Substance Abuse and Mental Health Services Administration, and Office of the Assistant Secretary for Planning and Evaluation (1999), *Blending Perspectives and Building Common Ground. A Report to Congress on Substance Abuse and Child Protection*, U.S. Government Printing Office, Washington, DC.

U.S. Department of Health and Human Services, Children's Bureau (2000), *National Child Abuse and Neglect Data System (NCANDS) Summary Data Components Survey, 1999 Data Year*, U.S. Government Printing Office, Washington, DC.

Walsh, C., H. MacMillan and E. Jamieson (2002), "The relationship between parental psychiatric disorder and child physical and sexual abuse: findings from the Ontario Health Supplement", *Child Abuse & Neglect*, Vol. 26(1), pp. 11–22.

Widom, C.S. (1989), "The cycle of violence", *Science*, Vol. 244(4910), pp. 160–166.

Wooldridge, J.M. (2002), *Econometric Analysis of Cross Sections and Panel Data*, Cambridge, MA: MIT Press.

Appendix A. State liquor sales status

Monopoly states (markup)	License states (excise tax)
Alabama	Alaska
Idaho	Arizona
Iowa	Arkansas
Maine	California
Michigan	Colorado
Mississippi	Connecticut
Montana	Delaware
New Hampshire	District of Columbia
North Carolina	Florida
Ohio	Georgia
Oregon	Hawaii
Pennsylvania	Illinois
Utah	Indiana
Vermont	Kansas
Virginia	Kentucky
Washington	Louisiana
West Virginia	Maryland
Wyoming	Massachusetts
	Minnesota
	Missouri
	Nebraska
	Nevada
	New Jersey
	New Mexico
	New York
	North Dakota
	Oklahoma
	Rhode Island
	South Carolina
	South Dakota
	Tennessee
	Texas
	Wisconsin

CHAPTER 3

Child Care Choices and Childhood Obesity

Resul Cesur*, Chris M. Herbst and Erdal Tekin

Abstract

Over the past three decades, the U.S. economy experienced a sharp increase in the labor-force participation of women, causing a similar increase in the demand for non-parental child care. Concurrent with these developments has been a dramatic rise in the prevalence of childhood obesity, prompting the question as to what extent the increase in child-care utilization is responsible for the growth in obesity. This chapter examines the impact of various child-care arrangements on school-age children's weight outcomes using panel data from the Early Childhood Longitudinal Study, Kindergarten Cohort (ECLS-K). An advantage of the ECLS-K for our purposes is that it tracks children's child-care arrangements between Kindergarten and the 5th grade. Our fixed-effects' results suggest that non-parental child-care arrangements are not strongly associated with children's weight outcomes. Our findings are robust to numerous sensitivity and subgroup analyses.

Keywords: childhood, obesity, child care

JEL classifications: I12, I18, J13

---

* Corresponding author.

CONTRIBUTIONS TO ECONOMIC ANALYSIS
VOLUME 290 ISSN: 0573-8555
DOI:10.1108/S0573-8555(2010)0000290006

1. Introduction

Over the past three decades, the prevalence of obesity has increased from 5 percent to 10.4 percent among two- to five-year olds and from 6.5 percent to 19.6 percent among 6–11-year olds (Ogden *et al.*, 2008, 2010). Childhood obesity is identified by public health officials as one of the most pressing health problems in the United States (U.S. Department of Health and Human Services, 2001). This alarming trend is also a growing source of concern among the public. In a 2008 nationwide public opinion survey, obesity was identified as the number one health problem among children (Mott, 2009).

This anxiety is justified given the immediate and long-term health and social consequences associated with childhood obesity. For example, obese children and adolescents are more likely to have the precursors of cardiovascular disease, including high cholesterol and blood pressure.[1] Such children are also found to perform worse academically and experience such social and psychological problems as stigmatization, depression, and poor self-esteem (Strauss, 2000; U.S. Surgeon General, 2001; Daniels *et al.*, 2005; Mocan and Tekin, 2010). Finally, obese children are likely to remain obese as adults, and therefore risk developing an array of health problems in the future, including heart disease, type 2 diabetes, stroke, several types of cancer, and osteoarthritis (U.S. Surgeon General, 2001). These health problems impose substantial costs on the U.S. health care system. According to one estimate, the direct medical costs from prescription drugs, emergency room visits, and outpatient services total $14.1 billion annually (Trasande and Chatterjee, 2009). The scale of the economic cost becomes more serious if one also considers the estimated $147 billion per year spent on treating obesity-related illnesses among adults (Finkelstein *et al.*, 2009).

The health and economic costs associated with childhood obesity have spurred a tremendous amount of attention by the research and policy communities devoted to exploring factors that contribute to it. For example, recent studies investigate the role of decreasing food prices (Lakdawalla and Philipson, 2002), the rise in maternal employment (Anderson *et al.*, 2003; Ruhm, 2008), changes in agricultural policies (Cawley and Kirwan, 2005), the development of technology to mass produce and preserve food (Philipson and Posner, 1999), and school-based policies (e.g., school breakfast and lunch program) (Hofferth and Curtin, 2005).

Interestingly, the growing prevalence of childhood obesity coincides with a substantial increase in the percentage of mothers participating in the labor force. Between 1970 and 2000, the labor force participation rate of

---

[1] In a sample of 5- to 17-year olds, 70 percent of obese youth had at least one risk factor for cardiovascular disease (Freedman *et al.*, 2007).

women with children almost doubled, rising from 38 percent to 68 percent (Story *et al.*, 2006). The sharp increase in labor force participation has been followed by an equally dramatic rise in the demand for non-parental child care. Today, of the 35 million children aged six to fourteen, 63 percent spend an average of 21 h per week in the care of someone other than a parent before and after school (Story *et al.*, 2006).

Motivated by the coincident rise in maternal employment and childhood obesity, a strand of empirical work has been devoted to exploring this relationship. Findings from these studies generally suggest that maternal employment is associated with an increase in children's weight outcomes (Anderson *et al.*, 2003; Courtemanche, 2007; Ruhm, 2008; Fertig *et al.*, 2009). For example, Anderson *et al.* (2003) find that increases in hours of maternal work raise the likelihood that children are obese. The authors also find greater effects among children of white mothers, of mothers with more education, and of mothers at higher income levels. Fertig *et al.* (2009) examine the mechanisms through which maternal employment influences children's weight outcomes and find that changes in supervision and nutrition play statistically significant but small roles in the relationship between maternal employment and childhood obesity. Cawley and Liu (2007) find that employed mothers spend significantly less time cooking and playing with their children and are more likely to purchase precooked meals.

The concurrent increase in childhood obesity and the utilization of formal child care raises the relevant question as to what extent the two developments are related to each other. There are numerous reasons why one might observe such a relationship. Given that millions of children spend substantial time in non-parental arrangements before and after they start school, the child care environment has the potential to play an important role in laying the foundation for children's food consumption and exercise patterns. Menu options available in child care settings expose children to a variety of new foods and flavors, which can influence food preferences at home and school (Deckelbaum and Williams, 2001). Structural and process features of the child care environment determine the types and frequency of physical activities in which children are engaged. Finally, child care providers can serve as an effective bridge to aid parents in making healthy food choices at home (Story *et al.*, 2006).

Despite this potential association, research on the effect of child care choices on childhood obesity is limited. An exception is Hubbard (2008), who examines the impact of maternal employment and child care choices on children's weight outcomes using data from the Early Childhood Longitudinal Study, Kindergarten Cohort (ECLS-K). Modeling the employment and child care decisions in a dynamic framework and using a discrete factor random effects estimator, she finds that among the cases of mothers working full-time, the use of non-parental child care significantly increases children's likelihood of being obese and overweight.

The impact of non-parental care on childhood obesity is insignificant among the cases of part-time working mothers. Contrary to previous research, she finds that maternal employment has a negative and statistically significant effect on the likelihood of being obese.

A number of studies focus on the relationship between Head Start attendance and children's weight outcomes. For example, Frisvold (2007) examines the effect of Head Start participation on childhood obesity using data from the Panel Study of Income Dynamics. He finds that Head Start attendance reduces the likelihood of obesity in late-childhood among black children. Similarly, Carneiro and Ginja (2008) find that participation in Head Start reduces the incidence of childhood obesity. Frisvold and Lumeng (in press) use administrative data from Michigan to examine the obesity effects of full-day Head Start attendance compared to half-day attendance. They find that full-day enrollment significantly reduces the proportion of obese children at the end of the academic year. Such findings are not surprising given that Head Start emphasizes quality through the provision of comprehensive child development services. For example, Whitaker *et al.* (2009) show that most Head Start programs report doing more to support healthy eating and gross motor activity than required by federal performance standards in these areas. Also the children enrolled in the Head Start program mostly come from low-income families due to the means-tested nature of Head Start eligibility. Therefore, the findings from these studies cannot necessarily serve as a guide for the impact of parental decisions about child care on childhood obesity.

Several descriptive studies examine the nutritional quality of foods offered in child care settings.[2] A review of these studies suggests that the quality of foods offered in center-based care typically falls below the standards recommended by *The Dietary Guidelines for Americans*.[3] For example, Padget and Briley (2005) compare the dietary intake of children attending center-based care with the recommendations of the Food Guide Pyramid for Young Children. They find that such children generally do not receive an adequate diet, and the intake at home does not compensate for the insufficient consumption of fresh fruits, vegetables, and grains during the time spent in child care. Furthermore, a number of studies show that preschool-age children in various non-parental child care settings do not

[2] Story *et al.* (2006) provide a comprehensive summary of these studies.

[3] A publication put forth every five years by the U.S. Department of Health and Human Services, the *The Dietary Guidelines for Americans,* provide authoritative advice for people aged two and above about the relationship between increased healthy dietary habits and the reduction in the risk of major chronic diseases. This publication also serves as the basis for Federal food and nutrition education programs. Additional information may be found at http://www.health.gov/DietaryGuidelines/.

meet the recommended guidelines for physical activity (Story *et al.*, 2006).[4] However, research suggests that preschools implementing practices aimed at increasing quality in general and physical activity in particular can be successful at reaching this goal. For example, in a study of 266 preschoolers, Dowda *et al.* (2004) find that children in high-quality preschools, as measured by child–staff ratios, teacher education, and structural attributes of the facility, participate in greater amounts of moderate to vigorous physical activity.

In this chapter, we examine the impact of various child care arrangements on school-age children's weight outcomes using panel data from the ECLS-K. We address the potential endogeneity of child care choices using a fixed-effects estimator. Our study differs from Hubbard (2008) in several respects. First, we utilize ECLS-K data from the fall of kindergarten, and the spring of first, third, and fifth grades, while she excluded data from kindergarten wave. Second, she uses a single binary indicator for non-parental child care, which does not allow her to distinguish among various types of arrangements. In particular, her measure is based on the total number of hours children spend in three modes of settings (informal care from a relative, informal care from a babysitter, and center care). She then constructs an indicator for whether a given arrangement was utilized for more than 5 h per week. In this chapter, we employ mutually exclusive and exhaustive groupings of child care arrangements. Specifically, we code children as attending relative care (which includes caregiving inside and outside the child's home), non-relative care (nanny, babysitter, or family-based), center-based care (daycare center), and parental care. Since a non-trivial number of children receive care in multiple arrangements, we focus on the primary arrangement, defined as the one from which the child receives the greatest number of hours of care per week. Third, Hubbard (2008) focuses only on body mass index (BMI) and indicators of overweight and obesity, while we also examine the effect of child care choices on the likelihood of being underweight. Finally, her analysis draws upon the balanced sample of children. Limiting the analyses to a balanced sample may be problematic if sample attrition is non-random. Therefore, we retain observations in the fixed-effects analysis as long as the obesity and child care variables are non-missing for at least two periods.

---

[4] *The Dietary Guidelines for Americans* of 2005 recommend that children and adolescents engage in no less than 60 min of physical activity each day. Furthermore, the National Association for Sport and Physical Education (NASPE) recommends that toddlers receive at least 30 min of structured physical activity and 60 min of unstructured activity each day. Preschoolers should receive 60 min of structured play and another 60 min of unstructured play each day.

The remainder of this chapter is organized as follows. Section 2 describes the empirical specification. Section 3 introduces the data used in the analyses and Section 4 discusses the results. Section 5 concludes the chapter.

2. Empirical specification

Our goal is to investigate the relationship between the choice of child care arrangements and school-age children's weight outcomes. This relationship can be expressed by the following regression model:

$$W_{it} = \alpha_0 + C_{it}\alpha_1 + X_{it}\alpha_2 + \omega_t + v_i + \varepsilon_{it} \tag{1}$$

where W_{it} is one of our weight outcomes for child i in grade t; C_{it} is a vector of child care arrangements; X_{it} is a vector of exogenous determinants of children's weight at the child and family level; and ω_t represents a vector of grade fixed effects that account for national curriculum changes influencing children's weight. For example, as more children become obese during the analysis period, concerns about the problem are likely to be heightened and become more widely known to policy-makers and the public. If, as a result, child care policy was assigned an increased role in the fight against obesity during the same period, the grade fixed effects would account for such nationwide effects.

Finally, the v_i represents a vector of child- or family-specific time-invariant unobserved characteristics that may be associated with children's weight outcomes. For example, there may be unobserved genetic characteristics that predispose some children to weight problems (Ding *et al.*, 2006). Alternatively, the v_i represents unobserved family resources or parenting style that influences the development of overweight and obesity. Some of these unobservables may also be correlated with parental decisions regarding child care arrangements. For example, a parent who understands the role of TV exposure or other sedentary activities in influencing children's weight may have a preference for center-based care over relative or family day care if she believes that the former is more effective at promoting physical activity and limiting TV exposure. Failure to control for these unobserved preferences may lead to biased estimates of the impact of child care arrangements on childhood obesity. Finally, there might be unobserved demographic, economic, and policy differences across states and localities that are correlated with both child care choices and children's weight outcomes.[5] For example, if a given state identifies childhood obesity as a particularly serious

[5] There are very few parents moving to other states during the analysis period in ECLS-K and a majority of these parents drop from the sample automatically as they are not followed.

problem, it may require certain child care establishments to implement formal practices to ensure healthy eating and physical activity patterns. Failure to account for this policy heterogeneity would further bias the estimates on child care arrangements if parents respond to these policies by placing their children in the regulated services.

We therefore account for time-invariant individual- and family-level unobserved heterogeneity by including child fixed effects in Eq. (1). The fixed-effects approach requires panel data, or repeated observations on children, so that the set of individual time-permanent unobservables can be eliminated. While the child-fixed effects approach effectively removes all unobserved heterogeneity that is stable over time, this method does have a number of limitations. First, it does not eliminate time-varying heterogeneity. For example, if a parent becomes more aware of the health risks associated with obesity, she may adjust her parenting style at home or choose different child care arrangements so that her child is exposed to less TV, becomes more physically active, and consumes more fresh fruits and vegetables. Such time-varying changes in parental preferences would still bias the estimated effects of child care arrangements on childhood obesity. Second, child fixed effects produce coefficient estimates only for variables that vary over time, thereby eliminating from the model some factors of interest to the researcher. Finally, measurement error in the explanatory variables can exacerbate attenuation bias when using child fixed effects.

In order to assess the extent of bias from time-invariant unobserved heterogeneity, we estimate versions of Eq. (1) with and without the child fixed effects. We also take a number of steps to guard against sources of time-varying unobservables that may bias our estimates of child care arrangements in the child fixed-effects models. First, we exploit the richness of the ECLS-K and control for a large number of time-varying child and family characteristics, including children's age, the presence of disabilities, and family structure and socioeconomic status (SES). Second, we incorporate period (or grade) effects to capture year-specific policy or economic shocks that may influence parental decisions on child care and children's weight outcomes.[6]

In some of our pooled Ordinary Least Squares (OLS) specifications, we incorporate county fixed effects to account for unobserved differences across states and localities that might be correlated with both parents' child care choices and children's weight outcomes. Given that state-level economic and policy conditions are identical for children in the same

[6] See Table A.1 for a full list of the time-variant and -invariant variables used in the OLS. The ECLS-K produces an index of SES, which combines mother's and father's education, mother's and father's occupational status, and total family income.

county, these factors are automatically controlled for and are not needed in the model. This is particularly important for states' social policy environment, including recent welfare reforms, expansions to the Earned Income Tax Credit (EITC), and pre-kindergarten initiatives, all of which may influence parents' decisions on child care and children's well-being. In addition, to the extent that the availability of fast food restaurants, supermarkets, and parks is unevenly distributed across the states, inclusion of county fixed effects will control for these factors as well. Another advantage is that any substate-level variation in families' demographic characteristics, physical activity and food options, or the social policy environment is captured by the county fixed effects.

3. Data

The data used in this chapter come from the ECLS-K, a nationally representative survey of 21,260 children entering kindergarten in the fall of 1998.[7] Children in the ECLS-K are followed through the eighth grade, with detailed parent, child, and teacher interviews conducted in the fall of kindergarten (1998) and the spring of first (2000), third (2002), fifth (2004), and eighth (2007) grades. An average of more than 20 children per school from over 1,200 public and private schools are included in the sample.

The analyses in this chapter use data from the fall of kindergarten and the spring of first, third, and fifth grades. Observations with data missing on BMI and child care arrangements are excluded from the sample. We further limit our sample to children living in one- or two-parent households in which the biological mother is present for the entire survey period.[8] The models also include binary variables for the missing data. Applying these criteria results in a sample of 48,870 observations.[9] About 33 percent of these observations come from fall of kindergarten, while the percentage of observations from the spring of first, third, and fifth grades represent about 26 percent, 22 percent, and 19 percent of the full sample, respectively. Therefore, our analysis sample is unbalanced. Any child appearing at least twice in our sample with non-missing obesity and child care variables

---

[7] The ECLS-K is sponsored by the U.S. Department of Education. For more information, see the ECLS-K website at http://nces.ed.gov/ecls/kindergarten.asp.

[8] Specifically, the children in our sample either lived with their biological mother or with their biological father and a biological or step father. Therefore, children in father-only households or those in households in which the mother figure is someone other than the biological mother are excluded from the analyses sample.

[9] The National Center for Educational Statistics requires number of observations to be rounded to the nearest ten when the restricted version of the ECLS-K is used without sample weights.

contributes to the fixed-effects analysis. Thus, child-specific fixed effects control for any time-invariant unobserved factors leading to some children dropping out of the sample. If sample attrition is non-random, then limiting the sample to a balanced sample would lead to biased estimates. In robustness analyses, we therefore estimate the main model using a balanced sample to assess the impact of sample attrition. Results from this balanced sample are consistent with the main findings. Since the identification of child care effects relies on within-child variation in child care arrangements, it is important to confirm that there is sufficient variation in these variables over time. Of the 48,870 child-time observations, only 11,480 (23.5 percent) come from children who never changed their child care arrangement.[10]

Our outcome variables are based on the BMI, which is calculated as weight in kilograms divided by height in meters squared. In addition to using the BMI, we estimate models using binary indicators of underweight, overweight, and obesity. One advantage of the ECLS-K is that children's BMI is available in each wave and is based on measured values of height and weight. For children aged 2–19, the BMI values are plotted on age- (in months) and gender-specific growth charts from the Centers for Disease Control and Prevention (CDC) to determine the corresponding BMI-for-age percentile. Children at or below the fifth percentile of the gender- and age-specific BMI distribution are coded as underweight. Children are coded as overweight or obese if their age- and gender-specific BMIs exceed the 85th percentile and 95th percentiles, respectively.

Our key independent variable is the primary child care arrangement used for the child during that survey year. The ECLS-K produces a composite variable indicating the primary child care arrangement in which the child spends the most time per week at the time of the interview. The values of this variable are: (0) no non-parental care; (1) relative care in child's home; (2) relative care in another home; (3) non-relative care in child's home; (4) non-relative care in another home; (5) center-based care; (6) two or more programs; and (7) varying location of care. Using these categories, we create mutually exclusive groupings of child care arrangements in the following manner: Children in no non-parental care arrangement are defined as using parental care. We combine categories (1) and (2) for relative care arrangements, such as care by a grandparent. Categories (3) and (4) are merged into a single group called non-relative care, which includes nanny or babysitter and family day care, and category

---

[10] Of the 11,480 observations, 7,640 belong to parental care, 1,760 observations are from relative care, and the remaining 600 and 1,480 are from non-relative/non-parental and center care, respectively.

Table 1. Summary statistics for obesity and child care arrangements

	Full sample	Parent care	Relative care	Non-relative care	Center care
Variable					
Body mass index	17.760	17.787	18.172	17.193	17.426
	(3.699)	(3.698)	(4.020)	(3.158)	(3.468)
Child is overweight (percent)	0.309	0.300	0.360	0.288	0.288
	(0.462)	(0.458)	(0.480)	(0.453)	(0.453)
Child is obese (percent)	0.154	0.149	0.190	0.135	0.138
	(0.361)	(0.356)	(0.393)	(0.341)	(0.345)
Child is underweight (percent)	0.032	0.033	0.029	0.034	0.033
	(0.177)	(0.179)	(0.167)	(0.181)	(0.178)
Primary type of child care					
Parent care (percent)	0.595	1	0	0	0
	(0.491)				
Relative care (percent)	0.184	0	1	0	0
	(0.387)				
Non-relative care (percent)	0.075	0	0	1	0
	(0.263)				
Center care (percent)	0.147	0	0	0	1
	(0.354)				
Survey wave dummies					
Kindergarten – fall dummy (percent)	0.325	0.292	0.330	0.453	0.390
	(0.469)	(0.455)	(0.470)	(0.498)	(0.488)
First grade – spring dummy (percent)	0.262	0.256	0.267	0.285	0.265
	(0.439)	(0.436)	(0.443)	(0.452)	(0.442)
Third grade – spring dummy (percent)	0.224	0.239	0.210	0.163	0.208
	(0.417)	(0.427)	(0.407)	(0.370)	(0.406)
Fifth grade – spring dummy (percent)	0.190	0.213	0.193	0.099	0.137
	(0.392)	(0.409)	(0.395)	(0.299)	(0.343)
Observations	48,870	29,050	8,980	3,660	7,180

Note: Standard deviations in parentheses.

(5) remains center care. We delete children in categories (6) and (7), which account for less than 2 percent of the overall sample.

Table 1 presents summary statistics for the weight outcomes and child care arrangements. The average BMI in our full sample is 17.8. Approximately 31 percent of children in our sample are overweight and 15 percent are obese. The proportion of children who are underweight is 3 percent. These figures are consistent with the national statistics cited earlier. Approximately 60 percent of the school-age children do not participate in any non-parental child care as their primary arrangement. Relative care constitutes the primary child care arrangement for about 18 percent of children, followed by center-based care, which is used by 15 percent of children. The remaining 7.5 percent of children enroll in non-relative care. A comparison of the weight outcomes by child care type reveals that children cared for by relatives have higher BMIs, are more likely to be overweight and obese, and are less likely to be underweight than those in other child care environments. For example, fully 36 percent of such children are overweight and 19 percent are obese, compared to 29 percent and 14 percent, respectively, for children in other non-parental child care modes. Interestingly, there appears to be no significant differences in overweight, obesity, and underweight prevalence across the other child care arrangements.

Our OLS models include a large set of control variables. The list includes child's age, gender, race, birthweight, and indicator for whether the child was born prematurely, disability status of the child, whether the child lives in a single or two parent household, mother's work status, indicators of families' SES, parents' expectations regarding the child's prospects for finishing high-school and college, number of siblings, indicators of the type of the residential location (city, suburban, town, or rural), and grade dummies. In some of the OLS specifications, we also control for county fixed effects. Note that any of these control variables that are time-invariant drop out of the child fixed-effects models.

Descriptive statistics for the covariates by the type of child care mode are displayed in Table 2. Raw differences in the means suggest that children cared for by their relatives come from poor social and economic backgrounds, which is consistent with their relatively high rates of overweight and obesity as presented in Table 1. For example, relative care is the dominant arrangement among black children and those living with low-educated mothers. On the other hand, relative care is the least utilized mode of care by white children, who are primarily cared for in non-relative care settings. Center care appears to be more common among children living with their biological mother only. It is also more heavily utilized by mothers employed full-time and more common among children from high SES.

4. Results

Our discussion of the empirical results begins with several OLS regressions constituting a baseline for the estimates obtained from child fixed-effects regressions. In all cases, we report robust standard errors clustered at the child level. As displayed in Table 3, we present the OLS results in different panels, each containing estimates for the relationship between child care choices and children's weight outcomes for a different specification. In Panel A, we use a single binary indicator for any participation in a non-parental child care. Panel B disaggregates the single binary indicator used in Panel A into three categories: relative care, non-relative care, and center care. Parental care serves as the omitted category. Panel C adds a rich vector of family and child characteristics that might be correlated with

Table 2. Descriptive statistics

Variable	Full sample	Parent care	Relative care	Non-relative care	Center care
Number of hours spent in non-parental care	5.732 (10.181)	0.000 (0.000)	15.325 (13.353)	14.523 (12.022)	12.448 (8.746)
Child has disability (percent)	0.172 (0.377)	0.175 (0.380)	0.159 (0.366)	0.161 (0.368)	0.177 (0.382)
Child lives with bio mother and father (omitted, percent)	0.718 (0.450)	0.793 (0.406)	0.555 (0.497)	0.689 (0.463)	0.636 (0.481)
Child lives with bio mother and other father (percent)	0.087 (0.282)	0.079 (0.270)	0.103 (0.303)	0.098 (0.298)	0.094 (0.291)
Child lives with bio mother (percent)	0.195 (0.396)	0.129 (0.335)	0.343 (0.475)	0.212 (0.409)	0.270 (0.444)
Boy (percent)	0.508 (0.500)	0.511 (0.500)	0.501 (0.500)	0.485 (0.500)	0.513 (0.500)
Child age in months	95.362 (24.931)	97.646 (25.167)	94.949 (25.075)	86.982 (21.876)	90.911 (23.684)
Race/Ethnicity: white (omitted, percent)	0.602 (0.490)	0.627 (0.484)	0.463 (0.499)	0.718 (0.450)	0.615 (0.487)
Race/Ethnicity: black (percent)	0.117 (0.321)	0.087 (0.283)	0.203 (0.402)	0.069 (0.253)	0.153 (0.360)
Race/Ethnicity: Hispanic (percent)	0.174 (0.379)	0.179 (0.383)	0.200 (0.400)	0.142 (0.349)	0.136 (0.343)
Race/Ethnicity: Asian (percent)	0.056 (0.230)	0.056 (0.230)	0.071 (0.256)	0.033 (0.179)	0.048 (0.214)
Race/Ethnicity: other (percent)	0.051 (0.219)	0.049 (0.217)	0.063 (0.243)	0.038 (0.191)	0.047 (0.212)
Birth weight in 250 g	13.487 (2.355)	13.536 (2.361)	13.333 (2.364)	13.550 (2.326)	13.445 (2.326)
Child is born more than two weeks premature (percent)	0.164 (0.371)	0.161 (0.367)	0.168 (0.374)	0.160 (0.367)	0.176 (0.381)
Current mother does not work (omitted, percent)	0.289 (0.453)	0.434 (0.496)	0.084 (0.277)	0.056 (0.229)	0.077 (0.266)
Current mother works full-time (percent)	0.479 (0.500)	0.303 (0.460)	0.731 (0.443)	0.713 (0.452)	0.755 (0.430)
Current mother works part-time (percent)	0.232 (0.422)	0.263 (0.440)	0.185 (0.388)	0.231 (0.421)	0.169 (0.375)
Family SES in first quintile (percent)	0.159 (0.366)	0.176 (0.381)	0.184 (0.388)	0.104 (0.305)	0.091 (0.288)
Family SES in second quintile (percent)	0.184 (0.387)	0.176 (0.381)	0.245 (0.430)	0.168 (0.374)	0.145 (0.352)
Family SES in third quintile (percent)	0.197 (0.398)	0.182 (0.386)	0.238 (0.426)	0.205 (0.403)	0.202 (0.402)
Family SES in fourth quintile (percent)	0.216 (0.412)	0.214 (0.410)	0.195 (0.396)	0.225 (0.418)	0.246 (0.431)
Family SES in fifth quintile (omitted, percent)	0.244 (0.429)	0.252 (0.434)	0.137 (0.344)	0.299 (0.458)	0.316 (0.465)
Parent expects HS or less for child (omitted, percent)	0.087 (0.282)	0.093 (0.290)	0.102 (0.303)	0.062 (0.242)	0.058 (0.234)
Parent expects some college for child (percent)	0.143 (0.350)	0.139 (0.346)	0.170 (0.375)	0.157 (0.364)	0.117 (0.322)

Table 2. (Continued)

Variable	Full sample	Parent care	Relative care	Non-relative care	Center care
Parent expects BA for child (percent)	0.510	0.508	0.476	0.526	0.553
	(0.500)	(0.500)	(0.500)	(0.499)	(0.497)
Parent expects >BA for child (percent)	0.260	0.261	0.252	0.255	0.272
	(0.439)	(0.439)	(0.434)	(0.436)	(0.445)
Only child (omitted, percent)	0.134	0.096	0.174	0.160	0.229
	(0.341)	(0.294)	(0.379)	(0.367)	(0.420)
One sibling (percent)	0.429	0.404	0.422	0.496	0.500
	(0.495)	(0.491)	(0.494)	(0.500)	(0.500)
Two siblings (percent)	0.282	0.312	0.260	0.256	0.203
	(0.450)	(0.463)	(0.438)	(0.436)	(0.402)
Three siblings (percent)	0.103	0.125	0.094	0.068	0.046
	(0.304)	(0.330)	(0.292)	(0.251)	(0.209)
Four or more siblings (percent)	0.052	0.064	0.051	0.021	0.022
	(0.222)	(0.244)	(0.219)	(0.144)	(0.148)
Large or midsize city (omitted, percent)	0.384	0.375	0.396	0.336	0.435
	(0.487)	(0.484)	(0.489)	(0.472)	(0.496)
Large or midsize suburb (percent)	0.395	0.400	0.357	0.414	0.413
	(0.489)	(0.490)	(0.479)	(0.493)	(0.492)
Large or small town, or rural (percent)	0.221	0.226	0.247	0.251	0.153
	(0.415)	(0.418)	(0.431)	(0.434)	(0.360)
Observations	48,870	29,050	8,980	3,660	7,180

Note: Standard deviations in parentheses.

children's weight outcomes. Finally, Panel D incorporates county fixed effects to further account for local policy, economic, and demographic differences affecting childhood obesity. In each panel, we present estimates on the continuous measure of BMI as well as binary indicators of overweight, obese, and underweight categories. To economize on space, we only present coefficients on the child care choice variables. Full results from the most comprehensive specification (Panel D) are displayed in Table A.1.

In Panel A of Table 3, in which all three non-parental child care modes are aggregated into one category, the estimates indicate that non-parental care is associated with a higher BMI, a higher likelihood of being overweight and obese, and a lower likelihood of being underweight. However, these estimates impose the assumption that all types of non-parental child care have the same association with children's weight outcomes.

When we allow the effects to differ by the type of care in Panel B, the estimates suggest that it is the relative care that is associated with a higher BMI and a higher likelihood of being obese and overweight compared to parental care. The estimates on non-relative and center care are small and statistically insignificant. A comparison of estimates in Panels B, C, and D implies that the effect sizes become smaller as control variables are added to the models for all the outcomes except for underweight. Specifically,

Table 3. OLS results for the relationship between child care choices and children's weight outcomes

	(1)	(2)	(3)	(4)
	BMI	Overweight	Obese	Underweight
Panel A				
Any non-parental care	0.264***	0.031***	0.021***	−0.004**
	(0.040)	(0.005)	(0.004)	(0.002)
Child and family characteristics	No	No	No	No
County fixed effects	No	No	No	No
R^2	0.186	0.013	0.012	0.002
Panel B				
Relative care	0.531***	0.065***	0.046***	−0.005**
	(0.055)	(0.007)	(0.006)	(0.002)
Non-relative care	0.053	0.009	0.002	−0.003
	(0.063)	(0.010)	(0.007)	(0.003)
Center care	0.032	−0.000	−0.001	−0.003
	(0.053)	(0.007)	(0.006)	(0.003)
Child and family characteristics	No	No	No	No
County fixed effects	No	No	No	No
R^2	0.188	0.015	0.014	0.002
Panel C				
Relative care	0.328***	0.041***	0.028***	−0.006**
	(0.055)	(0.007)	(0.006)	(0.002)
Non-relative care	0.094	0.010	0.005	−0.003
	(0.061)	(0.009)	(0.007)	(0.003)
Center care	0.046	−0.003	−0.002	−0.004
	(0.053)	(0.007)	(0.006)	(0.003)
Child and family characteristics	Yes	Yes	Yes	Yes
County fixed effects	No	No	No	No
R^2	0.224	0.046	0.039	0.012
Panel D				
Relative care	0.304***	0.039***	0.025***	−0.005**
	(0.055)	(0.007)	(0.006)	(0.002)
Non-relative care	0.058	0.007	0.003	−0.001
	(0.062)	(0.009)	(0.007)	(0.003)
Center care	0.068	−0.000	−0.000	−0.005*
	(0.054)	(0.007)	(0.006)	(0.003)
Child and family characteristics	Yes	Yes	Yes	Yes
County fixed effects	Yes	Yes	Yes	Yes
R^2	0.240	0.065	0.055	0.040
Observations	48,870	48,870	48,870	48,870

Note: Robust standard errors, clustered at child level, are in parentheses.
*, **, *** indicate that the coefficient is statistically significant at the 0.10, 0.05, and 0.01 levels, respectively.

between the specifications with no control variables (Panel B) and those with both county fixed effects and child and family controls (Panel D), the estimates decline in magnitude by 40–45 percent for BMI, overweight, and underweight. The estimates in the underweight model, on the other hand, remain fixed as more controls are added to the model.

Focusing on the estimates in Panel D, relative care is associated with a higher BMI by 0.304 points compared to parental care. Children in relative care are 4 and 2.5 percentage points more likely to be overweight and obese, respectively, than children in parental care. These children are also 0.5 percentage points less likely to be underweight than their counterparts in parental care. None of the other estimates are statistically significant in any of the weight models, except for the center care, which is statistically significant at the 10 percent level and associated with a small decrease in the likelihood of underweight. All other coefficients are statistically insignificant and too small in magnitude to have any noteworthy implications.

Results from the OLS models are consistent with the descriptive statistics suggesting that relative care is associated with a higher BMI and a higher likelihood of becoming overweight and obese. There appear to be no statistically significant differences in the obesity outcomes of children in parental care and those in non-relative or center environments. However, these estimates may be biased due to unobserved heterogeneity correlated with both child care arrangements and children's weight outcomes. Even after controlling for a large number of covariates and county fixed effects, it is no guarantee that one eliminates potential biases.

In Table 4, we present results from the child-fixed effects model, which eliminates all sources of time-invariant unobserved heterogeneity. To guard against potential bias from any remaining time-varying heterogeneity, we

Table 4. The fixed-effects estimates of the effect of child care choices on children's weight outcomes

	(1)	(2)	(3)	(4)
	BMI	Overweight	Obese	Underweight
Relative care	0.004	0.001	0.008	0.002
	(0.046)	(0.007)	(0.006)	(0.004)
Non-relative care	0.061	0.005	−0.000	0.001
	(0.059)	(0.010)	(0.007)	(0.005)
Center care	0.055	−0.008	0.002	−0.005
	(0.052)	(0.008)	(0.006)	(0.004)
Observations	48,870	48,870	48,870	48,870
R^2	0.872	0.779	0.788	0.566

Note: Robust standard errors, clustered at child level, are in parentheses.

*, **, *** indicate that the coefficient is statistically significant at the 0.10, 0.05, and 0.01 levels, respectively.

Table 5. The fixed-effects estimates of the effect of child care choices on children's weight outcomes-balanced panel

	(1)	(2)	(3)	(4)
	BMI	Overweight	Obese	Underweight
Relative care	0.009	0.007	0.009	0.005
	(0.058)	(0.009)	(0.007)	(0.004)
Non-relative care	0.069	0.009	0.001	−0.002
	(0.074)	(0.012)	(0.009)	(0.006)
Center care	0.118*	0.002	0.008	−0.009*
	(0.063)	(0.010)	(0.007)	(0.005)
Observations	24,060	24,060	24,060	24,060
R^2	0.849	0.731	0.745	0.466

Note: Robust standard errors, clustered at child level, are in parentheses.
*, **, *** indicate that the coefficient is statistically significant at the 0.10, 0.05, and 0.01 levels, respectively.

Table 6. The fixed-effects estimates of the effect of child care choices on children's weight outcomes

	(1)	(2)	(3)	(4)
	BMI	Overweight	Obese	Underweight
Mother's employment status controlled				
Relative care	0.014	0.002	0.008	0.001
	(0.047)	(0.007)	(0.006)	(0.004)
Non-relative care	0.071	0.006	−0.000	−0.000
	(0.059)	(0.010)	(0.007)	(0.005)
Center care	0.064	−0.007	0.002	−0.005
	(0.052)	(0.008)	(0.006)	(0.004)
Observations	48,870	48,870	48,870	48,870
R^2	0.872	0.779	0.788	0.566
Number of hours spent in non-parental care controlled				
Relative care	0.114	−0.010	0.008	0.007
	(0.083)	(0.013)	(0.010)	(0.007)
Non-relative care	0.172*	−0.006	−0.001	0.006
	(0.092)	(0.015)	(0.011)	(0.008)
Center care	0.162*	−0.018	0.001	−0.000
	(0.085)	(0.013)	(0.010)	(0.007)
Observations	48,870	48,870	48,870	48,870
R^2	0.872	0.779	0.788	0.566

Note: Robust standard errors, clustered at child level, are in parentheses.
*, **, *** indicate that the coefficient is statistically significant at the 0.10, 0.05, and 0.01 levels, respectively.

Table 7. The fixed-effects estimates of the effect of child care choices on children's weight outcomes

	(1)	(2)	(3)	(4)
	BMI	Overweight	Obese	Underweight
Boys				
Relative care	−0.016	0.003	0.012	0.002
	(0.067)	(0.011)	(0.008)	(0.005)
Non-relative care	0.033	−0.003	−0.008	−0.002
	(0.085)	(0.015)	(0.011)	(0.008)
Center care	−0.020	−0.019	−0.007	−0.006
	(0.072)	(0.012)	(0.008)	(0.006)
Observations	24,800	24,800	24,800	24,800
R^2	0.869	0.771	0.788	0.545
Girls				
Relative care	0.026	−0.000	0.005	0.002
	(0.064)	(0.010)	(0.007)	(0.005)
Non-relative care	0.086	0.012	0.007	0.004
	(0.081)	(0.013)	(0.010)	(0.007)
Center care	0.132*	0.004	0.010	−0.004
	(0.074)	(0.011)	(0.009)	(0.006)
Observations	24,060	24,060	24,060	24,060
R^2	0.876	0.787	0.789	0.586

Note: Robust standard errors, clustered at child level, are in parentheses.
*, **, *** indicate that the coefficient is statistically significant at the 0.10, 0.05, and 0.01 levels, respectively.

include in these models the control variables that vary between grades, such as socioeconomics. According to the estimates presented in Table 4, any non-parental child care participation, regardless of the type, appears to have no effect on children's weight outcomes once the time-invariant unobserved heterogeneity is accounted for. Unlike the OLS results presented in Table 3, estimates on relative care become zero and no longer statistically significant. In fact, none of the coefficients in Table 4 are large enough to have any significant policy implications. Taken together, the fixed-effects results suggest that the raw differences observed in children's weight outcomes are not the result of child experiences, but rather due to differences in observed and unobserved characteristics of children and their families.[11]

In order to assess the sensitivity of our results to using a balanced panel, we estimate the child fixed effects models after limiting the sample to children who participated in all four waves of the ECLS-K. This results in

[11] Adding child-specific linear time trends to our fixed-effects model does not change any of the current results.

Table 8.* *The fixed-effects estimates of the effect of child care choices on children's weight outcomes

	(1) BMI	(2) Overweight	(3) Obese	(4) Underweight
Whites				
Relative care	−0.059	0.002	0.001	0.002
	(0.062)	(0.010)	(0.008)	(0.005)
Non-relative care	−0.049	0.007	−0.007	−0.000
	(0.069)	(0.012)	(0.009)	(0.006)
Center care	0.012	−0.010	−0.001	−0.008
	(0.063)	(0.010)	(0.008)	(0.005)
Observations	29,420	29,420	29,420	29,420
R^2	0.862	0.765	0.776	0.542
Blacks				
Relative care	0.094	0.001	0.018	−0.004
	(0.138)	(0.019)	(0.016)	(0.009)
Non-relative care	−0.033	−0.031	0.013	0.001
	(0.238)	(0.036)	(0.030)	(0.018)
Center care	0.006	−0.011	−0.000	−0.002
	(0.170)	(0.023)	(0.019)	(0.013)
Observations	5,710	5,710	5,710	5,710
R^2	0.888	0.805	0.791	0.629

Note: Robust standard errors, clustered at child level, are in parentheses.
*, **, *** indicate that the coefficient is statistically significant at the 0.10, 0.05, and 0.01 levels, respectively.

a reduction of the sample size by about half. As presented in Table 5, the estimates from the balanced panel are largely consistent with those from the unbalanced panel, suggesting that the effects of non-parental child care modes on children's weight outcomes are small and not different from those of parental child care. The only exception to this is center care, which is now associated with a reduction in the likelihood of underweight by 0.9 percentage points and significant at the 10 percent level. Center care is also associated with an increase in BMI of 0.12 points. Even though two of the coefficients for center care are now estimated with some precision, they are nevertheless still small in magnitude, and do not change the implications obtained from the unbalanced panel.

In Table 6, we continue to check the robustness of our findings by including two key control variables in the fixed-effects model. In the upper panel, we control for the mother's employment status. Since child care decisions are typically made in conjunction with the employment decision, one of the primary channels through which child care choices can exert an influence on children's weight outcomes is through maternal employment. By controlling for the mother's employment status, we attempt to obtain the effect of child care choices on children's weight

Table 9. The fixed-effects estimates of the effect of child care choices on children's weight outcomes

	(1)	(2)	(3)	(4)
	BMI	Overweight	Obese	Underweight
Non-working mothers				
Relative care	0.023	0.010	0.023	0.004
	(0.195)	(0.031)	(0.022)	(0.016)
Non-relative care	0.116	0.058	0.011	0.004
	(0.273)	(0.048)	(0.036)	(0.035)
Center care	0.149	0.003	−0.005	0.021
	(0.208)	(0.032)	(0.025)	(0.020)
Observations	14,010	14,010	14,010	14,010
R^2	0.910	0.846	0.855	0.705
Working mothers				
Relative care	0.040	0.009	0.009	0.001
	(0.056)	(0.009)	(0.007)	(0.004)
Non-relative care	0.111	0.005	0.000	−0.002
	(0.069)	(0.012)	(0.008)	(0.006)
Center care	0.081	−0.005	0.002	−0.009*
	(0.061)	(0.010)	(0.007)	(0.005)
Observations	34,510	34,510	34,510	34,510
R^2	0.887	0.799	0.810	0.591

Note: Robust standard errors, clustered at child level, are in parentheses.
*, **, *** indicate that the coefficient is statistically significant at the 0.10, 0.05, and 0.01 levels, respectively.

outcomes net of the influence of mothers' labor force decisions. As illustrated in Table 6, this exercise does not produce any different results. All of the estimates on non-parental child care arrangements continue to be small and imprecisely estimated. However, one should interpret these results with caution, as the maternal employment is likely to be endogenous.[12]

The models so far assume that the intensity of non-parental care is the same across all three types. That is, once a child uses a certain type of care as the primary arrangement, it does matter how many hours he or she spends in it. However, there are slight differences in the average number of hours spent in non-parental child care modes as illustrated in Table 2. For example, children whose primary arrangement is center care spend about 12.4 h per week on average in this care, while those in relative and non-relative care spend about 15.3 and 14.5 h per week in these modes,

[12] See Hubbard (2008) for an exercise accounting for the endogeneity of both maternal employment and child care arrangements.

Table 10. ***The fixed-effects estimates of the effect of child care choices on children's weight outcomes***

	(1)	(2)	(3)	(4)
	BMI	Overweight	Obese	Underweight
Bottom quintile				
Relative care	−0.001	−0.015	0.004	0.019*
	(0.140)	(0.021)	(0.017)	(0.010)
Non-relative care	−0.184	−0.080**	−0.016	0.001
	(0.223)	(0.039)	(0.030)	(0.022)
Center care	0.014	−0.020	0.001	0.000
	(0.188)	(0.031)	(0.022)	(0.012)
Observations	7,790	7,790	7,790	7,790
R^2	0.910	0.827	0.844	0.690
Top quintile				
Relative care	0.020	0.008	−0.000	−0.012
	(0.112)	(0.020)	(0.014)	(0.011)
Non-relative care	0.022	0.019	0.014	−0.009
	(0.111)	(0.019)	(0.015)	(0.012)
Center care	0.016	−0.003	0.007	−0.016*
	(0.096)	(0.016)	(0.013)	(0.009)
Observations	11,920	11,920	11,920	11,920
R^2	0.876	0.790	0.787	0.615

Note: Robust standard errors, clustered at child level, are in parentheses.
*, **, *** indicate that the coefficient is statistically significant at the 0.10, 0.05, and 0.01 levels, respectively.

respectively. To account for these differences, we control for the number of hours spent in non-parental care in the fixed-effects models. As presented in the bottom panel of Table 6, controlling for this variable does not lead to any meaningful changes in the estimates.

In the next five tables, we present results from a number of subgroup analyses. In Table 7, we present the fixed-effects results separately for boys and girls. There appear to be no appreciable differences in the impact of child care choices on weight outcomes across boys and girls. For both groups, the estimates continue to be very small and statistically indistinguishable from zero. In Table 8, we present results separately across white and black children. Again, allowing the effects of child care choices on weight outcomes to be different between white and black children does not cause any changes to our main findings. In our third subgroup analysis, we estimate models separately for working and non-working mothers. As presented in Table 9, the current findings largely hold when we estimate models separately for working and non-working mothers, except that there is a small reduction in the likelihood of underweight for children using center care as their primary mode of care.

Table 11. The fixed-effects estimates of the effect of child care choices on children's weight outcomes

	(1)	(2)	(3)	(4)
	BMI	Overweight	Obese	Underweight
Single mothers				
Relative care	−0.005	−0.008	0.023	0.006
	(0.116)	(0.018)	(0.015)	(0.009)
Non-relative care	0.162	0.022	0.032	0.021
	(0.173)	(0.030)	(0.025)	(0.015)
Center care	−0.125	−0.017	−0.009	−0.004
	(0.144)	(0.021)	(0.018)	(0.012)
Observations	9,530	9,530	9,530	9,530
R^2	0.911	0.836	0.835	0.691
Married mothers				
Relative care	−0.001	0.006	0.002	0.001
	(0.055)	(0.009)	(0.007)	(0.005)
Non-relative care	0.046	0.006	−0.011	−0.004
	(0.067)	(0.011)	(0.008)	(0.006)
Center care	0.105*	−0.003	0.003	−0.006
	(0.060)	(0.009)	(0.007)	(0.005)
Observations	39,340	39,340	39,340	39,340
R^2	0.876	0.786	0.795	0.577

Note: Robust standard errors, clustered at child level, are in parentheses.
*, **, *** indicate that the coefficient is statistically significant at the 0.10, 0.05, and 0.01 levels, respectively.

In Table 10, we present results separately for children in the bottom and top quintiles of the SES distribution. This exercise reveals that children from the bottom quintile of the SES distribution are about 2 percentage points more likely to be underweight than children in parental care if their primary mode of care is relative care. In addition, the children in the bottom quintile are 8 percentage points less likely to be overweight if their primary mode of care is non-relative care. The coefficients on center care are very small and statistically insignificant. For children in the top quintile of the SES distribution, the only statistically significant effect applies to center care in the underweight model, which indicates that center care is associated with a reduction in the likelihood of underweight by 1.6 percentage points. Again, the remaining coefficients are small and imprecisely estimated.

Finally, we report results separately for children living with single biological mothers and married biological mothers. As shown in Table 11, allowing the effects of child care choices on children's weight outcomes to differ between children of single and married mothers does not cause any changes to our main findings. None of the estimates are large enough to have any meaningful implications and statistically significant at conventional levels.

5. Conclusion

Motivated by the simultaneous rise in the use of non-parental child care arrangements and childhood obesity in the United States over the last three decades, this chapter seeks to understand to what extent non-parental child care is responsible for the sharp increase in childhood obesity. We do not find evidence to support the hypothesis that the two developments are related. Although the OLS findings point to a positive association between relative care and obesity and a negative association between relative care and the likelihood of underweight among school-age children, we show that this relationship is due to the endogeneity of the child care choice; parents and children using relative care differ in many ways that are also likely to be correlated with children's weight outcomes. Once we control for these characteristics, we find no evidence that relative care is more harmful for school-age children's weight outcomes than any other type of care. Our findings are robust to numerous sensitivity and subgroup analyses.

Our data do not provide information on the exact nature of experiences that children have in various child care environments. For example, physical activity patterns may play a more important role in one type of arrangement and the dietary conditions may matter more in another type. Therefore, it would be interesting to analyze this question using data with detailed information on the environments in each of these arrangements. Furthermore, the relationship between child care and children's weight outcomes may be non-linear. For example, using quantile regression techniques, Herbst and Tekin (in press) show that child care subsidy is associated with a higher likelihood of obesity for children who are already overweight and obese, but not for other children. An interesting avenue for future research could be to implement a similar analysis for the association between child care choices and children's weight outcomes.

References

Anderson, P.M., K.F. Butcher and P.B. Levine (2003), "Maternal employment and overweight children", *Journal of Health Economics*, Vol. 22, pp. 477–504.

Carneiro, P. and R. Ginja (2008), "Preventing behavior problems in childhood and adolescence: evidence from Head Start", University College London Working Paper.

Cawley, J. and B. Kirwan (2005), "U.S. agricultural policy and obesity", Unpublished manuscript, Cornell University.

Cawley, J. and F. Liu (2007), "Mechanisms for the association between maternal employment and child cognitive development", NBER Working Paper, No. 13609.

Courtemanche, C. (2007), "Working yourself to death The relationship between work hours and obesity", Washington University in St. Louis Working Paper.

Daniels, S.R., D.K. Arnett, R.H. Eckel, *et al.* (2005), "Overweight in children and adolescents: pathophysiology, consequences, prevention, and treatment", *Circulation*, Vol. 111, pp. 1999–2002.

Deckelbaum, R. and C. Williams (2001), "Childhood obesity: the health issue", *Obesity Research*, Vol. 9, pp. 239S–243S.

Ding, W., S.F. Lehrer, J.N. Rosenquist and J. Audrain-McGovern (2006), "The impact of poor health on education: new evidence using genetic markers", National Bureau of Economic Research Working Paper, No. 12304.

Dowda, M., R. Pate, S. Trost, M. Joao, C. Almeida and J. Sirard (2004), "Influences of preschool policies and practices on children's physical activity", *Journal of Community Health*, Vol. 29, pp. 183–196.

Fertig, A.R., G. Glomm and R. Tchernis (2009), "The connection between maternal employment and childhood obesity: inspecting the mechanisms", *Review of Economics of the Household*, Vol. 7(3), pp. 227–255.

Finkelstein, E.A., J.G. Trogdon, J.W. Cohen and W. Dietz (2009), "Annual medical spending attributable to obesity: payer- and service-specific estimates", *Health Affairs*, Vol. 28(5), pp. w822–w831.

Freedman, D.S., M. Zuguo, S.R. Srinivasan, G.S. Berenson and W.H. Dietz (2007), "Cardiovascular risk factors and excess adiposity among overweight children and adolescents: the Bogalusa Heart Study", *Journal of Pediatrics*, Vol. 150, pp. 12–17.

Frisvold, D. (2007), "Head Start participation and childhood obesity: does investing in early childhood education reduce obesity", Working Paper, University of Michigan.

Frisvold, D. and J. Lumeng (in press), "Expanding exposure: can increasing the daily duration of Head Start reduce childhood obesity", *Journal of Human Resources*.

Herbst, C. and E. Tekin (in press), "Child care subsidies and childhood obesity", *Review of Economics of Household*.

Hofferth, S. and S. Curtin (2005), "Poverty, food programs and childhood obesity", *Journal of Policy Analysis and Management*, Vol. 24, pp. 703–726.

Hubbard, M. (2008), "The effect of mothers' employment and child care decisions on the body mass status of young children", The University of North Carolina at Chapel Hill Working Paper, November.

Lakdawalla, D. and T. Philipson (2002), "The growth of obesity and technological change: a theoretical and empirical examination", NBER Working Paper No. 8946.

Mocan, N. and E. Tekin (2010), "Obesity, self-esteem, and wages", NBER Working Paper No. (15101). Forthcoming in: M. Grossman and N. Mocan, editors, *Economic Aspects of Obesity*, University of Chicago Press.

Mott, C.S. (2009), "Children's hospital", *National Poll on Children's Health*, Vol. 7(2), p. 1.

Ogden, C.L., M.D. Carroll and K.M. Flegal (2008), "High body mass index for age among US children and adolescents, 2003–2006", *The Journal of American Medical Association*, Vol. 299, pp. 2401–2405.

Ogden, C.L., M.D. Carroll, L.R. Curtin, M.M. Lamb and K.M. Flegal (2010), "Prevalence of high body mass index in US children and adolescents, 2007–2008", *The Journal of American Medical Association*, Vol. 303, pp. 242–249.

Padget, A. and M. Briley (2005), "Dietary intakes at child-care centers in central Texas fail to meet food guide pyramid recommendations", *Journal of the American Dietetic Association*, Vol. 105, pp. 790–793.

Philipson, T.J. and R.A. Posner (1999), "The long-run growth in obesity as a function of technological change", NBER Working Paper No. 7423, Cambridge (MA): National Bureau of Economic Research.

Ruhm, C. (2008), "Maternal employment and adolescent development", *Labour Economics*, Vol. 15, pp. 958–983.

Story, M., K. Kaphingst and S. French (2006), "The role of child care settings in obesity prevention", *The Future of Children*, Vol. 10, pp. 143–168.

Strauss, R. (2000), "Childhood obesity and self-esteem", *Pediatrics*, Vol. 105, p. E15.

Trasande, L. and S. Chatterjee (2009), "The impact of obesity on health service utilization and costs in childhood", *Obesity*, Vol. 17, pp. 1745–1749.

U.S. Department of Health and Human Services (2001), *The Surgeon General's Call to Action to Prevent and Decrease Overweight and Obesity*, Rockville, MD: U.S. Department of Health and Human Services, Public Health Service, Office of the Surgeon General.

U.S. Surgeon General (2001), *Overweight and Obesity: Health Consequences*, Rockville, MD: Office of the Surgeon General (US).

Whitaker, R.C., R.A. Gooze, C.C. Hughes and D.M. Finkelstein (2009), "A national survey of obesity prevention practices in Head Start", *Archives of Pediatrics and Adolescent Medicine*, Vol. 163(12), pp. 1144–1150.

Appendix

Table A.1. OLS estimates – full sample

	(1)	(2)	(3)	(4)
	BMI	Overweight	Obese	Underweight
Relative care	0.304***	0.039***	0.025***	−0.005**
	(0.055)	(0.007)	(0.006)	(0.002)
Non-relative care	0.058	0.007	0.003	−0.001
	(0.062)	(0.009)	(0.007)	(0.003)
Center care	0.068	−0.000	−0.000	−0.005*
	(0.054)	(0.007)	(0.006)	(0.003)
Child has disability (percent)	0.099*	0.012*	0.010*	0.007***
	(0.053)	(0.007)	(0.005)	(0.002)
Child lives with bio mother and other father (percent)	−0.146*	−0.013	−0.017**	0.001
	(0.082)	(0.011)	(0.008)	(0.003)
Child lives with bio mother (percent)	0.031	−0.000	−0.000	−0.004
	(0.070)	(0.008)	(0.007)	(0.003)
Boy (percent)	−0.012	0.010	0.020***	−0.001
	(0.049)	(0.006)	(0.005)	(0.002)
Child age in months	0.032***	−0.001	−0.000	0.000*
	(0.006)	(0.001)	(0.001)	(0.000)
Race/Ethnicity: black (percent)	0.738***	0.074***	0.049***	−0.002
	(0.103)	(0.012)	(0.010)	(0.004)
Race/Ethnicity: Hispanic (percent)	0.774***	0.099***	0.072***	−0.004
	(0.083)	(0.011)	(0.009)	(0.003)
Race/Ethnicity: Asian (percent)	−0.021	0.012	0.026**	0.028***
	(0.110)	(0.014)	(0.011)	(0.006)
Race/Ethnicity: other (percent)	0.412***	0.041***	0.031**	0.009
	(0.124)	(0.015)	(0.013)	(0.006)
Birth weight in 250 g	−0.050	−0.017**	−0.015**	−0.015***
	(0.069)	(0.009)	(0.007)	(0.004)
Birth weight in 250 g^2	0.010***	0.002***	0.001***	0.000**
	(0.003)	(0.000)	(0.000)	(0.000)
Child is born more than two weeks premature (percent)	0.200***	0.024**	0.013*	−0.003
	(0.074)	(0.010)	(0.008)	(0.004)
Family SES in first quintile (percent)	0.779***	0.085***	0.065***	−0.004
	(0.089)	(0.011)	(0.009)	(0.004)
Family SES in second quintile (percent)	0.846***	0.093***	0.072***	−0.007**
	(0.077)	(0.010)	(0.008)	(0.003)
Family SES in third quintile (percent)	0.545***	0.065***	0.045***	−0.004
	(0.067)	(0.009)	(0.007)	(0.003)
Family SES in fourth quintile (percent)	0.271***	0.029***	0.020***	−0.003
	(0.058)	(0.008)	(0.006)	(0.003)
Parent expects some college for child (percent)	0.005	0.009	−0.003	−0.000
	(0.082)	(0.010)	(0.009)	(0.004)
Parent expects BA for child (percent)	−0.097	−0.003	−0.010	0.001
	(0.078)	(0.010)	(0.008)	(0.003)

Table A.1. (Continued)

	(1) BMI	(2) Overweight	(3) Obese	(4) Underweight
Parent expects >BA for child (percent)	−0.011	0.012	−0.006	0.002
	(0.084)	(0.010)	(0.009)	(0.004)
One sibling (percent)	−0.367***	−0.048***	−0.036***	−0.003
	(0.076)	(0.009)	(0.008)	(0.003)
Two siblings (percent)	−0.505***	−0.068***	−0.056***	−0.007**
	(0.081)	(0.010)	(0.008)	(0.003)
Three siblings (percent)	−0.632***	−0.079***	−0.061***	−0.006
	(0.096)	(0.012)	(0.010)	(0.004)
Four or more siblings (percent)	−0.872***	−0.124***	−0.089***	−0.011**
	(0.118)	(0.015)	(0.012)	(0.005)
Large or midsize suburb (percent)	0.008	0.005	0.000	−0.000
	(0.067)	(0.009)	(0.007)	(0.003)
Large or small town, or rural (percent)	0.324***	0.028**	0.022**	−0.002
	(0.105)	(0.012)	(0.010)	(0.004)
Observations	48,870	48,870	48,870	48,870
R^2	0.240	0.065	0.055	0.040

Note: Robust standard errors, clustered at child level, are in parentheses.
*, **, *** indicate that the coefficient is statistically significant at 0.10, 0.05, and 0.01 levels, respectively.

CHAPTER 4

Individual Time Preferences and Health Behaviors, with an Application to Health Insurance

W. David Bradford* and James F. Burgess Jr.

Abstract

One of the fundamental tasks in optimal insurance design is mitigating the moral hazard effects inherent in insurance mechanisms. Empirically, relatively little is known about how individual-level time preferences affect selection of insurance options. We use several waves of the Health and Retirement Survey to explore the relationship between revealed time preferences at the individual level and the selection of insurance options for both the under-age-65 population and the Medicare-eligible population. Our results suggest that time preferences are not likely to be fixed across the life cycle, and that they appear to be important predictors of health insurance decisions.

Keywords: health care demand, health insurance, intertemporal choice

JEL classifications: I10, D12, D91

* Corresponding author.

CONTRIBUTIONS TO ECONOMIC ANALYSIS
VOLUME 290 ISSN: 0573-8555
DOI:10.1108/S0573-8555(2010)0000290007

1. Introduction

Time preferences are considered a fundamental characteristic of economic behavior, and dynamic models of utility maximization have strong predictions about the effects of different rates of discounting on individual behavior. In general, we expect that higher rates of discounting will lead an individual to shift consumption of economic goods more strongly to the present and economic bads to the future, relative to a person with lower rates of preference for the present. While time preferences are clearly fundamental to all choices, economists have devoted surprisingly little attention to understanding their origins. Some of the earliest modern theoretical works on the subject were conducted by Paul Samuelson. He proposed a discount factor that indicates a strength of preference for the present over the future. For several decades after Samuelson's work, his model of discounted utility was the standard conceptual basis for economists' understanding of intertemporal choice. Since this time, additional research has been conducted to explore what factors might contribute to an individual's level of discounting.

While some progress has been made in understanding how time preferences might be endogenized, and substantial effort has been devoted to exploring the impact of time preferences on many aspects of economic life, surprisingly little attention has been paid to the effect of time preferences on health and health care – despite the fact that many aspects of health care reflect strongly time-dependent choices. There are strong conceptual reasons to expect a relationship between an individual's rate of discounting the future and their current demand for, for example, preventive health services. Prevention requires patients to engage in activities they do not enjoy today (e.g., reducing the intake of high-fat and high-sodium foods, exercising, losing weight, and consuming pharmaceutical products) in order to prevent the onset of disease. Interestingly, secondary prevention involves screening intended to detect disease that may already be present, and care to prevent its advancement. Thus, while people who have high rates of discounting would still prefer to shift unpleasant health care into the future, their past neglect of primary prevention may raise the likelihood of disease such that the increased clinical need outweighs the economic tendency toward procrastination.

Individual rates of discounting may affect many other aspects of choices in health economics as well. For example, one of the fundamental tasks in optimal insurance design is mitigating the moral hazard effects inherent in insurance mechanisms. Empirically, relatively little is known about how individual-level time preferences affect selection of insurance options possessing varying degrees of riskiness balanced against expected future net medical costs. Health care reform efforts to standardize health insurance coverage options and add more homogeneity to the system may force many individuals to make suboptimal choices if these individual-level time preferences vary substantially. If health insurance and other health choices have significant feedback effects on behavioral preferences, then health care policies may have substantial spillover effects – for good or ill – on a wide range of substantive time-dependent economic choices (e.g., rational addiction, educational attainment, employment, and retirement behavior).

We have two goals for this chapter. First, we present a survey of some of what is known about the role of time preferences in health-related choices, ranging from risky behaviors (smoking and illicit drug use), to preventive health care. Second, we present some original research that focuses on one area of discounting and health: how do individual time preferences, measured as discount rates, affect health insurance choices? Finally, the chapter highlights promising areas for future research.

2. Background

2.1. Foundations of time preferences

Standard utility theory, set in a dynamic model, presents strong predictions about the effect of different rates of discounting on an individual's behavior. In general, we expect that higher rates of discounting for an individual will lead him or her to shift consumption of economic goods more strongly to the present and economic bads to the future, relative to a person with lower rates of preference for the present.

Grossman (1972) introduced the concept of health as a component of human capital, which depreciates and in which investments can be made. Since that seminal contribution, a number of economists have investigated many dynamic aspects of health production and health care demand (e.g., Wagstaff, 1986; van Doorslaer, 1987; Wagstaff, 1993; Grossman and Kaestner, 1997; Zweifel and Breyer, 1997). Theoretically, there have been a number of contributions that have explicitly modeled the role of time preferences on general human capital investments, of which health care is one. Ehrlich and Chuma (1990) explore the general implications of the Grossman model more completely and pay particular attention to the impact of time preference. They find that increasing the rate of discounting the future tends to reduce investments in health capital – though this result holds only on average.

While time preferences are clearly fundamental, economists have devoted surprisingly little attention to understanding their origins. Some of the earliest modern theoretical works on the subject were conducted by Samuelson (1947), as he proposed a model of discounted utility as a useful analog of individual decision making under uncertainty and across time. Samuelson did not propose this model as normative, though he believed it useful. In this framework, Samuelson argued that people chose consumption to maximize a flow of separate utilities, where future utilities were weighted less heavily compared to the current level of utility. Thus individuals were assumed to select some level of consumption, x_t, in order to maximize

$$U^t(x_1, ..., x_T) = \sum_{t=0}^{T} \beta(t)u(x_t)$$

subject to some income/wealth constraint. This weighting factor, $\beta(t)$, is assumed to be constant across all time periods in this model and corresponds to our understanding of a "discount rate." As such, it simply indicates a strength of preference for the present over the future.

For several decades after Samuelson's work, this model of discounted utility was the standard conceptual basis for economists' understanding of intertemporal choice. However, the model simply assumes that the discount factor/strength of time preference is a given, and is not affected by an individual's environment or choices. Consequently, additional research has been conducted to explore what factors might contribute to the *level* of discounting that each individual might have. Among the most influential of these efforts are those by Koopmans *et al.* (1960, 1964), Thaler and Shefrin (1981), and Becker and Mulligan (1997). Each of these contributions attempted to incorporate the idea that people's environment and decisions affect their preference in predictable and orderly ways. Thus Koopmans' contributions demonstrated that a very simple and basic set of assumptions about the nature of utility would require that people have some positive rate of time preference (i.e., $\beta(t)$ must be less than one, such that they are impatient and prefer the present to the future). Thaler and Shefrin develop a neoclassical theory of intertemporal decision making where people are thought to act as current consumers and also agents for their future selves. This need to be an agent for themselves in the future sets up an internal conflict that leads to a discount rate. Since agency relationship models are well established in economics, this assumption leads Thaler and Shefrin to make predictions about how various environmental factors might affect $\beta(t)$.

With respect to understanding how time preferences change for people from a theoretical perspective, Becker and Mulligan (1997) propose (and indirectly test) a theoretical model of how individuals' time preferences change as a consequence of each person's choices. Thus, they endogenize time preferences in equilibrium. To do this, Becker and Mulligan add four assumptions to the typical neoclassical set: (1) people are not equally patient; (2) any differences in patience across individuals can be explained by initial conditions and the individual's choices; (3) preferring the present too much relative to the future is widely understood to be undesirable; and (4) people know their weaknesses (such as having too strong a preference for the present) and will exert effort to overcome these weaknesses.

The model assumes that individuals seek to maximize the happiness they receive from consuming goods and services in all of the time periods in their life (present and future). Let c_i represent the level of consumption in each time period, where $i = 0, \ldots, T$ ($i = 0$ reflects the present, and $i = T$ reflects the last time period of life). Further, Becker and Mulligan posit that people will reduce the importance of future happiness according to a function $\beta(S)$. This function, $\beta(S)$, is a key component of their model. $\beta(\cdot)$ is a relationship between the variable S and the amount by which the future is discounted. Consistent with the typical economic production relationship, this function is concave, which implies $\partial\beta/\partial S \geq 0$, $\partial^2\beta/\partial S^2 \leq 0$, and $\beta(S) > 0$, for all S. Generally, $\beta(\cdot) < 1$ – that is, people consider the future to be less important than the present. As $\beta(\cdot)$ approaches 1, then people begin to value the future more like the present. We will refer to the value of this function as the discount factor for the future.

The actual value of $\beta(\cdot)$ – or how much people value the future less than the present – will depend upon the value of S. This variable, S, represents investments by individuals in learning how to make the future seem more like the present. Becker and Mulligan argue that accumulating higher levels of S involves investments that build skills for committing to future outcomes (both good and bad). As they point out, such investments are very common in society. For example, people trying to improve their health by losing weight or starting an exercise regime often understand that they "lack willpower" and so may pay money to join a health club or weight loss program. This is fundamentally an investment aimed at increasing the value of the future to the individual, motivated because the person understands that their discount factor for the future is "too high" from their own perspective; consequently, the person undertakes an action to reduce their own discount rate. As Becker and Mulligan (somewhat comically) point out, Christmas clubs and piggy banks also represent actions with positive opportunity costs (foregone current consumption and interest income) aimed at improving one's appreciation of the future. Higher levels in S may also be associated with more certain future outcomes. A student may learn about the attributes college admissions officers look for in a successful application. In doing so, the probability of being admitted to college is more certain, and thus rewards for current studying are more certain, leading to a lower discount rate.

Mathematically, the Becker and Mulligan model assumes that an agent will choose a program of consumption ($c_0, c_1, \ldots, c_T$) and will choose an ability to value the future (S) in order to maximize

$$V = \sum_{i=0}^{T} f_i(c_i) \cdot \beta(S)^i$$

subject to a wealth constraint. The equilibrium conditions for optimality reveal a particularly strong result: anything that raises future utility will increase the optimal investment in S and lower the person's discount factor for the future.

This has direct implications for the expected relationships between (1) a number of important choices a person makes/parameters a person faces and (2) the strength of their discounting of the future. Omitting the mathematical proofs and other questions they address, Becker and Mulligan show how higher levels of health can cause a person to invest more heavily in *S* and therefore have a lower discount factor for the future. This raises the theoretical and empirical question of whether lower discount rates can lead to better health choices, which would set up a positive feedback loop.

While there has been less theoretical work done on the origins of time preferences by economists, there is a long literature that examines predictors for time preferences and what factors are associated with changes in the rate of time preference. Again, in the economic literature, this is typically couched in terms of a "discount rate." (As will be discussed below, the economists' construct of "discount rate" has been shown to be equivalent to the psychologists' construct of "delayed gratification" – at least in terms of measurement.) Consequently, there is a great deal of guidance for this project from the literature with respect to measuring time preferences and modeling predictors of an individual's rate of time preference (discount rate).

2.2. Measuring time preferences

The empirical economic literature that estimates discount rates for individuals can be divided generally into three groups: research that takes advantage of natural experiments; research utilizing laboratory-based experimental methods; and research that uses survey (contingent valuation (CA)) methods for eliciting discount rates. An article in the *Journal of Economic Perspectives* (2002) reviews this literature in great detail. We will only highlight a few archetypical examples of this broad literature in order to motivate the research we propose.

The first approach mentioned is to use natural experiments in which individuals must choose between alternatives with differential time dimensions, such that a discount rate can be inferred. An example of this literature is the work by Warner and Pleeter (2001), which took advantage of data generated from an early retirement program in the U.S. military to estimate discount rates for enlisted men and officers. Retirees were required to decide whether to take their retirement benefit as a lump sum or as an annuity payment. The value of each depended on rank, years of service, and other factors. Since the retirees were choosing between an immediate and a delayed payout, which had a fixed rate of return, it is possible to use that information to infer the strength of preference for the present vs. the future (i.e., the discount rate) of the retirees. Warner and Pleeter estimate discount rates in the 25% per year range for officers and in the 45% per year range for enlisted men. Other researchers have used this method (existing data from natural experiments) to estimate individual-level discount rates and find similar results (1980, 1979, 1996); though some results using natural experiments find much lower rates of discount (1990). One explanation for the persistence of individual rates of discounting that are much higher than market rates is that capital markets are incomplete. If borrowing were costless, one would expect individuals to arbitrage their own discount rates until they drove them to equilibrium with the market. Imperfect capital markets preclude this from occurring.

A second methodology is to present individuals with hypothetical or real payouts that vary in their time dimension in an experimental setting. The work by Collier and Williams (1999) represents an example of this research. In this study, the authors offered their subjects payouts of real money under controlled laboratory settings. Their principal interest was in determining whether providing subject information about the actual discount rates implied in their experimental choices, or the real discount rates available in the market at the time were factors in people's choices. They found that providing the information was important, and presumably yields superior estimates. But they also estimated rates in the 20% per year range. There are numerous other examples of experimental methods used to assess individual discount rates (1994, 1999, 1995, 1994, 1995).

The third methodology employed is to present survey subjects with a set of hypothetical present and future payouts and estimate discount rates using a CV-method based upon their answers. This method will be employed in our empirical analysis, and discussed in more detail below. There are additional studies that utilize the survey method (1997, 1995, 1989, 2000, 1998, 1997, 1988, 1993, 2001, 1996).

The literature also contains warnings regarding the method that should be employed. A number of studies have found that the answers that people give to surveys or experiment, and the behaviors they exhibit, are not consistent with a single, constant, discount rate. Rather, alternative structures such as the hyperbolic (an example of which is Eq. (3)) have been found to be consistent with the data (1989, 1994, 1995). Since in empirical applications framing effects (where a respondent is led to believe a certain response is the correct one because it's close to some value they were offered by the surveyor) are important, and also because declining marginal utility of income may alter behavioral responses in ways unrelated to time, selecting appropriate dollar values has also been shown to be important (1989, 1994). Also, behavior is dependent upon whether respondents are offered a series of options that are improving (becoming more lucrative) vs. depreciating (becoming less lucrative) (1995) – with success dependent upon offering improving series (2004). Finally, while some authors find that discounting behavior is consistent for money and health (1988, 1989, 2001), others find that discounting behavior varies depending upon what is being discounted (1995, 2000, 1997).

2.3. Dynamic questions in time preferences

One issue that the existing literature has not settled is whether time preferences are stable across a person's life, whether they evolve in a relatively fixed manner as a person develops, or whether they are mutable. Some early conceptual work by economists on the issue asserts that time preferences ought to be relatively stable for a person, neither evolving nor subject to conscious change (1991, 1977). The basis for these theoretical assertions, however, is not empirical, but rather a theoretical desire to rule out any potential inconsistencies in intertemporal choice. On the other hand, psychologists who have constructed theoretical models to explain delay of gratification have not viewed time preferences as necessarily stable. For example, Metcalfe and Mischel (1999) incorporate a theory of time preferences into a "hot/cool" decision-making framework and conclude that the ability to delay gratification should vary depending upon the presence or absence of hot cues, and that individuals should be able to learn to adopt cool decision-making tools and so permanently enhance their ability to delay gratification. To date, there is no published research that seeks to follow individuals longitudinally and assess the stability or mutability of their time preferences. However, some research is suggestive that time preferences should be permitted to change in models. Nurmi (2005) and Strathman and Joireman (2005) survey the literature on the subject and find that a number of factors that are themselves modifiable have been found to contribute to higher or lower rates of future orientation (such as parental involvement or developmental stage). Finally, Bishai (2004) uses a longitudinal data set to infer time preferences (though not measure them directly) and finds that time preferences appear to change with both a person's age and years of schooling.

2.4. Time preferences and health

People who discount the future more heavily should be less likely to demand health insurance coverage that covers primary preventive health care than patients with low rates of time discounting. However, insurance also covers secondary prevention that involves screening and medical care intended to detect disease that may already be present, and to prevent its advancement. Thus, while people who have high rates of discounting would still prefer to shift unpleasant health care into the future, their past neglect of primary prevention may raise the likelihood of disease such that the increased clinical need outweighs the economic tendency toward procrastination. This may increase the current demand for health insurance and could lead to complex non-linear reaction functions such that more complex interactions between time preferences and the use of secondary prevention and screening and derived demand for health insurance are possible. Despite the potential importance of these complex time discounting effects on the demand for health insurance options, the issue has not been heavily studied to date.

Since the seminal contribution of Grossman (1972), a number of economists have investigated many dynamic aspects of health production and health care demand (e.g., Wagstaff, 1986; van Doorslaer, 1987; Wagstaff, 1993; Grossman and Kaestner, 1997; Zweifel and Breyer, 1997). Theoretically, there have been a number of contributions that have explicitly modeled the role of time preferences on general human capital investments, of which health care is one. The Becker and Murphy (1988) model of rational addiction is perhaps the most prevalent of these models in the literature. In that model, agents have foresight, and make human capital (and other consumption) decisions based upon the current utility and future utility generated. They find that higher rates of time preference tend to lead to lower current consumption of goods, but will increase current consumption of addictive products. As Grossman (2000) notes, the Becker/Murphy model predicts a discount rate effect only under certain circumstances. (The result is generally ambiguous in sign and uncertain in magnitude.) Ehrlich and Chuma (1990) explore the general implications of the Grossman (1972) model more completely, and do pay particular attention to the impact of time preference. They find that increasing the rate of discounting the future tends to reduce investments in health capital – though this result holds only on average. The empirical research we present below will test these "average" predictions from the Grossman and the Ehrlich and Chuma models in a wider context.

While the theoretical guidance is relatively clear with respect to the impact of time preference in health care demand, direct empirical tests of these predictions are notably absent from the literature. A number of authors have tested the effect indirectly, by demonstrating a schooling/health investment relationship that is consistent with an inverse relationship between discounting and human capital investment (1989, 1982). However, these are only indirect tests and subject to multiple interpretations. Consequently, in the words of Grossman (2000) (page 401), "definitive evidence with regard to the time preference hypothesis is still lacking." While *definitive* evidence may be long in coming, we will at least present *direct* evidence in this work.

One paper that does examine time and risk preferences impacts on the use of medical screening exams is by Picone *et al.* (2004) – though again the test with respect to time preferences is necessarily indirect. The authors propose a simple two-period model of expected utility maximization over the decision to undergo cancer screening. They predict that higher rates of discounting would lead to a reduction in the demand for screening. However, in their model the likelihood of disease does not depend upon the health state, there is no long-term clinical benefit from early detection (either in terms of likelihood of successful treatment or mortality), and they do not explicitly model time preferences (rather they make inferences about time preferences by assuming specific functional forms for utility). From a data perspective as well, the authors lack a direct measure of time preferences. Using the Health and Retirement Survey (HRS), they are only able to categorize individuals into short time-horizon or long time-horizon groups, which may or may not be directly correlated with having high or low time preferences over the long run. Despite these limitations, which the authors discuss, they find that women with longer life expectancies and self-identifying as having a long time horizon are more likely to undergo cancer screening. We will improve upon this work in two areas. Theoretically, we will expand their model to permit more direct assessment of the role of time preferences, which generates a somewhat more complex set of results. Empirically, we will have a direct estimate of each person's underlying discount rate, which we can then use as an explanatory variable in models that track their actual use of several types of screening (not just mammography and PAP smears among women).

More recently, three contributions by Bradford and colleagues have examined the impact of a direct measure of discounting on various measures of preventive health choices. Bradford *et al.* (2010) conducted a nationally representative survey of 2,000 adults and asked questions about their health states, medical care usage, and socioeconomic status. In addition, the respondents were asked to consider whether they would rather receive the payout from a hypothetical sweepstake prize as $10,000 in one year, or some larger amount in six years. Consistent with the findings in the study by Coller and Williams (1999), the respondents were informed about the implied interest rate. As an improvement on the usual approach, each respondent was offered a different, randomly assigned, prize value. Additionally, individuals were asked follow-up questions offering higher or lower interest rates, depending on their answers to the first question. The authors then employed a one and one-half bound dichotomous choice model to estimate discount rates for each individual. The imputed discount from the CV survey were then compared to respondents' utilization of five common disease screens (prostate exam, PAP smear, mammogram, dental exams, and cholesterol testing). The results suggest that the average respondent in the survey has an underlying discount rate of around 25% per year. The likelihood of screening within the past two years did depend upon the imputed discount rate (directly and interacted with respondent age) and other patient characteristics. Completely interacted results indicate that higher rates of discount are associated with lower use of all studied screening technologies except prostate exams, where the effect was positive. Similar results were seen in the study by Bradford (2010), which used a subsample from the HRS. Axon *et al.* (2009), using a sample of participants in a hypertension control study, examine the relationship between individual discount rates and patients knowledge of, and adherence to, physician advice. There, patients with higher discount rates are less likely to follow physician advice with regard to hypertension control.

3. Discounting and health insurance choice

3.1. Conceptual model of health insurance demand

Before beginning the process of evaluating the empirical relationship between time preferences and health insurance choices, it will be helpful to consider what guidance may be available from existing theory. As noted above, theoretical models of health insurance demand have not generally focused on the impact (if any) of time discounting behavior. As a side note, few researchers have explicitly treated the impact of risk preferences in insurance demand at all, though assumptions about the curvature of individuals' utility functions lie at the heart of all such models. To see how individual discount rates may affect insurance demand, consider a simple model, such as put forward in the studies by Feldman and Dowd (1991) and Cutler and Zeckhauser (2000). Our notation will adhere most closely to the latter.

To isolate the impact of preferences, assume that a person maximizes a standard utility function $U(Y)$, which is twice differentiable with the usual convexity assumptions, and where Y is disposable income. This person also faces a risk of illness, which if it occurs can be treated by purchasing m units of health care – and that this health care returns the individual to full health with certainty. This is an admittedly strong assumption and is made to focus attention solely upon the health insurance decision, without confounding the model with heterogeneity of care issues. Thus, the only risk in this simple model is to an individual's income. If the individual is not sick, all income, Y, is spent on a utility-generating numeraire good; if the individual is sick, then he or she will only have $Y{-}m$ available for utility generation. Assume further that insurance against the risk to income from health shocks can be purchased at an actuarially fair value (i.e., we abstract away from administrative costs and market competitive structure) of $\pi = \rho m$.

In this case, the individual's expected utility if he or she does not purchase insurance is

$$V_N = [1 - \rho] \times U(Y) + \rho \times U(Y - m) \tag{1}$$

where $\rho = \Pr(\text{Illness})$. The value of this function in the neighborhood of insurance purchase can be approximated by a second order Taylor's series expansion around $Y{-}\pi$ (recalling that $\rho m = \pi$), which when simplified reduces to

$$V_N \approx U(Y - \rho m) + [1 - \rho] \times U'(Y - \rho m) \times \rho m + \frac{1}{2}[1 - \rho] \times U''(Y - \rho m) \times [\rho m]^2 \tag{2}$$

Contrarily, if the individual is insured then she will have income equal to $Y{-}\pi$ with certainty, and an associated utility of

$$V_I = U(Y - \rho m) \tag{3}$$

So, the value of insurance is

$$V_I - V_N \approx -\pi \times [1-\rho] \times U'(\cdot) \times \left[1 + \frac{1}{2}\pi \times \frac{U''(\cdot)}{U'(\cdot)}\right] \tag{4}$$

Clearly, for a person to have a positive demand for (health) insurance, it must be true that the difference in Eq. (4) is positive. Since $U''(\cdot)<0$, for insurance demand to be positive, it must be true that

$$-\frac{1}{2} \times \pi \times \frac{U''(\cdot)}{U'(\cdot)} > 1 \tag{5}$$

In a static world, this implies that as the (Arrow–Pratt) coefficient of absolute risk aversion (here, $|R| \equiv |U''(\cdot)/U'(\cdot)|$) increases – i.e., as the person becomes more risk averse – then the value of insurance should rise.

The next question is what might be expected to happen to the value of insurance to a person when there are dynamic spillovers. Insight into this question can be achieved even without exploring a fully dynamic model. Assume that a person essentially faces a stream of choices each time period, such as those defined in Eqs. (2) and (3), each of which is discounted at a constant discount rate, e^{-dt}, where d represents the individual's private discount rate. Further, assume that the purchase of insurance carries additional benefits in that it subsidizes health investments (for simplicity we can consider insurance instruments that offer full insurance on preventive services). Consequently, if a person chooses the time path involving insurance purchases, the probability of insurance falls over time such that if $\rho(t)$ is the time-dependent insurance-supported trajectory of illness probabilities, $\rho'(t)<0$. Conversely, if the person chooses not to purchase insurance, the probability of illness remains constant at $\bar{\rho}$. Again, we consider dynamic decision processes where a person chooses a time path that either always involves insurance purchases, or never does.

Under these assumptions, the Taylor series expansion of the present value of the no insurance trajectory around $Y-\rho(t)m$ becomes

$$V_N \approx \sum_{t=0}^{T} \left\{ \begin{array}{l} e^{dt} U(Y-\rho(t)m) + [1-\bar{\rho}] \\ \times U'(Y-\rho(t)m) \times \bar{\rho}m + \frac{1}{2}[1-\bar{\rho}] \times U''(Y-\rho(t)m) \times [\bar{\rho}m]^2 \end{array} \right\} \tag{6}$$

whereas the present value of the insurance option is

$$V_I = \sum_{t=0}^{T} e^{-dt} U(Y-\rho(t)m) \tag{7}$$

such that the difference in present values is

$$V_I - V_N \approx \sum_{t=0}^{T} e^{-dt}\{-\bar{\rho}m \times [1-\bar{\rho}] \times U'(Y-\rho(t)m) \times \left[1+\frac{1}{2}\bar{\rho}m \times \frac{U''(Y-\rho(t)m)}{U'(Y-\rho(t)m}\right]\} \quad (8)$$

The question then becomes, what happens to the term in braces as time progresses? Essentially, as one looks further into the future the advantages of selecting insurance over no insurance grow, as the gap between $\rho(t)$ and $\bar{\rho}$ grows. However, this advantage of insurance is offset by the fact that those future higher benefits are discounted. The derivative of the difference in the present value of insurance over no insurance with respect to time is

$$\frac{\partial[V_I - V_N]}{\partial t} = m\bar{\rho}[1-\bar{\rho}]\sum_{t=0}^{T}\left\{e^{-dt}\left[d+\frac{1}{2}dm\bar{\rho}\frac{U''(Y-\rho(t)m)}{U'(Y-\rho(t)m)} + m\rho'(t)\frac{U''(Y-\rho(t)m)}{U'(Y-\rho(t)m)}\right]\right\} \gtreqless 0 \quad (9)$$

The sign is indeterminate, since the first term in brackets (d) is positive and the second two terms are negative; it would depend upon two things: the rate at which $\rho(t)$ and $\bar{\rho}$ diverge, and the relative magnitudes of the individuals (always positive) discount rate and (always negative) ratio of risk aversion. Thus, in a simplistic dynamic sense, the impact of discounting over time may be positive or negative – and generally will be non-linear.

Intuitively, this is a straightforward relationship. At the most fundamental level, future outcomes are "future" in large part because (1) we can't have them now and (2) things at a temporal distance are less predictable than things temporally proximate. In other words, the future is risky – and the further in the future something is, the riskier it is. Behaviorally, then, if a person is very risk averse then his or her valuation of temporally distant benefits should be lower than a person who is not very risk averse. Irrespective of any effects from "pure" time preferences – which recall happen in a world of certainty – we should expect to see a strong correspondence between risk-aversion/insurance option choice relationships and discounting/insurance option choice relationships. Time discounting has a complex effect on the net value of health insurance; whether the net effect is positive or negative remains an empirical question.

3.2. Discounting and health insurance choice

3.2.1. Data

Data for this study were taken from the 2004, 2006, and 2008 waves of the HRS, which is a longitudinal survey of mostly older Americans begun in 1992. Currently, the survey follows (primarily) four cohorts of individuals, representing a population of persons 50 years and older and their spouses, partners, and resident children. Data elements include demographics, housing, health insurance, income and net worth, employment status, and so forth. In addition, specific information about time preferences was asked in the 2004 wave. We use the time preference measures in 2004 as (predetermined) predictors of insurance choices in 2006 and 2008. Thus, we examine people who appear in the 2006 and 2008 waves and who also answered the time preference questions in 2004. After imposing this restriction and dropping a small number of observations whose insurance options could not be modeled (those over 65 who report no Medicare coverage, and the Medicare – Medicaid dually eligible respondents, whose numbers were too small to model), we arrive at a final sample of 854 respondents.

3.2.2. Discount rate variables

This section has two major aims. The first is to add to the literature that models time preferences at the individual level. Second – and principally – we wish to determine what impact time preferences have on insurance option decisions of individuals as an example of one of the major health-related decisions that people make incorporating time preferences that are generally not considered in studies. Given the potential for endogeneity of time preferences in the insurance choice models (discussed below), we will not estimate a full system between the two, but rather estimate determinants of the time preferences first and then use predetermined (2004 wave) responses to time preference questions to predict current (2006 and 2008 wave) insurance decisions.

Of those respondents completing the core survey items in 2004, 1,039 were randomly selected to be asked questions in an experimental module on annuity preferences. This subset of respondents was selected randomly from all age, race, and socioeconomic groups who participated in the HRS. The availability of the time preference measure will serve as the major limitation on the sample we are able to study.

A set of time preference questions was asked as part of the supplemental annuities module of the 2004 HRS. The time preference questions were of the general form:

> Suppose that you won a prize that is worth $1000 if you take it today. Or you could wait one year to claim the prize and be guaranteed to receive $1100. Would you claim the $1000 dollars today, or would you wait one year for $1100?

Follow-up questions were posed, which asked respondents to compare $1,000 today vs. $1,200 and $1,050 in one year. Given the answers to the HRS time preference questions, one can infer the ranges in which the latent discount rate must lie. Given the rates of return implicit in the questions, one can translate the responses into the following intervals:

SCHEMA

Prefer \$1050 in one year $\Leftrightarrow 0 < D^* \leq 0.05$
Prefer \$1100 in one year $\Leftrightarrow 0.05 < D^* \leq 0.10$
Prefer \$1200 in one year $\Leftrightarrow 0.10 < D^* \leq 0.20$
Prefer \$1000 today $\Leftrightarrow 0.20 < D^* \leq \infty$

where D^* represents the latent individual rate of discounting. We assign each individual to a 2004 discount category, where Category 1 has the lowest discount rate and Category 4 has the highest. Table 1 presents the distribution of discount rate groups in our sample.

Two things are of note in the raw distributions. First, the set of questions asked in the HRS is such that most respondents fall in the highest discount grouping – with implied discount rates of over 20% per year. Ideally, then, we will want an estimator that can accommodate the censored nature of the responses, without having to discard the censored observations. As shown in the study by Stewart (1983), interval regression (also called grouped regression) can accomplish this goal, in addition to more naturally modeling the interval nature of the responses. Nonetheless, it will be important to consider that 67% of the sample lies in the highest, censored, region, such that we know the lower bound, but not the upper bound on their implied discount rates. Second, note that there is relatively little attrition between 2004 and 2008 such that this distribution of imputed discount rates is quite comparable (Table 1).

We assume that the underlying individual discount rate can be represented as a latent variable D^*, where

$$D_{it}^* = [Z_{it}, C_{it}, H_{it}, X_{it}] \cdot \beta + \varepsilon_i \tag{10}$$

Table 1. ***Distribution of population in each discount group***

	2006		2008	
	Mean	Sum	Mean	Sum
1st discount category	0.069	58	0.068	54
2nd discount category	0.134	112	0.134	107
3rd discount category	0.128	107	0.123	98
4th discount category	0.669	561	0.675	539

Note: "mean" = percent of population in that discount category; "sum" = number in that discount category.

The matrix of variables represents characteristics that affect that latent rate, discussed below. This model is estimated for $t = 2004$ only. While we cannot observe this latent construct directly, given the ranges in which the latent discount rate must lie, a parametric method is available to take advantage of the information contained in the discount rate groups to model discounting behavior for each person, and thus identify important predictors. Since we know the actual cut-points for the intervals, this process can be most efficiently modeled as an interval regression, or grouped regression.

3.2.3. Explanatory variables for discount responses

In summary, the explanatory variables appearing in our estimates of Eq. (10) are as follows:

Z_{it}: the respondents' subjective probability that he or she will live to age 95, whether the respondent feels religion is very important, whether the respondent smoked as an adolescent, whether the respondent's parents smoked when the respondent was a child, the percent of words correctly recalled on a cognitive test administered as part of the HRS each wave, whether the respondent is able to correctly subtract 7 twice from 100;

C_i: individual out-of-pocket expenditures in 2004 wave of HRS data for outpatient visits and prescription drug;

H_{it}: dummy variables indicating whether the respondent reports having a diagnosis of diabetes, cancer, heart disease, or stroke, in the current wave (2006 or 2008);

X_{it}: respondent age, gender (male = 1), good or excellent self-reported health, race (African American, Hispanic, Other, with Caucasian as the excluded category), marital status (married = 1), education (less than a high school education, high school diploma, with any college as the excluded category), employment status (currently employed, retired, with not employed as the excluded category), and household income, all measured as of the current wave (2006 or 2008).

3.2.4. Insurance decisions

The HRS captures comprehensive information on health insurance choices for all respondents in each wave. Thus, we measure health insurance choices for 2006 and 2008 for all respondents, without the need for imputation. For insurance options, respondents fall into one of two important groups: those under age 65 – and thus not eligible for Medicare – and those over age 65 – all of which have Medicare, and some of which have supplemental insurance. Since the incentives facing these two groups differ substantially, we analyze their insurance choices separately.

Before outlining the types of insurance decisions we model, we must consider what distinctions we can fruitfully make between them. For our purposes we will note that a traditional private non-health maintenance organization (HMO) insurance plan, which will typically involve significant deductibles and per-use copayments, offers less complete financial coverage than the typical private HMO insurance plan, which may have no deductible and will generally have nominal (fixed) copayments. Clearly, HMO mechanisms also may come with greater utilization management restrictions and more active gatekeeping roles for providers whose financial incentives are to economize on care. In that sense, HMOs may be "less generous" than fee-for-service-based plans. But, it is beyond the scope of this chapter to explore a comprehensive measure of plan generosity. Thus, in what follows, we will focus on only one dimension across which different types of insurance mechanisms differ – the degree to which they fully insure against financial loss, which represents the major financial implication of health insurance that is vivid to enrollees in any case. Recent research has indicated that people generally understand the cost-sharing requirements of the health insurance plans they hold in a general sense (Lischko and Burgess, 2010) – though perhaps not in fine detail; however, their knowledge is such that they should be able to distinguish between the broad categories of plans we model.

For the under 65 years old group, we capture three distinct choices.

- First, respondents may report that they have private, non-HMO health insurance. For this research, we do not distinguish between private insurance obtained from an employer, as a self-employed person, or on the individual market. Our primary concern here is about the comprehensiveness of the coverage. In that sense, irrespective of the source, private non-HMO coverage will generally involve payment of copayments and deductibles and is therefore not complete.
- Second, respondents may report that they have private HMO insurance. Again, no distinction is made between the sources of that coverage. Since HMOs generally charge nominal copayments and small to no deductibles, we anticipate that HMO coverage will be more complete in this cost/risk sense than non-HMO coverage.
- Third, respondents may report having no health insurance coverage.

There are also respondents who report having Medicaid coverage – however, the number of such respondents in the HRS modules who were asked the time preference questions is quite low, and consequently we are unable to analyze their choices. We therefore exclude all Medicaid covered individuals (both below and above age 65) from the analysis.

For the 65 years and older group, we also define three insurance choices.

- First, respondents may report having private non-HMO coverage. This corresponds to non-HMO supplemental (Medigap) plans, incurring deductibles and copayments. They may also cover categories of care (e.g., pharmaceuticals in 2006) not covered at all by Medicare. While these plans are regulated at the federal level with respect to the benefit packages, they nonetheless represent less than full coverage.

- Second, respondents may report having private HMO coverage. In general, there are two ways that a Medicare enrollee can have HMO coverage. First, through private purchase as a form of Medigap policy, but one with distinctly lower cost sharing – and thus generally more complete coverage. Second, enrollees may enroll in an HMO as part of their base Medicare package. This type of coverage is as complete as the Medigap HMO plans, but since it is part of the Medicare system directly, it is accessible with lower out-of-pocket premiums (since an additional premium is not needed to purchase the coverage beyond what is paid to Medicare for Part B coverage). Ideally, we would distinguish between these two in the choice set, but given limitations on sample size, we will combine them.
- Third, respondents may report having only Medicare FFS coverage, without supplemental care. This type of coverage requires no premiums in addition to Part B premiums, but also leaves the respondent exposed for substantial inpatient deductibles and copayments. Further in 2006, prior to the introduction of Medicare Part D, respondents choosing this portfolio would have no coverage for pharmaceutical products. (It is perhaps worth noting that we examine insurance choice in 2006 and 2008 – and it is possible that the increase in Medicare FFS only choices between these two years reflects the full implementation of Part D which had occurred by 2008.)

Note that there is one additional type of coverage option for the over-65 population: joint coverage by Medicare and Medicaid. These dually eligible individuals have complete coverage, in the sense that they have no additional premiums, have no deductibles, and have no or very low copayments. As with Medicaid for the under-65-year-old population, eligibility is restricted based upon low income and asset levels. However, the HRS sample that was asked the discount rate questions contains very few dually eligible respondents, and we are unable to analyze their choices. Table 2 presents the distribution of insurance choices in 2006 and 2008 in our sample.

Empirically, we will assume that the current choice regarding health insurance coverage will depend upon factors that affect the expected value of that insurance in the present period. Taking our lead from the conceptual framework presented and discussed above,

$$\Pr[k\text{th insurance option is chosen}] = \Pr[y_{it}^k = 1] = G(D_{it}, C_{it}, H_{it}, X_{it}) \tag{11}$$

where D_{it} is the subjective discount rate, C_{it} represents expected expenditures on health care, H_{it} represents underlying health state measures, and X_{it} represents other characteristics of the individual, such

Table 2. Distribution of insurance choices, 2006 and 2008

	Under Age 65		Age 65 and Over	
	Mean	Sum	Mean	Sum
Rates of insurance in sample, 2006				
Has private non-HMO insurance	0.477	326	0.494	76
Has HMO insurance	0.291	199	0.305	47
Has no health insurance	0.114	78		
Has medicare FFS only			0.188	29
Rates of insurance in sample, 2008				
Has private non-HMO insurance	0.475	261	0.472	117
Has private HMO insurance	0.285	157	0.294	68
Has no health insurance	0.125	69		
Has medicare FFS only			0.246	61

Note: "mean" = rate of insurance; "sum" = number in insurance group.

as age, gender, race, income, and so forth. We estimate three separate probit models for the population under age 65 (private non-HMO coverage, HMO coverage, and no coverage) and three separate probit models for the aged 65 and over population (non-HMO medigap, HMO medigap, and traditional Medicare FFS only).

Ideally, one would want to model insurance choice in a way that permits the probability of choice k to be affected by the probability of choice j (where $j \neq k$). In the current context this would imply a multinomial probit or logit (since the underlying insurance choices are not naturally ordered). However, such models put a relatively high demand on the data, and we have a relatively small sample. Consequently, we will model each option separately, using simple probits – recognizing that the resulting models are inefficient, and that comparing effects across all three simultaneously may be misleading – and so should be avoided.

Econometrically, we must confront the contemporaneous endogeneity of the discount and medical expenditure measures. (Technically, one may also consider the potential for endogeneity of the health measures as well; however, we will only be capturing chronic health states such as diabetes or serious health shocks such as cancer, which can reasonably be viewed as predetermined in the model.) In order to estimate a simultaneous system, identifying instruments would be necessary between the factors that affect insurance choice and the discount preference relationships, and between the expected medical expenditures and insurance choice. The latter would be difficult to justify theoretically. Consequently, we will use the panel structure of our data to aid identification.

We will estimate these models for the 2006 and 2008 waves of the HRS and include the reported discount preferences categories from 2004. To the extent that 2004 discount/risk preferences are correlated with 2006 and 2008 values, these variables will serve as good proxies. While we do have plausible exclusion restrictions between the time preferences and the insurance choices, since they are predetermined in our 2006 and 2008 choice models, endogeneity will not be an issue. We will take two approaches to examining the relationship between discounting and insurance choices. First, we will use the point estimates for each individual (recovered from Eq. (10)) to examine the raw relationships between these preference measures and insurance choices. For the regression models, however, we will want to permit non-linear relationships – for empirical and theoretical reasons – and so will just use indicator variables corresponding to the raw response categories reported in the 2004 sample-discount categories 2–4, with the lowest discount category as the excluded group.

Similarly, we will use the actual out-of-pocket expenditures for outpatient visits, inpatient visits, outpatient surgery, pharmacy, home health, and other medical care from 2004 as proxies for C_{it} in the 2006 and 2008 wave regressions.

3.2.5. Explanatory variables for insurance choice models

In summary, the explanatory variables appearing in our six estimates of Eq. (11) are as follows:

D_i: either dummy variables for the highest discount category, or dummy variables for discount categories 2, 3, and 4 as listed in the Schema, from 2004 wave of HRS data;

C_i: individual out-of-pocket expenditures in 2004 wave of HRS data for outpatient visits and prescription drug;

H_{it}: dummy variables indicating whether the respondent reports having a diagnosis of diabetes, cancer, heart disease, or stroke, in the current wave (2006 or 2008);

X_{it}: respondent age, gender (male = 1), good or excellent self-reported health, race (African American, Hispanic, Other, with Caucasian as the excluded category), marital status (married = 1), education (less than a high school education, high school diploma, with any college as the excluded category), employment status (currently employed, retired, with not employed as the excluded category), and household income, all measured as of the current wave (2006 or 2008).

3.3. Discounting and health insurance choice results

The results from the grouped regression models of the determinants of individual discount rates are presented in Table 3. Imputed discount rates are presented in Figure 1. The first column reflects a model that only contains cognitive and child experience variables; the second column reflects the full model. Several estimated effects are significant and consistent with past findings. The results do address – but by no means

Table 3. Discount models on all respondents, 2004

	Cognitive and Child Risk Only	Full Models
Subjective probability respondent live to 95	−0.00011	−0.00026
Respondent feels religion is very important	0.0029	−0.015
Smoked as adolescent	0.0020	0.0061
Parents smoked when a child	0.026**	0.019
% words correctly recalled in memory test	−0.027	0.024
Correctly answered second subtraction question	−0.014	0.0058
Age of respondent		−0.00013
Respondent is male		−0.021*
Good or excellent self-reported health		−0.0040
Respondent is African American		0.071***
Respondent is Hispanic		0.044*
Respondent is other race, non-Caucasian		−0.037
Respondent is married		−0.0063
Less than high school education		0.031
Only high school diploma		0.023*
Respondent is employed		−0.010
Respondent is retired		−0.017
Imputed household income (in $10K)		−0.00084**
Respondent has diabetes		0.030
Respondent has cancer		−0.046**
Respondent has heart disease		−0.0097
Respondent has had a stroke		−0.0038
Constant	0.27***	0.26***
Lnsigma		
Constant	−1.98***	−2.02***
Pseudo-R^2		
Chi^2	7.43	61.66
LnL	−863.53	−839.65
Observations	815	815

*$p<0.10$.
**$p<0.05$.
***$p<0.01$.

resolve – one long-standing debate in the economic and psychological literature about time preferences: whether time preferences are determined in early youth (prior to, say, age 8) and then remain fixed thereafter. Interestingly, with respect to early life impacts, only whether a parent smoked when the respondent was a child is significant, and that variable loses significance in the full model. Some authors (e.g., Becker and Mulligan, 1997) have argued that religious views may affect revealed time preferences, though we find no support for that. Some fixed traits of the respondent – namely gender, African-American race, and Hispanic ethnicity – do have a significant impact on time preferences. As with past studies, and for some, a bit counterintuitively, men are found to have lower discount rates than women. Of most interest for those who argue in favor

Figure 1. Imputed discount rate from HRS module, 2004

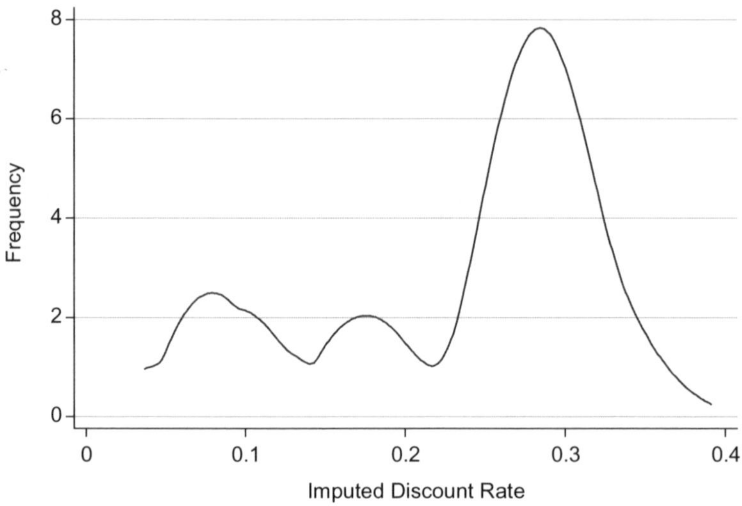

Note: Imputed discount rate ranges from 0.036 to 0.408.

of varying time preferences, we find that the life event of cancer and the time-varying factor of household income are significant predictors of time preferences. If these associations are causal, then it would be difficult to reconcile the evidence with hypotheses of fixed time preferences. To determine causality, however, longitudinal measures of time preferences across individuals are needed. To our knowledge, such data does not currently exist.

The next step in the analysis – and the primary focus of this section – is to assess what the underlying relationship is between the revealed time and the respondents' insurance decisions. As a first pass, we plot the predicted discount values against the percent of the populations that make the different insurance choices – separately for the under-65-year-old and over-65-year-old populations in 2006 and 2008. Figures 2 and 3 present these raw relationships for 2006. (The figures for 2008 are essentially identical.) Interestingly, in most cases, we do observe a non-linear association between discounting and insurance choice. Figures 2 and 3 also provide 95% confidence intervals, which are often – though not universally – broad. The apparent non-linear relationships are visually most striking for the discount vs. private FFS and no insurance choices in the under-65 group and the discount vs. HMO choice for the over-65-year-old group. These graphs more immediately raise the question of whether we might find statistically significant bivariate relationships between discounting and insurance choice regression-based tools.

Figure 2. ***Insurance choices vs. imputed discount, 2006 aged less than 65 years***

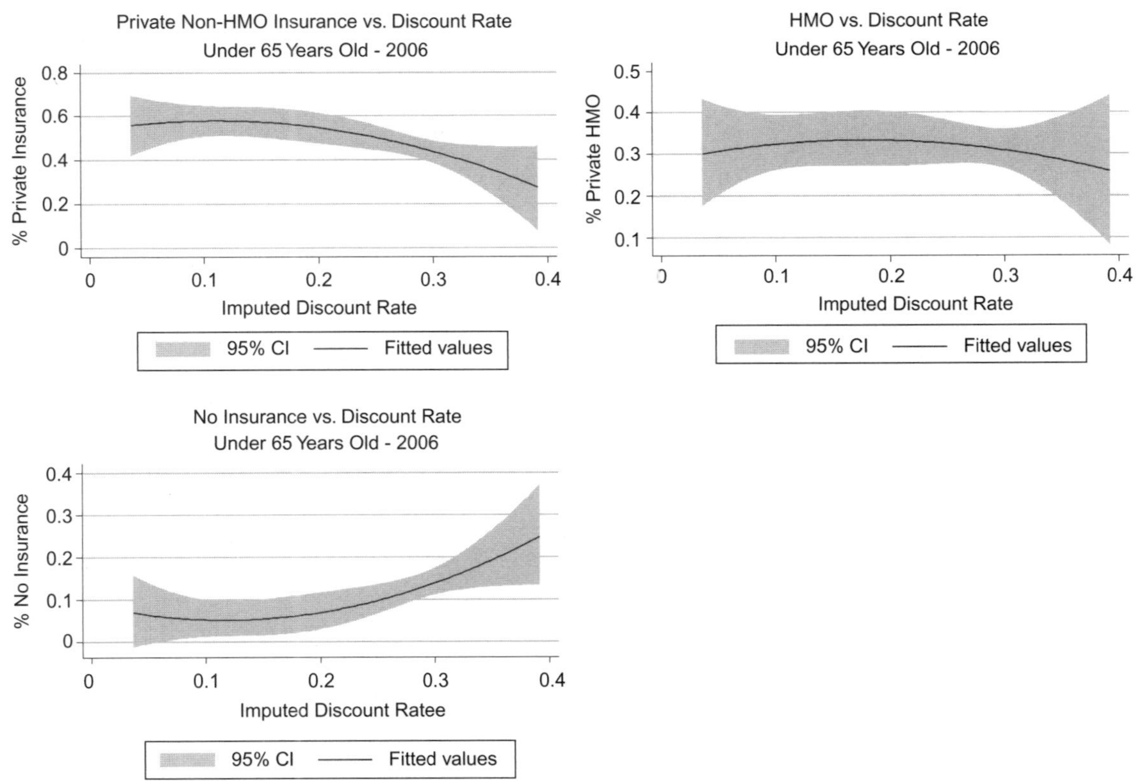

Figure 3. ***Insurance choices vs. imputed discount, 2006 aged greater than 65 years***

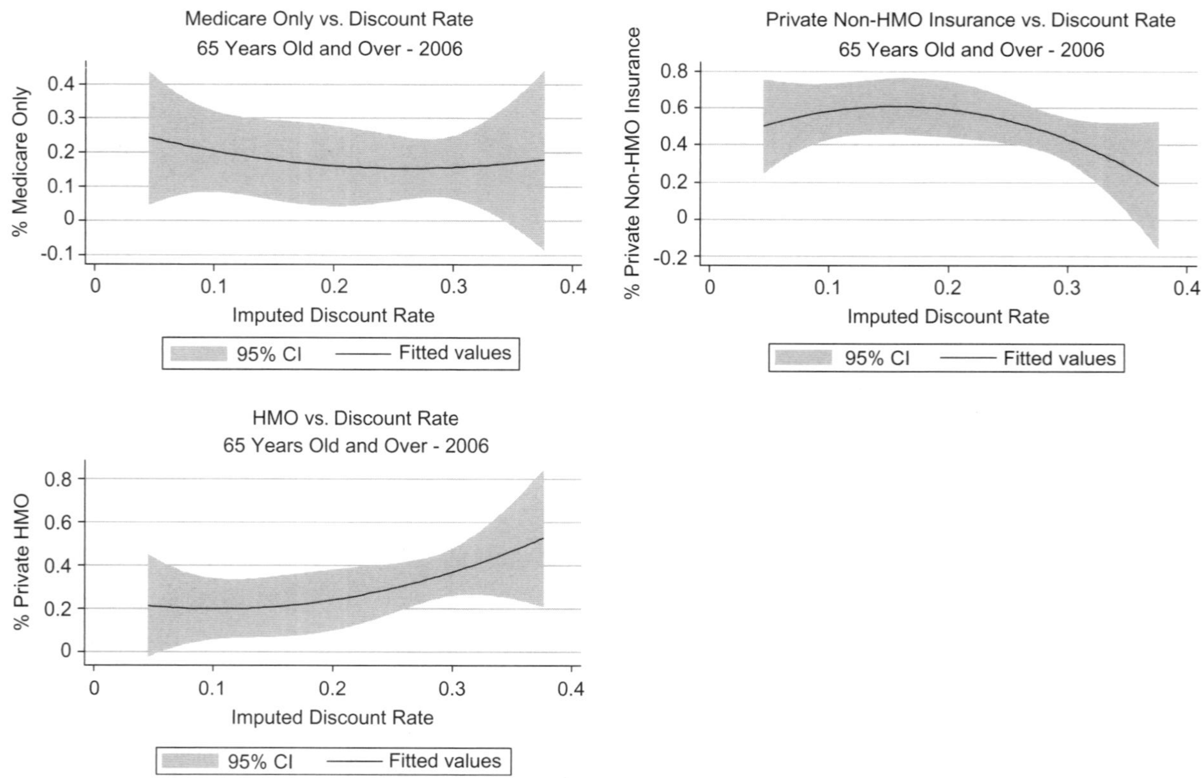

We will take two approaches to looking for non-linear relationships between time preferences and insurance choice. First, we create two dummy variables – one of which equals one if the respondent has an imputed discount rate or risk-aversion ratio in the highest 25% of the imputed values. The second will be a series of dummy variables for each of the raw dichotomous discount responses from 2004.

Table 4 presents simple probit models explaining insurance choice where the only predicted values are the high discount indicator variables (no constant). These results correspond to simple correlations between being in the highest preference groups and the probability of choosing each insurance option. Note that the two-way associations are generally statistically quite strong. With the exception of private Medigap coverage for the over-65-year-old population, being in the highest imputed discount rate group is a significant predictor of insurance choice. Recall, however, that the raw relationships between time preferences are generally non-linear – so that these bivariate relationships are incomplete.

We therefore run two versions of our models of insurance coverage decisions using multivariate probits. The results are presented in Tables 5–8. Note that each model contains the full set of regressors listed above, but we suppress the presentation of the non-time preference coefficients for presentational simplicity. These parameters are presented separately in the Appendix.

Our full models tend to find the strongest results for the relationship between time preferences and health insurance coverage using the simple "highest predicted group" measure. In 2006 (Table 5) private FFS and no health insurance coverage respond most strongly to time preferences. The

Table 4. ***Simple probits of insurance choices for highest discount group vs. all others***

	Under age 65			Age 65 and over		
	Private Insurance	HMO	No Insurance	Private Insurance	HMO	Medicare FFS Only
High discount group only, 2006						
Highest discount rate category	−0.15*	−0.50**	−1.10**	−0.037	−0.47**	−0.97*
Observations	684	684	684	154	154	154
High discount group only, 2008						
Highest discount rate category	−0.19**	−0.47**	−1.05**	−0.12	−0.63**	−0.67**
Observations	550	550	550	248	248	248

*$p<0.05$.
**$p<0.01$.

***Table 5.* Probit regressions for insurance status 2006, age < 65**

	All discount and risk categories			Top discount and risk categories		
	Has private FFS insurance	Has HMO insurance	Has no health insurance	Has private FFS insurance	Has HMO insurance	Has no health insurance
Highest discount rate category				−0.18*	−0.027	0.27*
2nd discount category	−0.17	0.22	−0.36			
3rd discount category	−0.17	0.050	0.092			
4th discount category	−0.31	0.083	0.20			
Pseudo-R^2	0.081	0.049	0.172	0.081	0.047	0.168
Chi^2	62.93	36.98	67.49	62.95	36.16	57.67
LnL	−433.72	−402.82	−199.22	−434.02	−403.39	−200.16
Observations	682	682	667	682	682	667

*$p < 0.10$.

***Table 6.* Probit regressions for insurance status 2006, age> = 65**

	All discount and risk categories			Top discount and risk categories		
	Has private FFS insurance	Has HMO insurance	Has medicare only	Has private FFS insurance	Has HMO insurance	Has medicare FFS only
Highest discount rate category				0.070	0.36	−0.49*
2nd discount category	0.18	−0.53	0.82			
3rd discount category	0.00080	−0.17	0.81			
4th discount category	0.15	0.088	0.18			
Pseudo-R^2	0.133	0.132	0.231	0.132	0.127	0.219
Chi^2	27.27	25.66	34.02	27.31	24.50	32.24
LnL	−90.14	−76.47	−56.65	−90.24	−76.97	−57.50
Observations	150	145	150	150	145	150

*$p < 0.10$.

over-65-year-old population exhibits a statistically significant concave (inverted "U") response of the probability of having only Medicare coverage to time preferences – again, confirming Figure 2. This is seen in the statistically significant negative effect on the highest discount rate category when it is entered alone, and the statistically significant positive effects on the middle two categories when the whole set of discount indicators are included. The results from 2008 are largely consistent with those from 2006. The highest predicted discount rates are negatively

Table 7. ***Probit regressions for insurance status 2008, age<65***

	All discount and risk categories			Top discount and risk categories		
	Has private FFS insurance	Has HMO insurance	Has no health insurance	Has private FFS insurance	Has HMO insurance	Has no health insurance
Highest discount rate category				-0.22^{*}	0.11	0.21
2nd discount category	−0.15	0.63^{**}	-0.68^{*}			
3rd discount category	0.036	0.42	-0.77^{**}			
4th discount category	−0.27	0.55^{**}	−0.31			
Pseudo-R^2	0.093	0.068	0.188	0.092	0.062	0.177
Chi^2	70.61	35.93	87.92	69.99	31.92	75.00
LnL	−344.40	−315.08	−168.54	−344.79	−317.28	−170.87
Observations	549	549	549	549	549	549

$^{*}p<0.10$.
$^{**}p<0.05$.

Table 8. ***Probit regressions for insurance status 2008, age> = 65***

	All discount and risk categories			Top discount and risk categories		
	Has private FFS insurance	Has HMO insurance	Has medicare only	Has private FFS insurance	Has HMO insurance	Has medicare FFS only
Highest discount rate category				−0.016	0.061	0.10
2nd discount category	0.15	0.48	−0.51			
3rd discount category	0.022	0.76	-0.80^{*}			
4th discount category	0.053	0.56	−0.35			
Pseudo-R^2	0.078	0.138	0.145	0.077	0.130	0.135
Chi^2	32.54	38.43	42.67	32.74	38.31	38.85
LnL	−157.57	−119.99	−116.76	−157.66	−121.13	−118.19
Observations	247	247	242	247	247	242

$^{*}p<0.10$.

associated with private FFS insurance in the under-65-year-old group. In 2008, the convex relationship to discount rates is also exhibited in the no insurance choice for this age group as well. Time preferences do seem related, though not in a completely consistent way, with the decision to opt for HMO coverage in this age group, when considering the full indicator variable models.

4. Summary

Economists view health as a type of human capital – decisions across which are made under the influence of myriad factors common across many types of investments for health and welfare. One factor that is ubiquitous across such investments is the role that the timing of payoffs plays in determining whether an investment is worthwhile. Despite this fundamental nature of time preferences in decision making, the role such preferences have on health-related decisions has not been studied heavily.

For example, interventions aimed at educating people on the benefits of cardiovascular prevention will be ineffective for those people who strongly prefer the present over the future. This is because the problem lies not in the fact that such people don't appreciate the benefit that might occur in 5 or 10 years from reduced coronary heart disease – the problem lies in the fact that the person cares substantially less about what happens in the distant future than in the present. These tendencies to engage in present-oriented consumption could affect a wide array of health choices – preventive care, weight management, cancer screening, or even health insurance decisions. Despite this relatively obvious observation, there have been few attempts in the economic literature to directly assess how individuals' time preferences affect the demand for health services or insurance.

In the second half of this chapter, we used three waves of the HRS to explore the determinants of individual-level discounting, and the relationship between discounting and choices regarding insurance coverage. To avoid concerns about simultaneity, we model the impact of discounting responses in 2004 on categorical health insurance outcomes from 2006 to 2008. Driven by theoretical considerations, the probit models of insurance choice permit non-linear responses to time and risk preferences. Our findings are generally supportive of the theoretical prediction that individuals' time preferences should exhibit non-linear relationships between health insurance choices.

While the results here are supported by a relatively small sample size (682 in the under-65-year-old population and only 150 in the over-65-year-old population), they are nonetheless significant for several reasons. First, we add to the growing body of literature that indicates that time preferences are determined by time-varying events and personal characteristics. Thus, rather than being fixed endowments – like genes, or like personality traits, according to many psychologists – time preferences appear to at least evolve, and may be directly malleable. Second, we find that preferences for insurance coverage (or at least the latent variables that represent them) do depend upon individual's rates of discounting the future. These time responses are consistent with a theoretical description that assumes dynamic effects of health choices on health expectations.

That time preferences appear both to respond to health states and appear to affect health insurance decisions in our analysis suggests that important feedback loop effects are possible. When designing insurance benefit structures and policies that independently affect coverage, policy makers often consider the consequences on health. Our results suggest that policy considerations should be significantly more comprehensive. If health – among other things – affects time preferences as Becker and Mulligan hypothesize, then the dynamic impact on insurance decisions and future health outcomes are potentially large. In addition, if health does affect time preferences, then the spillover effects from insurance policy decisions to other aspects of life (e.g., savings rates, educational attainment, and addictive behaviors) may themselves become first-order considerations.

Clearly, much research remains to be conducted – and the results in this chapter on the relationship between time preferences and insurance should be taken as suggestive. New data is needed, which tracks revealed time (and risk) preferences alongside health care consumption, health insurance coverage, and health outcomes. The research we present here points toward the potential value in understanding these relationships more precisely and indicates intriguing avenues for policies aimed at improving a broad range of social ills.

Acknowledgment

The authors would like to thank Avi Dor, Randall Ellis, and participants at the Allied Social Sciences Association Annual Meetings, Atlanta, GA, January 3–5, 2010 for their helpful comments on a version of this chapter.

References

Axon, R.N., W.D. Bradford and B.M. Egan (2009), "The role of individual time preferences in health behaviors among hypertensive adults: A pilot study", *Journal of the American Society of Hypertension*, Vol. 3(1), pp. 35–41.

Becker, G. and K. Murphy (1988), "A theory of rational addiction", *Journal of Political Economy*, Vol. 96(4), pp. 675–700.

Becker, G.S. and C.B. Mulligan (1997), "The endogenous determination of time preference", *Quarterly Journal of Economics*, Vol. 1123(3), pp. 729–758.

Bishai, D.M. (2004), "Does time preference change with age?", *Journal of Population Economics*, Vol. 17, pp. 583–602.

Bradford, W.D. (2010), "Association between individual time preferences and health maintenance habits", *Medical Decision Making*, Vol. 30, pp. 99–112.

Bradford, W.D., J. Zoller and G. Silvestri (2010), "Estimating the effect of individual time preferences on the demand for preventative healthcare", *Southern Economic Journal*, Vol. 76(4), pp. 1005–1031.

Coller, M. and M. Williams (1999), "Eliciting individual discount rates", *Experimental Economics*, Vol. 2, pp. 107–127.

Cutler, D.M. and R.J. Zeckhauser (2000), "The anatomy of health insurance", pp. 563–643 in: A.J. Culyer and J.P. Newhouse, editors, *Handbook of Health Economics*, Amsterdam: North Holland.

Ehrlich, I. and H. Chuma (1990), "A model of the demand for longevity and the value of life extension", *Journal of Political Economy*, Vol. 98(4), pp. 761–782.

Feldman, R.M. and B. Dowd (1991), "A new estimate of the welfare loss of excess health insurance", *American Economic Review*, Vol. 81(1), pp. 297–301.

Grossman, M. (1972), "On the concept of health capital and the demand for health", *Journal of Political Economy*, Vol. 80(2), pp. 223–255.

Grossman, M. (2000), "The human capital model", in: A. Culyer and J. Newhouse, editors, *Handbook of Health Economics*, Amsterdam: Elsevier Science B.V.

Grossman, M. and R. Kaestner (1997), "Effects of education on health", pp. 69–123 in: J. Behrman and N. Stacey, editors, *The Social Benefits of Education*, Ann Arbor: University of Michigan Press.

Koopmans, T.C. (1960), "Stationary ordinal utility and impatience", *Econometrica*, Vol. 28(2), pp. 287–309.

Koopmans, T.C., P.A. Diamond and R.E. Williamson (1964), "Stationary utility and time perpsective", *Econometrica*, Vol. 32(1–2), pp. 82–100.

Lischko, A.M. and J.F. Burgess (2010), "Knowledge of cost sharing and decisions to seek care", *The American Journal of Managed Care*, Vol. 16(4), pp. 298–304.

Metcalfe, J. and W. Mischel (1999), "A hot/cool system analysis of delay of gratification: Dynamics of willpower", *Psychological Review*, Vol. 106(1), pp. 3–19.

Nurmi, J.-E. (2005), "Thinking about and acting upon the future: Development of future orientation across the lifespan", pp. 31–57 in: A. Strathman and J. Joireman, editors, *Understanding Behavior in the Context of Time: Theory, Research, and Application*, Mahwah, NJ: Lawrence Erlbaum Associates.

Picone, G., F. Sloan and D. Taylor (2004), "Effects of risk and time preference and expected longevity on demand for medical tests", *Journal of Risk and Uncertainty*, Vol. 28(1), pp. 39–53.

Samuelson, P. (1947), *Foundations of Economic Analysis*, Cambridge, MA: Harvard University Press.

Stewart, M.B. (1983), "On least squares estimation when the dependent variable is grouped", *Review of Economic Studies*, Vol. 50(4), pp. 737–753.

Strathman, A. and J. Joireman (eds.) (2005), *Understanding Behavior in the Context of Time: Theory, Research, and Application*, Mahwah, NJ: Lawrence Erlbaum Associates.

Thaler, R.H. and H.M. Shefrin (1981), "An economic theory of self control", *Journal of Political Economy*, Vol. 89(2), pp. 392–406.

van Doorslaer, E. (1987), *Health, Knowledge, and the Demand for Medical Care: An Econometric Analysis*, Maastricht, The Netherlands: van Gorcum and Comp.

Wagstaff, A. (1986), "The demand for health: Some new empirical evidence", *Journal of Health Economics*, Vol. 5(2), pp. 195–233.

Wagstaff, A. (1993), "The demand for health: An empirical reformulation of the Grossman model", *Health Economics*, Vol. 2(2), pp. 189–198.

Warner, J.T. and S. Pleeter (2001), "The personal discount rate: Evidence from military downsizing programs", *American Economic Review*, Vol. 91(1), pp. 33–53.

Zweifel, P. and F. Breyer (1997), *Health Economics*, New York: Oxford University Press.

CHAPTER 5

Disparate Effects of CHIP Premiums on Disenrollment for Minorities☆

James Marton*, Cynthia S. Searcy and Jennifer Ghandhi

Abstract

This chapter examines whether or not the introduction of a new $20 family premium in Kentucky's Children's Health Insurance Program (CHIP) program in late 2003 had a differential impact on the enrollment duration of children in different demographic groups, with a special focus on any potential differences by race or ethnicity. A competing risk hazard model is estimated in order to differentiate between children exiting CHIP via a transfer to Medicaid and children who exited public coverage completely. We find that non-white children are generally more likely to exit than white children. This general white/non-white difference increases immediately following the introduction of the $20 premium

Keywords: CHIP, minorities, public policy, child health

JEL classifications: I18, I38, J13

☆ This chapter is based on the research Jennifer Ghandhi conducted as James Marton's intern during the Andrew Young School of Policy Studies: Research Experiences for Undergraduates Summer Internship Program in the summer of 2009.

* Corresponding author.

CONTRIBUTIONS TO ECONOMIC ANALYSIS
VOLUME 290 ISSN: 0573-8555
DOI:10.1108/S0573-8555(2010)0000290008

1. Introduction

In 1997, Congress passed the State Children's Health Insurance Program (CHIP) to provide financial assistance to states for offering health insurance benefits to lower-income children who do not qualify for Medicaid coverage. As of 2009, all 50 states and the District of Columbia offer CHIP programs – together comprising 5.6 million enrollees (CMMS, 2009). While early studies focused on characteristics of new CHIP enrollees and those eligible who are not enrolled (Dick *et al.*, 2003, 2004; Shone *et al.*, 2003), more recent studies have concentrated on evaluating quality of care for children in CHIP, program retention, and measuring program costs (Shone and Szilagyi, 2005). A number of studies have explored characteristics of disenrollees and reasons for disenrolling from CHIP, although few have focused on race or ethnicity as a determinant of leaving a state program (Miller *et al.*, 2004; Sommers, 2005). This is a curious gap in the literature, given evidence of the link between lack of health insurance and poor health among minorities (Lantz *et al.*, 1998). Although studies of eligible non-enrollees capture these children in some time periods, it is important to understand if race or ethnicity is a predictor of churn in CHIP enrollment, especially if continuous access to health care promotes better health.

Children leaving CHIP may retain health insurance by qualifying for Medicaid or shifting into private coverage. Those leaving CHIP without health insurance despite being eligible, however, are of concern to policymakers. Reasons for dropping out of CHIP may include the costs of redetermining eligibility, dissatisfaction with prior or available care, availability of more affordable health care alternatives (e.g., low cost, out-of-pocket clinics), and the stigma of receiving public assistance (Sommers, 2005). More recently, states have introduced explicit costs for enrolling in CHIP to offset growth in program expenditures – monthly premiums. Some worry that requiring premiums to retain CHIP might create inequity among vulnerable subgroups in the program, particularly minorities who disproportionately lack health insurance and report higher unmet needs and being in poorer health compared to their non-white peers (Stevens *et al.*, 2006; Flores and Tomany-Korman, 2008).

The purpose of this study is to examine the differential short-run effects of premiums on disenrollment based on sociodemographic characteristics of CHIP recipients after the introduction of a $20 per family per month premium in Kentucky's CHIP program in late 2003. In this study, we examine various exit routes from CHIP in order to differentiate between exits to other forms of public insurance coverage and an exit to no public coverage. While previous studies have examined differential exit patterns of non-whites within CHIP, this chapter focuses on the differential impact of premiums on minorities. To the extent that the introduction of premiums puts minorities at greater risk for dropping out of CHIP, policymakers should consider the benefit of cost sharing relative to the potential cost of interrupted access to health care.

2. *Background*

Investigations into the demographic characteristics and prior access to health care of CHIP enrollees have interesting associations with race and ethnicity. Shone *et al.* (2003) examine demographic characteristics and enrollees in four states' CHIP programs. They find black and Hispanic children, prior to enrolling in CHIP, to be more likely to lack health insurance and to have poorer health status despite the fact that eligibility for CHIP requires family income to fall within a similar, narrow range. After gaining access to health care via CHIP, however, the program is associated with decreases in disparities among minorities in access to and receipt of medical care, although differences in quality of care still exist (Shone and Szilagyi, 2005). The authors point out that differential care should not be surprising since CHIP only eliminates financial barriers to care – not non-financial ones that could result in inequity.

Less is known about the relationship between race and disenrollment from CHIP. One major study for New Jersey finds that minority children are more likely to disenroll from CHIP. Miller *et al.* (2004) find that black, non-Hispanic children in New Jersey's CHIP program are more likely to disenroll compared to their white counterparts, although this result only applies to families with incomes between 150 and 350 percent of the federal poverty level (FPL) where premiums for cost sharing are in place.[1] The authors suggest that black families may be more likely to disenroll because they live in regions with poor access to health care, so they attach a lower value to remaining enrolled in the program. Alternatively, they suggest that differences in treatment might lead blacks to have a more dissatisfying experience with their health care providers. Lastly, they propose that black families have lower mean income than white families despite being in the same qualifying income bracket, potentially making the premium unaffordable.

In contrast, several studies find that race has no association with disenrollment. Sommers (2005) uses national data from the Current Population Survey March Supplement and finds black children no less likely compared to whites to exit CHIP or Medicaid to become uninsured when they should still be eligible. Using enrollees in Texas' CHIP program,

---

[1] Although non-payment of premiums was the primary reason for disenrollment among this group, the authors cannot determine if children left the program to enroll in private plans or for some other reason (e.g., dissatisfaction with care).

Shenkman *et al.* (2004) find that proportions of minorities among groups of established enrollees, new enrollees, and disenrollees are similar, indicating no disproportionate rate of disenrollment among minorities. A more recent study of New York CHIP enrollees also finds no association between race and disenrollment within 2 months of receipt of benefits (Liu *et al.*, 2009). Failure to find race or ethnicity to be a significant determinant of disenrollment could result from the difficulty of disentangling their independent effects from socioeconomic factors that also affect retention of health insurance.

Although few studies find associations between race and disenrollment, it is worth noting that the disproportional disenrollment trend among black families observed in New Jersey's CHIP program occurs in the eligibility category (between 150 and 350 percent of the FPL) with a cost-sharing premium (Miller *et al.*, 2004). As a result of increased budgetary pressure, cost sharing has become a common feature of many CHIP programs. By January 2008, 34 states charged premiums for some or all CHIP enrollees. Furthermore, states often change cost-sharing levels either by changing premiums or by changing the income thresholds at which families must pay premiums (Marton, 2007).

Several papers in the literature have tested the relationship of premium increases on disenrollment based on health status and sociodemographic characteristics such as age and number of siblings. Herndon *et al.* (2008) study this topic but do not include child race or ethnicity as a variable in their analysis, nor do they control for specific illnesses and conditions. Kenney *et al.* (2006/2007) study the effects of premium increases on disenrollment in CHIP in Kansas, Kentucky, and New Hampshire. They find that non-white children were more likely to disenroll from the premium-paying category of CHIP after a premium increase in Kentucky; however, no associations between race and disenrollment exist for children in Kansas and New Hampshire. The extent to which these non-white children left public coverage completely versus transferring to other forms of public coverage, such as Medicaid, is not clear.

Both lack of research and mixed results from prior studies warrant continued investigation into the differential impacts of premiums on children in various demographic groups, particularly minorities. This chapter extends the literature on CHIP disenrollment patterns among minorities and their associations with cost-sharing premiums by examining exits to other forms of public coverage and exits to no public coverage. We use a competing risk model to estimate duration of a child's enrollment in CHIP after a \$20 premium was introduced for families with incomes between 151 and 200 percent of the FPL in Kentucky. We also control for health status using three different chronic health characteristics. The competing risk model suggests that non-white children are 52 percent more likely to exit public coverage than their white counterparts in the three months after the introduction of the premium. The implication is that minority children are more likely to become uninsured than white children, suggesting that the policy change adversely affects non-whites.

3. KCHIP program and data

Kentucky's CHIP program (known as KCHIP) is a combination Medicaid expansion program for children in families with incomes at or below 150 percent of the FPL (hereafter called KCHIP 2) and a separate CHIP program (hereafter called KCHIP 3) for children in families with incomes between 151 and 200 percent of the FPL.[2] Due in part to challenging state economic conditions, Kentucky implemented a $20 monthly family premium for children enrolled in KCHIP 3 starting in December 2003. Note that because KCHIP 2 is a Medicaid expansion program, premiums cannot be implemented within that eligibility category without a federal waiver.

In order to analyze this policy change, the Kentucky Cabinet for Health and Family Services provided enrollment and claims microdata for each child enrolled in KCHIP and Medicaid programs from December 2001 to August 2004. Figure 1 provides monthly KCHIP enrollment counts by eligibility category. Unadjusted enrollment trends may mask potential differences among recipients by demographic characteristics or health status. We investigate the impact of this new premium in greater depth by constructing a dataset that consists of all new enrollment spells in KCHIP 3 initiated during our 33-month study period (51,649 spells). Enrollment is defined on a monthly basis, and we focus on new enrollment spells to avoid problems with left-censoring. A new KCHIP 3 enrollment spell is defined to begin the month a child moves into KCHIP 3. We record if the spell begins via a transfer from Medicaid coverage (40 percent), a transfer from KCHIP 2 coverage (31 percent), or from no public health insurance coverage (29 percent). Table 1 presents a summary of spell characteristics.

We follow these enrollees over time and define their KCHIP 3 enrollment spell to end if they transfer into Medicaid, if they transfer into KCHIP 2, or if they exit public coverage completely for an "other" reason, such as obtaining private health insurance coverage. If a child is no longer covered by KCHIP 3 and we do not observe a transfer to another form of public coverage, then we classify them as exiting/ending their spell via the "other" exit route. Table 1 shows that 36,892 spells (71.43 percent) end in an exit. We treat children who exit due to turning 19 and those enrolled at the end of our study period (August 2004) as right-censored observations.

---

[2] Children over age 6 are eligible for Medicaid coverage if their family income is below the poverty line (100 percent FPL). If under age 6, the income eligibility cut-offs for Medicaid extend above 100 percent FPL. Medicaid thresholds are 185 percent FPL for children under age 1 and 133 percent FPL for children aged 1 to 5.

Figure 1. KCHIP 2 and KCHIP 3 enrollment by month

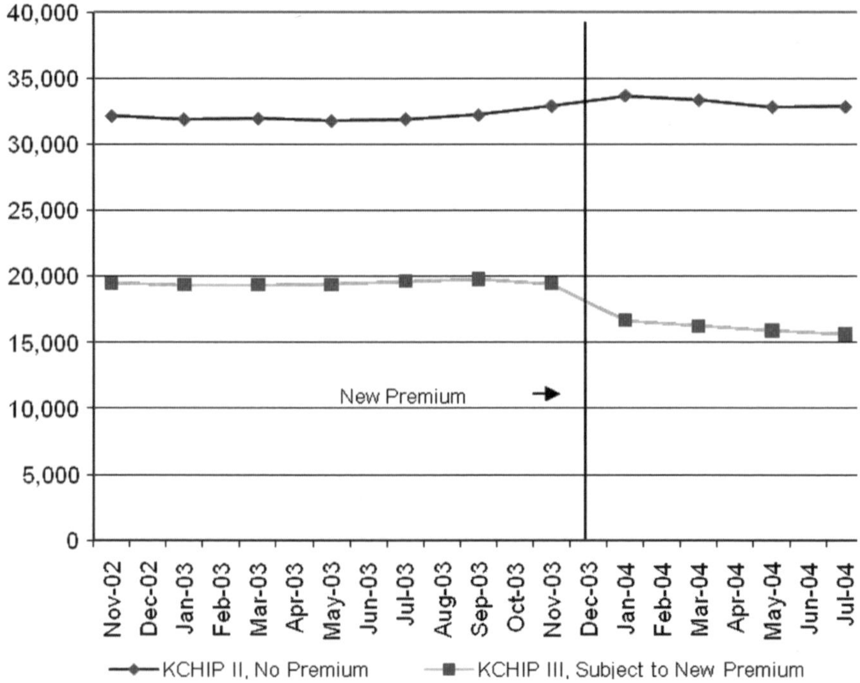

Source: Kentucky enrollment microdata provided by the Kentucky Cabinet for Health and Family Services.

The administrative enrollment database provides demographic information for these children, including age, gender, race or ethnicity, and region of residence. Figure 2 provides a map of these 16 regions. Because the Louisville area in Kentucky mandates that Medicaid and KCHIP enrollees receive care through the PASSPORT managed care program, we also create an indicator for managed care coverage. By matching this enrollment data to state administrative claims data for 2001–2005, we created a set of chronic condition indicators for children in our sample. We follow Shenkman *et al.* (2002), Marton and Talbert (2010), and Marton *et al.* (2010) and assign a chronic condition to a child in which we observe two or more appearances of the appropriate ICD-9 code in their claims records. The three main chronic conditions we analyze are asthma (ICD-9 code 493), diabetes (ICD-9 code 250), and the presence of a mental health condition (ICD-9 codes 290–319).

Table 1 shows that 48 percent of the spells in our sample are generated by females, 12 percent by non-whites, and the average number of siblings

Table 1. KCHIP 3 spell descriptive statistics

Spell characteristics	
Number of Spells	51,649
Number of Unique Children	46,222
% Multiple Spells	11
% Managed Care	23
Average Spell Length (months)	8.23
by origin	
% from Medicaid	40
% from KCHIP 2	31
% from Other	29
by exit route	
Number of Exits	36,892
% to Medicaid	33
% to KCHIP 2	24
% to Other	43
Number of Right-Censored Spells	14,757
Demographic characteristics	
% Female	48
% Non-white	12
% Age 1–5	36
% Age 6–12	37
% Age 13–18	27
Average Number of Siblings	1.16
% Diabetic	1
% Asthmatic	14
% Mental Health Problem	21
Region of residence	
% Purchase	4.32
% Pennyrile	5.87
% Green_river	5.05
% Barren_river	7.03
% Lincoln_trail	6.46
% North_central	16.60
% Northern_KY	5.61
% Buffalo_trace	1.42
% Gateway	2.49
% Fivco	4.37
% Big_sandy	6.51
% KY_river	4.93
% Cumberland_valley	8.99
% Lake_cumberland	8.21
% Bluegrass	12.15

per spell is 1.16 children. At the beginning of each spell, 36 percent are aged 1–5, 37 percent are aged 6–12, and 27 percent are aged 13–18. The most prevalent chronic health condition is a mental health problem (21 percent), followed by asthma (14 percent) and diabetes (1 percent).

Figure 2. A Map of Kentucky regions

Source: http://www.bgadd.org/index1.html.

4. Methods

We model the duration of a child's enrollment in KCHIP 3 and the relative risk of exiting via each of three exit routes (Medicaid, KCHIP 2, and no public coverage). As is common in the literature (Marton, 2007; Marton *et al.*, 2010), we assume that families compare the expected utility net of any monetary (i.e., premiums) or non-pecuniary costs (i.e., stigma) of remaining in KCHIP 3 with the net expected utility associated with each of these three exit routes. Our empirical model must allow for time-varying covariates in order to examine the impact of the change in premium level over time from $0 to $20.

We estimate a separate hazard equation as specified by Eq. (1) below for each exit route j. The competing risk model thus consists of the following set of hazard equation:

$$H_j(t) = \exp(X'_{1t}\beta_1)^* \exp(t\alpha_{j1} + t^2\alpha_{j2}) \quad \text{for } j = 1, 2, \text{or } 3 \qquad (1)$$

This equation implies that the impacts of the observable characteristics are estimated parametrically using the standard proportional hazards functional form ($\exp(X'_{1t}\beta_1)$). Rather than modeling the baseline hazard in the standard way (using the Weibull distribution), we include a quadratic in time on the right-hand side of our model ($\exp(t\alpha_{j1} + t^2\alpha_{j2})$).[3] In addition, we include as controls on the right-hand side of our model indicators for

[3] Lancaster (1992) is a seminal reference on the analysis of transition data.

spikes in the underlying KCHIP 3 hazard that occur every 12 months during periods of eligibility recertification.

Our primary research question of interest is whether or not the introduction of this new premium had a differential short-run impact on the enrollment duration of children in different demographic groups, with a special focus on any potential differences by race/ethnicity. In order to address this question, we first estimate a competing risk model as described in Eq. (1) without any interaction terms in order to assess the general relationship between demographic characteristics and KCHIP 3 enrollment duration. Next, we reestimate this model with interactions of an indicator for the first three months after the premium was introduced and the demographic variables described above. These interaction terms will tell us whether or not children in demographic groups of interest were differentially impacted in the short run by the new premium.

5. *Results*

5.1. *Main effects of the policy indicators*

Table 2 presents both a single risk (panel A) and a competing risk (panels B–D) hazard model for KCHIP 3 enrollment with no interaction terms in order to assess the primary effect of the new premium and demographics on the duration of KCHIP 3 enrollment spells. The single risk model given in panel A ignores differences in the three competing exit routes (exiting to KCHIP 2, exiting to Medicaid, exiting public health coverage completely for an "other" reason) and treats them as same. The competing risk model allows the covariates to differentially impact the likelihood of exit via each exit route.

We created an indicator (SR_3_months) for the first three months with the new premium (December 2003–February 2004) to capture the short-run impact of the policy change on enrollment. We also created a long-run indicator (LR_6_months) representing the remaining months to capture the longer run impact of the new premium. Panels B–D show that the hazard ratios for the short-run premium introduction for the three exit routes are 1.20, 1.07, and 3.35, respectively, and are all statistically significant. These imply that, compared to other months, in the months December 2003–February 2004, an "average" child is 20 percent more likely to exit via Medicaid, 7 percent more likely to exit via KCHIP 2, and 235 percent more likely to exit to no public health insurance coverage. Panel A shows that, when all exit routes are combined, an "average" child is 94 percent more likely to exit in each of these three months. More generally, a hazard ratio for an independent variable greater than 1 implies that the presence of (or an increase in) that variable leads to an increase in the likelihood of an exit (the end of a spell). The opposite is true if the estimated hazard ratio is less than 1. The *p*-values are for the test of

Table 2. ***Competing risk model for KCHIP 3 spells with no interactions (dependent variable: duration of KCHIP 3 enrollment spell)***

	(A) All exits				(B) To Medicaid				(C) To KCHIP 2				(D) To other exit			
	Haz. ratio	Std. err.	*p*-value	Abs. effect (%)	Haz. ratio	Std. err.	*p*-value	Abs. effect (%)	Haz. ratio	Std. err.	*p*-value	Abs. effect (%)	Haz. ratio	Std. err.	*p*-value	Abs. effect (%)
Policy/Spell Variables																
SR_3_months	1.94	0.03	0.00	14.11	1.20	0.03	0.00	3.39	1.07	0.04	0.03	2.03	3.35	0.06	0.00	8.61
LR_6_months	1.05	0.02	0.00	7.61	0.82	0.02	0.00	2.30	0.99	0.03	0.81	1.88	1.31	0.03	0.00	3.36
recert1	4.15	0.07	0.00	30.20	2.91	0.10	0.00	8.22	4.97	0.16	0.00	9.40	4.46	0.10	0.00	11.47
recert2	3.44	0.20	0.00	25.04	2.83	0.39	0.00	7.98	4.75	0.54	0.00	8.98	3.22	0.24	0.00	8.27
HMO_indicator	1.23	0.11	0.02	8.95	1.38	0.20	0.02	3.90	1.79	0.32	0.00	3.38	0.91	0.13	0.50	2.34
from_Medicaid	1.49	0.02	0.00	10.81	2.02	0.05	0.00	5.70	1.74	0.05	0.00	3.29	1.11	0.02	0.00	2.84
from_KCHIP2	1.19	0.02	0.00	8.68	1.05	0.03	0.06	2.97	2.23	0.06	0.00	4.21	0.90	0.02	0.00	2.32
Demographic Variables																
female	1.00	0.01	0.97	7.28	1.03	0.02	0.06	2.92	1.03	0.02	0.17	1.95	0.96	0.02	0.02	2.47
non_white	1.13	0.02	0.00	8.25	1.23	0.03	0.00	3.48	1.08	0.04	0.02	2.05	1.09	0.03	0.00	2.80
age 1 to 5	1.11	0.02	0.00	8.05	1.69	0.04	0.00	4.78	0.68	0.02	0.00	1.29	1.00	0.02	0.87	2.56
age 6 to 12	0.96	0.01	0.00	6.97	1.08	0.03	0.00	3.05	1.03	0.03	0.25	1.95	0.85	0.02	0.00	2.19
#siblings	1.07	0.01	0.00	7.77	1.11	0.01	0.00	3.12	1.17	0.01	0.00	2.20	0.98	0.01	0.03	2.52
diabetes	0.81	0.05	0.00	5.87	0.91	0.10	0.39	2.55	1.09	0.11	0.42	2.06	0.55	0.07	0.00	1.41
asthma	0.93	0.01	0.00	6.80	1.18	0.03	0.00	3.33	1.03	0.03	0.39	1.94	0.69	0.02	0.00	1.77
mental health problem	1.07	0.01	0.00	7.81	1.45	0.03	0.00	4.09	1.26	0.03	0.00	2.39	0.73	0.02	0.00	1.88
# spells	*51,649*				*51,649*				*51,649*				*51,649*			
# exits	*36,892*				*12,159*				*8,746*				*15,987*			
Avg. exit prob. (%)	*7.28*				*2.82*				*1.89*				*2.57*			
Log-likelihood	*−58,335*				*−34,921*				*−25,705*				*−33,579*			

Note: Each model also includes a linear and a quadratic time trend, as well as controls for region of residence and the monthly state unemployment rate. These coefficients are not reported above.

the hypothesis that the hazard ratio for the variable in question is equal to 1 (i.e., no effect).

As is well known in hazard analysis, the magnitudes of these effects can be difficult to interpret, because they are relative probabilities. Therefore, Table 2 also reports the absolute effect associated with each independent variable. For each exit route, these absolute effects can be compared to the average monthly probability of exiting via that exit route (calculated in the months prior to the introduction of the premium). As is reported at the bottom of Table 2, the average monthly probabilities of a child in KCHIP 3 moving into Medicaid, KCHIP 2, and no public health insurance coverage are 2.82 percent, 1.89 percent, and 2.57 percent, respectively. The absolute effect associated with the short-run premium introduction indicator suggests that the probability of a child moving into Medicaid in the months December 2003–February 2004 is 3.39 percent, which is larger than the average monthly probability of a child moving into Medicaid of 2.82 percent. Comparisons such as this one give a sense of the magnitude of the effect of the independent variable on the likelihood of an exit.

More generally, the short-run hazard ratios in Table 2 suggest that children in KCHIP 3 were more likely to move into Medicaid, slightly more likely to move into KCHIP 2, and much more likely to move to no public health insurance coverage in the first three months associated with the new KCHIP premium. The long-run indicators suggest that, conditional upon being enrolled as of March 2004 or starting a spell in that month or later (i.e., having demonstrated a willingness to pay the new premium), children were less likely to move into Medicaid or KCHIP 2 in the remaining seven months analyzed and continued to be more likely to exit to no public health insurance coverage.

Note that we are controlling for demographics, spell origin, the presence of chronic health conditions, and region of residence in order to isolate this premium impact. Most importantly, we control for other spikes in the hazard and include linear and quadratic time trends to model the baseline hazard. We also control for the state's economic climate and the availability of outside insurance options by including the monthly state unemployment rate as an additional explanatory variable.

5.2. Main effects of the demographic indicators

Turning to our demographic variables, Table 2 shows that non-white children are, in general, more likely than white children to exit KCHIP 3 by each of the exit routes. Younger children are more likely to move into Medicaid than to exit via the other exit routes, consistent with higher family income ceilings for Medicaid eligibility for younger children. Children with more siblings are more likely to transfer to both Medicaid and KCHIP 2 and slightly less likely to leave public coverage completely. Spell duration does not appear to vary to a large degree by gender.

Children with chronic health conditions are more likely to transfer into Medicaid or KCHIP 2 than to exit to no public health insurance coverage. Analysis of these chronic health conditions highlights the benefits of a competing risk approach. The combined risk approach in panel A suggests that children with a mental health condition are more likely to exit KCHIP 3 altogether. This result may concern policymakers and child health advocates alike. The competing risk model, however, suggests that this is a transfer effect. In other words, children with a mental health condition generally have a higher probability of exiting KCHIP 3 into Medicaid (panel B) or KCHIP 2 (panel C). In addition, they actually have a lower probability of exiting to no public health insurance coverage as compared to healthy children (panel D).

5.3. Differential impact of the new premium on minorities

In order to determine whether or not the new KCHIP 3 premium had a differential short-run impact on different demographic groups, we reestimated the models presented in Table 2 with interaction terms between the short-run premium indicator and all of our demographic variables. As in Table 2, we estimate both a single and competing risk version of this interacted model. The results are reported in Table 3.

Panel A of Table 2 tells us that non-white children are, in general, 13 percent more likely to exit KCHIP 3 than white children. Panel A of Table 3 reports a statistically significant 1.32 estimated hazard ratio for the non-white, short-run premium interaction term. This implies that the general white/non-white difference in the likelihood of exit from KCHIP 3 is even larger in the first three months after the new premium is put into place.

The competing risk model reported in Table 2 says that this white/non-white 13 percent relative difference in the likelihood of exiting KCHIP 3 is the average of a 23 percent relative difference in the likelihood of moving into Medicaid, an 8 percent relative difference in the likelihood of moving to KCHIP 2, and a 9 percent relative difference in the likelihood of exiting public coverage completely. The competing risk model results from Table 3 show that the increase in the general white/non-white difference in the likelihood of exiting KCHIP 3 in the first three months after the new premium is put into place is being driven by an increase in the relative likelihood of non-whites exiting public coverage completely. The hazard ratios associated with the non-white interaction terms in the "to Medicaid" and "to KCHIP 2" models are not statistically significant. Therefore, one consequence of the introduction of the new CHIP premium in Kentucky was a short-run increase in the likelihood that non-white children exit public coverage completely as compared to white children.

Panel A of Table 3 suggests no statistically significant differential short-run impact of the new premium on females or children aged 6–12. In addition, family size is not a significant predictor of a short-run differential

Table 3. Competing risk model for KCHIP 3 spells with demographic interactions (dependent variable: duration of KCHIP 3 enrollment spell)

	(A) All exits			(B) To Medicaid			(C) To KCHIP 2			(D) To other exit		
	Haz. ratio	Std. err.	*p*-value	Haz. ratio	Std. err.	*p*-value	Haz. ratio	Std. err.	*p*-value	Haz. ratio	Std. err.	*p*-value
Policy/Spell Variables												
SR_3_months	2.06	0.07	0.00	1.20	0.10	0.02	1.01	0.09	0.92	3.05	0.14	0.00
LR_6_months	1.04	0.02	0.00	0.82	0.02	0.00	0.99	0.03	0.81	1.30	0.03	0.00
recert1	4.15	0.07	0.00	2.91	0.10	0.00	4.98	0.16	0.00	4.46	0.10	0.00
recert2	3.43	0.20	0.00	2.83	0.39	0.00	4.77	0.54	0.00	3.20	0.24	0.00
HMO_indicator	1.23	0.11	0.02	1.38	0.20	0.02	1.79	0.32	0.00	0.91	0.13	0.51
from_Medicaid	1.48	0.02	0.00	2.02	0.05	0.00	1.74	0.05	0.00	1.11	0.02	0.00
from_KCHIP2	1.19	0.02	0.00	1.05	0.03	0.06	2.22	0.06	0.00	0.90	0.02	0.00
Demographic Variables												
female	1.00	0.01	0.80	1.02	0.02	0.31	1.03	0.02	0.14	0.97	0.02	0.13
non_white	1.07	0.02	0.00	1.22	0.04	0.00	1.07	0.04	0.09	0.96	0.03	0.19
age 1 to 5	1.13	0.02	0.00	1.72	0.05	0.00	0.68	0.02	0.00	1.02	0.02	0.40
age 6 to 12	0.96	0.01	0.01	1.10	0.03	0.00	1.03	0.03	0.31	0.83	0.02	0.00
# siblings	1.07	0.01	0.00	1.11	0.01	0.00	1.16	0.01	0.00	0.97	0.01	0.00
diabetes	0.82	0.06	0.01	0.98	0.12	0.85	1.04	0.12	0.70	0.50	0.07	0.00
asthma	0.96	0.02	0.01	1.18	0.03	0.00	1.02	0.03	0.62	0.69	0.02	0.00
mental health problem	1.10	0.02	0.00	1.44	0.03	0.00	1.29	0.03	0.00	0.71	0.02	0.00

Table 3. (Continued)

	(A) All exits			(B) To Medicaid			(C) To KCHIP 2			(D) To other exit		
	Haz. ratio	Std. err.	*p*-value	Haz. ratio	Std. err.	*p*-value	Haz. ratio	Std. err.	*p*-value	Haz. ratio	Std. err.	*p*-value
Demographic Interactions												
non_white × SR	1.32	0.05	0.00	1.06	0.08	0.44	1.13	0.11	0.20	1.52	0.08	0.00
female × SR	0.98	0.03	0.48	1.12	0.06	0.05	0.96	0.06	0.57	0.96	0.03	0.29
age 1 to 5 × SR	0.89	0.03	0.00	0.91	0.07	0.18	1.00	0.09	0.96	0.91	0.04	0.04
age 6 to 12 × SR	0.98	0.03	0.57	0.89	0.07	0.15	1.02	0.08	0.84	1.07	0.05	0.12
# siblings × SR	1.00	0.01	0.99	1.01	0.03	0.72	1.07	0.03	0.02	1.04	0.02	0.04
diabetes × SR	0.92	0.15	0.62	0.45	0.21	0.09	1.32	0.38	0.33	1.33	0.33	0.25
asthma × SR	0.89	0.04	0.00	1.00	0.07	0.94	1.09	0.10	0.37	1.00	0.06	0.94
mental × SR	0.88	0.03	0.00	1.06	0.07	0.38	0.81	0.06	0.01	1.10	0.05	0.05
# spells	*51,649*			*51,649*			*51,649*			*51,649*		
Log-likelihood	*−58,288*			*−34,915*			*−25,697*			*−33,530*		

response to the new premium. Children aged 1–5 are less likely than usual to exit KCHIP 3 coverage during the first three months after the introduction of the new premium. The chronic condition indicators suggest that children with asthma or a mental health problem are also less likely than usual to exit KCHIP 3 in these first three months. Thus, the largest differential demographic effect we observe is the increase in the relative likelihood that non-white children will exit KCHIP 3 in the short run after the introduction of the new $20 family premium. We conclude this section with a statement of our four primary results with respect to race:

(1) In general, non-white children are more likely to exit KCHIP 3 than white children.
(2) This difference holds across all exit routes and is the biggest in the "to Medicaid" exit route.
(3) In the three months after the introduction of the premium, the general white/non-white difference in the likelihood of exiting KCHIP 3 increased.
(4) This increase in the difference appears to be driven by a relative increase in the likelihood that non-whites were exiting all public coverage.

6. Discussion

Previous studies using data from the Current Population Survey (Sommers, 2005), Texas (Shenkman *et al.*, 2004), and New York (Liu *et al.*, 2009) did not find a relationship between race and disenrollment patterns. Therefore, our analysis appears to be only the second study, joining Miller *et al.* (2004), to demonstrate that non-white children are more likely than white children to exit CHIP coverage when cost-sharing premiums are in place. Further, our competing risk model shows that this difference appears to be driven by a relative increase in the likelihood that non-whites are exiting all public coverage, even after adding controls for child health status.

One hypothesis for this result discussed in Miller *et al.* (2004) is that non-whites may live in regions with poor access to health care, so they attach a lower value to remaining enrolled. The regional dummies we included in our models are intended to capture some of this regional variation in access to care. In results not reported, we interacted the regional indicators with the short-run premium indicator to investigate whether or not there were short-run differences in response to the premium by region of residence. For the most part, these interactions were insignificant. Another hypothesis discussed is that non-whites are more likely to experience dissatisfaction with their health care providers. Descriptive statistics from Kentucky's 2003 Medicaid and CHIP recipient surveys, however, do not suggest that minorities are less satisfied with their overall health care compared to whites. Without linking individual responses to enrollment data, we cannot be sure if this result holds for those who disenrolled after the introduction of the monthly premium.

Since KCHIP 3, KCHIP 2, and Medicaid each has different income-level requirements, one may wonder how children can exit so quickly (within three months) to a different form of public coverage. While actual income may not change right away, reported levels of income can change with an appointment or call. If family income levels change before recertification, it may be months before the family reports the change to the state. However, with the introduction of a premium, the family may take the time and effort to report the lower income right away in order to be eligible for Medicaid or the non-premium-paying eligibility category of CHIP. Marton *et al.* (2010) claim that a short-run response to the imposition of a new premium is that reported income becomes better aligned with contemporaneous income.

Even if contemporaneous income is more accurately measured when premiums are introduced, we cannot be sure how minority families respond to this new cost relative to their income because our data do not contain a variable measuring family income. Although eligibility for KCHIP 3 requires families to be between 151 and 200 percent of the FPL (roughly between $28,000 and $36,800 for a family of four in 2003), it is possible that the effects for minorities are confounded by income. Kenney *et al.* (2006/2007) and Miller *et al.* (2004) suggest that minority families may be more likely to be at the lower end of this income range compared to white families. Thus, the introduction of a monthly premium could impose a larger burden on minority families resulting in a greater likelihood of disenrollment. Similarly, not being able to control for parental education as a pathway for the effects of income could also confound the results we observe for minorities.

Absent variables to control for income or education, however, this study suggests that cost sharing does adversely impact minority children in CHIP in the short run. This could, as Shone *et al.* (2003) suggest, decrease the health of poorer families, who are more likely to be black or Hispanic, and keep them from getting adequate access to health care. Indeed, even if those who disenroll later reenroll, studies indicate that gaps in insurance coverage can have adverse health consequences for children. Federico *et al.* (2007) find that disruptions in health coverage of CHIP recipients result in unmet medical needs and less frequent preventive and sick care visits. Likewise, Cummings *et al.* (2009) find that children lacking health insurance even for short periods of time (1–4 months) lose consistency in health care providers and are more likely to delay in getting needed care compared to those with continuous coverage. To the extent that minorities in CHIP experience more churn in enrollment than whites, policymakers should consider the potential long-term costs of untreated medical conditions when attempting to share short-run costs via premiums.

Recent legislation for Medicaid and CHIP appears to recognize this trade-off, at least implicitly. The Patient Protection and Affordable Care

Act (111–148) requires states, starting in 2015, to report annually on changes in Medicaid enrollment by population, outreach and enrollment processes, and other data to monitor enrollment and retention of Medicaid eligible individuals. Legislation that renewed CHIP in 2009 (called CHIPRA) provides financial incentives to states to streamline enrollment and renewal procedures for Medicaid and CHIP (CCF, 2009). Time will tell how responsive states are to these incentives, particularly as states struggle in lean fiscal times to afford the health systems they currently have in place. Future research to quantify the costs of churn in CHIP will be important to state coffers and child health.

Acknowledgment

We like to thank Subha Basu for her work as a research assistant. We are responsible for any errors.

References

Center for Children and Families. (2009), "The Children's Health Insurance Program Reauthorization Act of 2009: overview and summary", Georgetown University Health Policy Institute (http://ccf.georgetown.edu/index/cms-filesystem-action?file = ccf%20publications/federal%20UschipU%20policy/chip%20summary%2003-09.pdfH). Accessed on May 31, 2010.

Centers for Medicare and Medicaid Services. (2009), "Table IV.8 Medicaid enrollment and beneficiaries, selected fiscal years" (http://www.cms.gov/DataCompendium/15_2009_Data_Compendium.asp#TopOfPage). Accessed on May 31, 2010.

Cummings, J.R., S.A. Lavarreda, T. Rice and E.R. Brown (2009), "The effects of varying periods of uninsurance on children's access to health care", *Pediatrics*, Vol. 123(3), pp. e411–e418.

Dick, A.W., J.D. Klein, L.P. Shone, J. Zwanziger, H. Yu and P.G. Szilagui (2003), "The evolution of the State Children's Health Insurance Program (SCHIP) in New York: changing program features and enrollee characteristics", *Pediatrics*, Vol. 112(6), pp. 542–550.

Dick, A.W., C. Brach, R.A. Allison, E. Shenkman, L.P. Shone, P.G. Szilagyi, J.D. Klein and E.M. Lewit (2004), "SCHIP's impact in three states: how do the most vulnerable children fare?", *Health Affairs*, Vol. 23(5), pp. 63–75.

Federico, S.G., J.F. Steiner, B. Beaty, L. Crane and A. Kempe (2007), "Disruptions in insurance coverage: patterns and relationship to health care access, unmet need, and utilization before enrollment in the State Children's Health Insurance Program", *Pediatrics*, Vol. 120(4), pp. e1009–e1016.

Flores, G. and S.C. Tomany-Korman (2008), "Racial and ethnic disparities in medical and dental health, access to care, and use of services in US children", *Pediatrics*, Vol. 121(2), pp. e286–e298.

Herndon, J.B., W.B. Vogel, R.L. Bucciarelli and E.A. Shenkman (2008), "Public premiums and benefit design", *Health Research and Educational Trust*, Vol. 43(2), pp. 458–477.

Kenney, G., R.A. Allison, J.F. Costich, J. Marton and J. McFeeters (2006/2007), "Effects of premium increases on enrollment in SCHIP: findings from three states", *Inquiry*, Vol. 43(4), pp. 378–392.

Lancaster, T. (1992), *The Econometric Analysis of Transition Data*, Cambridge, MA: Cambridge University Press.

Lantz, P.M., J.S. House, J.M. Lepkowski, D.R. Williams, R.P. Mero and J. Chen (1998), "Socio-economic factors, health behaviors, and mortality", *Journal of the American Medical Association*, Vol. 279, pp. 1703–1708.

Liu, H., C.E. Phelps, P.J. Veazie, A. Dick, J.D. Klein, L.P. Shone and P.G. Szilagyi (2009), "Managed care quality and disenrollment in New York SCHIP", *American Journal of Managed Care*, Vol. 15(12), pp. 910–918.

Marton, J. (2007), "The impact of the introduction of premiums into a SCHIP program", *Journal of Policy Analysis and Management*, Vol. 26, pp. 237–255.

Marton, J. and J.C. Talbert (2010), "CHIP premiums, health status, and the insurance coverage of children", *Inquiry*, Vol. 47(3), pp. 199–214.

Marton, J., P.G. Ketsche and M. Zhou (2010), "SCHIP premiums, enrollment, and expenditures: a two state, competing risk analysis", *Health Economics*, Vol. 19(7), pp. 772–791.

Miller, J.E., D. Gaboda, J.C. Cantor, T.M. Videon and Y. Diaz (2004), "Demographics of disenrollment from SCHIP: evidence from NJ KidCare", *Journal of Health Care for the Poor and Undeserved*, Vol. 15(1), pp. 113–126.

Shenkman, E., B. Vogel, J.M. Boyett and R. Naff (2002), "Disenrollment and re-enrollment patterns in a SCHIP", *Health Care Financing Review*, Vol. 23(3), pp. 47–63.

Shenkman, E.A., V. Schaffer and D. Vargas (2004), *An Analysis of Disenrollment Patterns in the Children's Health Insurance Program in Texas*, Gainesville, FL: Institute for Child Health Policy, Accessed on May 27, 2010 at: http://www.hhsc.state.tx.us/chip/reports/120304_disenroll.html

Shone, L.P. and P.G. Szilagyi (2005), "The state children's health insurance program", *Current Opinion in Pediatrics*, Vol. 17, pp. 764–772.

Shone, L.P., A.W. Dick, C. Brach, K.S. Kimminau, B.J. LaClair, E.A. Shenkman, J.F. Col, V.A. Schaffer, F. Mulvihill, P.G. Szilagyi, J.D. Klein, K. VanLandeghem and J. Bronsteint (2003), "The role of race and ethnicity in the State Children's Health Insurance Program (SCHIP) in four states: are there baseline disparities, and what do they mean for SCHIP?", *Pediatrics*, Vol. 112(6), pp. 521–532.

Sommers, B.D. (2005), "From Medicaid to uninsured: drop-out among children in public insurance programs", *Health Services Research*, Vol. 40(1), pp. 59–78.

Stevens, G.D., M. Seid and N. Halfon (2006), "Enrolling vulnerable, uninsured but eligible children in public health insurance: association with health status and primary care access", *Pediatrics*, Vol. 117(4), pp. e751–e759.

CHAPTER 6

Health Outcomes from Head Start Participation

Carolina C. Felix and David E. Frisvold*

Abstract

In this chapter, we discuss whether early-childhood investments in low-income children could lead to a lasting impact on health outcomes. We note that such investments could improve adolescent and adult health by increasing child health, increasing educational attainment, or influencing parents' behaviors. Model preschool programs, such as the High/Scope Perry Preschool Program and the Carolina Abecedarian Program, have been successful in increasing the educational attainment and health behaviors of low-income children. The Head Start program, which is the largest public investment in low-income, preschool-aged children in the United States, has also improved child health and educational attainment.

Although there is extensive research on the impact of Head Start participation, there has been little research on the impact on risky behaviors in adolescence. Using data from the Panel Study of Income Dynamics (PSID) and its Child Development Supplements (CDS), we examine the impact of Head Start participation on smoking, alcohol use, and drug use throughout adolescence and the extent to which varying degrees of selection on unobservables influence this relationship.

Keywords: Head Start, smoking, alcohol, drug use

JEL classifications: I12, I38, J13

---

* Corresponding author.

CONTRIBUTIONS TO ECONOMIC ANALYSIS
VOLUME 290 ISSN: 0573-8555
DOI:10.1108/S0573-8555(2010)0000290009

1. Introduction

Growing up in poverty has a persistent impact on a broad range of social and economic outcomes. Holzer *et al.* (2007) estimate the aggregate social costs of childhood poverty in the United States at approximately $500 billion per year. Childhood poverty is associated with lower levels of educational attainment (Duncan *et al.*, 1998) and higher rates of criminal activity (Holzer *et al.*, 2007). Additionally, childhood poverty is linked to a reduction in health outcomes during childhood, adolescence, and adulthood (Case *et al.*, 2002; Almond and Currie, 2010). Socioeconomic status during childhood is negatively related to a variety of adult health measures, including adult body mass index (BMI) (Blane *et al.*, 1996), the incidence of type 2 diabetes for women (Maty *et al.*, 2002), and mortality (Davey Smith *et al.*, 1998; Hayward and Gorman, 2004). Thus, public investments in the cognitive, social, and physical development of poor youths may significantly improve individual and social welfare.

This chapter focuses on whether early childhood education programs that emphasize cognitive, social, and physical development can reduce the negative impact of growing up in poverty. In particular, we focus our attention on whether the Head Start program improves health outcomes for poor children. The Head Start program, which began as a key component of the War on Poverty in 1965, has been one of the largest federal investments in the human capital of poor children. The program currently provides educational, health, nutritional, and social services to approximately 900,000 preschool-aged children and their families each year at an annual cost of $7 billion.

To address this topic, we begin by describing conceptually why early childhood education programs may influence health. Next, we review the literature on the impact of small, high-quality preschool programs, which suggests that early childhood intervention programs do have the potential to significantly influence adolescent and young adult outcomes. Next, we review the literature on the impact of the large-scale, publicly funded Head Start program on health outcomes. Finally, to supplement this literature, we examine the impact of Head Start participation on smoking, alcohol use, and drug use throughout adolescence.

2. Conceptual framework

Grossman's (1972) health capital model provides a conceptual basis for the hypothesis that participation in an early childhood education program might permanently influence participants' health: investments in childhood health and nutrition should augment current and future health capital, while investments in human capital should increase the efficiency with which health capital is produced over time. There is substantial evidence of a positive correlation between childhood and adult health. For example, Case *et al.* (2005) find that prenatal and childhood health, measured by prenatal smoking, birth weight, and the number of chronic conditions at age 7, directly influences adult health status. Thus, public investments for young children that improve childhood health should have a persistent impact throughout adolescence and adulthood. Case *et al.* (2005) find that chronic conditions at age 7 that do not exist by age 16 do not reduce health status in adulthood.

There is also substantial evidence of a positive effect of education on health outcomes. Grossman and Kaestner (1997) review the early research on the relationship between educational attainment and a variety of measures of health outcomes and conclude that the influence of education is most likely a causal effect. More recent research with a variety of different empirical strategies, with the exception of Clark and Royer (2010), corroborates this conclusion (Currie and Moretti, 2003; Lleras-Muney, 2005; Chou *et al.*, 2007; de Walque, 2007; Grimard and Parent, 2007; Mazumder, 2007; Fletcher and Frisvold, 2009a). Further, improvements in school quality and graduating from a selective college have a persistent influence on a variety of health measures throughout adulthood (Fletcher and Frisvold, 2009b; Frisvold and Golberstein, 2010a, 2010b). Thus, public investments for young children that improve educational attainment or school quality should have a persistent impact on health outcomes.

An important consideration, however, is that the impact of participation in an early childhood development program on childhood outcomes and, thus, for adolescent and adult outcomes as well, is the net result of the direct effect of the program and the augmenting or diminishing indirect effect of changes in parents' behavior (Behrman *et al.*, 2004; Frisvold and Lumeng, 2009). If publicly provided early-childhood education programs that offer child care and developmental services lower the marginal cost of child quality, then parental investment in children may increase (Becker and Tomes, 1976). Greater parental investment would magnify the impact of these programs on childhood outcomes. On the other hand, parents could also respond with compensating behaviors such as decreasing their investment in the child if the Head Start program leads to an endowment and not a price effect (Becker and Tomes, 1976). Thus, the total impact of participation in an early childhood education program on later health behaviors and health outcomes will likely be influenced by the impact of the program on childhood health, human capital development, and parental behaviors.

3. Small, high-quality preschool programs

There were a variety of small, high-quality preschool programs that began in the 1960s and 1970s that aimed to improve the social and educational development of low-income children. Many of these programs are reviewed in Currie (2001); here, we focus on the two most prominent examples, the High/Scope Perry Preschool Program and the Carolina Abecedarian Program. The Perry Preschool program occurred throughout the 1960s in Ypsilanti, Michigan (Schweinhart *et al.*, 2005). The program provided center-based care for 2.5 hours per weekday for 35 weeks for up to 2 years, home visiting for 1.5 hours per week, and group meeting for parents. The participants in the study were 123 black children aged 3 and 4 who lived in poverty and were assessed to be at risk of school failure; 58 of these children were randomly assigned to participate in the preschool program and the remaining children were the control group. The child–teacher ratio varied from 5 to 6.25 children per teacher throughout the program. The program costs were $15,166 per child in 2000 dollars, and the majority of the funds were directed to teachers' salaries (Schweinhart *et al.*, 2005). All teachers were trained in child development and had master's degrees (Currie, 2001). The short-term evaluation of the program focused primarily on cognitive outcomes (Currie, 2001), so it is unknown whether the program improved childhood health outcomes. There were significant improvements in educational attainment – Perry Preschool participants were three times more likely to graduate from high school (Belfield *et al.*, 2006) – which suggests that there may be persistent effects on health outcomes as well. Indeed, Schweinhart *et al.* (2005) and Belfield *et al.* (2006) note that program participants were less likely to smoke or use drugs; however, the prevalence of these behaviors for both the treatment and control groups greatly exceeded the prevalence of these behaviors among blacks nationally.

The Carolina Abecedarian program occurred throughout the 1970s and provided center-based care to poor, black infants and children as early as 6 weeks old through 5 years for 8 hours per day, 5 days per week, and 50 weeks per year (Currie, 2001). The program emphasized language development, and the child–teacher ratios were 3 to 1 for infants and 6 to 1 for children. This program was evaluated by randomly assigning 57 children to the program and 54 children to the control group (Currie, 2001). The program costs were $34,473 per child in 2000 dollars (Schweinhart *et al.*, 2005). The Abecedarian program increased IQ and achievement, as well as educational attainment (Barnett and Masse, 2007). Thus, it is likely that the program improved health outcomes as well. The effects on health have generally not been studied; however, Barnett and Masse (2007) do show that the prevalence of smoking among participants at age 21 is substantially less (16 percentage points) than the prevalence among the control group. Similar to the Perry Preschool program, the prevalence of smoking for both the treatment and control groups greatly exceeded the prevalence of smoking nationally.

The High/Scope Perry Preschool Program and the Carolina Abecedarian Program demonstrate that high-quality early-childhood interventions focused on cognitive development for low-income children can improve adult health behaviors. In the next section, we discuss whether Head Start, a large public program for low-income children that is less funded, can also have a lasting impact on health.

4. The Head Start program

The Head Start program is the largest public early education program in the United States for low-income and disadvantaged children. According to the Head Start Program Information Report (PIR) data, excluding Early Head Start and the Migrant and Seasonal Head Start programs, there were 792,454 funded enrollment slots in Head Start in 2009 and 46 percent of these slots were in a center-based full-day classroom that provided services for 5 days per week.[1] Due to turnover, 925,473 children participated in the Head Start program throughout the year. Fifty-seven percent of these children were 4 years old and 39 percent were 3 years old. Thirty-four percent of Head Start participants were Hispanic or Latino origin, 31 percent were black, and 39 percent were white. The average cost per child in 2009 was $7,600 (Office of Head Start, 2010a). More than 27 million children have participated in Head Start since it began in 1965 as part of the War on Poverty (Office of Head Start, 2010a).

Although Head Start is locally administered and operated primarily by community action agencies, public school systems, and non-profit organizations, the federal government regulates and funds the program. Federal regulations define eligibility criteria, the selection and recruitment of children, and the services provided to children and families in the program.

Eligibility for Head Start participation is determined primarily by family income, although children may also be categorically eligible. A child is eligible if the family's gross annual income, including unemployment compensation and other sources of transfer income, is less than or equal to the poverty guidelines (Office of Head Start, 2010b). Annual income can be determined using the previous year's tax returns or extrapolating from recent pay statements (Office of Head Start, 2010b). Children are categorically eligible if the family receives public assistance through Temporary Assistance for Needy Families or Supplemental Security Income, if the child is homeless, or if the child is in foster care. Each Head Start center may enroll up to 10 percent of children from families with incomes above the poverty guidelines and at least 10 percent of the

---

[1] In 2009, 127,532 children participated in the Early Head Start and Migrant and Seasonal Head Start programs. Of the 792,454 funded enrollment slots for Head Start, 98 percent were funded through the Administration for Children and Families and the remaining 2 percent were funded by other sources, which include state revenues.

enrollment opportunities must be available for children with disabilities. Further, after the recent reauthorization of the Head Start Act in 2007, each Head Start center may enroll up to an additional 35 percent of children from families with incomes between 100 and 130 percent of the poverty guidelines.[2] Finally, a child must be at least 3 years old to be eligible for Head Start participation, based on the date used by the community to determine public school eligibility. Once enrolled in Head Start, children may remain in the program until kindergarten or first grade is available in the community.

Head Start is not a fully funded program so that eligible applicants may not be admitted. Approximately half of 3- and 4-year-old children in families with incomes below the poverty line attend Head Start, which represents about 10 percent of all 3- and 4-year-old children nationwide.[3] Each Head Start program is required to widely recruit eligible children from the local community so that the number of applications exceeds the enrollment opportunities (Office of Head Start, 2010b). To determine which eligible applications are admitted, Head Start programs are required to establish a formal selection process to enroll children with the greatest need for the program's services (Office of Head Start, 2010b).[4]

To achieve the program's overall goal of improved school readiness, Head Start provides educational, nutritional, health, and social services to children and their families. To improve participants' cognitive skills, Head Start centers implement a curriculum that emphasizes age-appropriate literacy, numeracy, reasoning, problem solving, and decision-making skills (Office of Head Start, 2010b). Cognitive development is also fostered through creative activities, including art and music. Parents are encouraged to assist in developing the center's curriculum and an individualized developmental strategy for their child.

Head Start's federal guidelines emphasize nutritional health as an essential component of child development through screening, providing healthy meals, and nutrition education. At the beginning of the year, the

---

[2] According to PIR data, 2.7 percent of children who were not categorically eligible resided in families with incomes between 100 and 130 percent of the poverty guidelines and an additional 5.2 percent of children resided in families with incomes above 130 percent in 2009.

[3] Authors' calculations from Census data.

[4] This selection process ensures that children in families with incomes farthest below the poverty line are most likely to be chosen to enroll in the program, as well as children with more severe disabilities. Children without two parents are more likely to be selected into the program than children from two-parent families. Also, children in high-risk families are preferentially admitted into the program. Although high risk may be defined differently across programs, this category can include children in families with substance abuse or domestic violence; children in families afflicted by a crisis such as death, separation, terminal illness, or chronic health issues; children referred into Head Start by a community agency; or other special circumstances.

child's nutritional needs are assessed with the cooperation of family members and the measurement of hemoglobin/hematocrit, height, and weight. Children in a half-day program receive meals and snacks that provide at least one-third of their daily nutritional needs and children in a full-day program receive one-half to two-thirds. Parents also receive training on food preparation and nutrition to help them improve the nutritional content of the food consumed by Head Start participants.

In addition to nutrition, the physical development goals of Head Start target pediatric health care and health education (Office of Head Start, 2010b). Head Start centers determine if the child has an adequate source of ongoing, continuous, and accessible pediatric health care. If the child does not, then program administrators assist parents in finding one. Head Start staff members also help children and families develop an age-appropriate schedule of preventive and primary health care that includes child immunizations. The provision of health care services is monitored throughout the duration of the program. Children are screened for developmental problems upon program enrollment, and parents are notified of any concerns. Parents are familiarized with pediatric health care and developmental screening procedures and the importance of these procedures.

At the beginning of the year, Head Start administrators work with parents to design and implement an individualized family partnership agreement, which enables Head Start staff and teachers to understand the goals of the family and develop strategies to achieve these goals. Staff members identify sources of community assistance and, as needed, help parents gain access to emergency assistance for food, housing, clothing, and transportation; continuing education and employment training opportunities; and counseling programs for substance abuse, child abuse and neglect, and domestic violence (Office of Head Start, 2010b). Federal Head Start performance standards also require at least two home visits and at least two staff–parent conferences that focus on the educational and developmental progress of the child (Office of Head Start, 2010b).

Parents are encouraged to participate in the development of the program's curriculum and to visit, observe, and participate in their child's class (Office of Head Start, 2010b). Parents are also involved in the Head Start program as volunteers and employees. In 2009, more than 850,000 parents volunteered and 26 percent of staff members were parents of current or former Head Start children (Office of Head Start, 2010a). More than 228,000 fathers participated in regularly scheduled parent involvement and education activities in 2009 (Office of Head Start, 2010a). Further, parents are involved in the program's policy-making and operations (Office of Head Start, 2010b).

As outlined in the conceptual framework above, Head Start participation could influence adolescent and adult health behaviors and health outcomes by improving childhood health, increasing human capital, and influencing parental behaviors. The specific components of the Head Start program, as detailed above, target each of these mechanisms, which are expected to affect health.

Participation in the Head Start program has been shown to significantly improve childhood health. Ludwig and Miller (2007) demonstrate that, when the program began, counties that received additional Head Start funding because of technical grant writing assistance to the 300 poorest counties in the United States experienced a substantial decline in childhood mortality from causes of death that were preventable with vaccinations or screening. Hale *et al.* (1990) determine that Head Start participants are more likely than children on the Head Start waiting list or middle-class children to receive age-appropriate health screenings or dental examinations. Currie and Thomas (1995) find that Head Start participation does not have an effect on height-for-age, a long-run measure of health and nutrition, but that participation improves the probability of being immunized for the measles, relative to not attending preschool. This benefit of Head Start is not limited to the participant, as there is evidence that the younger siblings of Head Start participants are more likely to receive the immunization as well. The recent, national randomized evaluation of the Head Start program found that participants had greater access to dental care by the end of their first year in the Head Start, but that this impact did not persist, and that participants were more likely to have health insurance in the beginning of elementary school (U.S. Department of Health and Human Services, 2005, 2010). Additionally, Lumeng *et al.* (2010) show that there is a decrease in BMI for Head Start participants throughout the academic year, particularly among children who were obese in the beginning of the program. In contrast with the rising prevalence of obesity among young children nationally, this result suggests that Head Start participation might decrease obesity. Frisvold and Lumeng (2009) demonstrate that participation in a full-day class, which has become more common since the mid-1990s, reduces the prevalence of childhood obesity by approximately 25 percent, compared to attending a half-day class.

Participation in the Head Start program has also been shown to significantly improve educational attainment. Head Start participation is generally believed to be associated with short-term cognitive benefits; however, a few years after program completion, these benefits fade (McKey *et al.*, 1985; Aughinbaugh, 2001; Barnett, 1995; Currie and Thomas, 1995; Lee *et al.*, 1988, 1990; U.S. Department of Health and Human Services, 2005, 2010). On the other hand, Head Start participation leads to sizable increases in educational attainment (Garces *et al.*, 2002; Ludwig and Miller, 2007; Deming, 2009).

There is less evidence on whether Head Start participation influences parents' behavior. Keane *et al.* (1996), in a national survey of Head Start parents, center directors, and health coordinators, find that a lack of parenting skills is the second most commonly identified health risk factor by the center directors and health coordinators when children enter Head

Start. Keane *et al.* (1996) also note that two-thirds of parents report noticeable changes in their family's health behaviors as a result of their child's attendance in Head Start, including improved nutrition, increased safety at home, improved feelings and friendships, and better dental hygiene. The Head Start Impact Study found that children are less likely to be physically disciplined and more likely to be read to by parents, but these effects did not persist throughout elementary school and there was no impact on safety practices (U.S. Department of Health and Human Services, 2005, 2010). These studies suggest that parents are not likely to reduce their investments in children in response to the public investments through Head Start.

Given the evidence on the impact of Head Start participation on childhood health, human capital development, and parental behaviors, it is plausible that the program would influence adolescent and adult health. Head Start participation decreases the likelihood of smoking as an adult (Anderson *et al.*, 2010), being obese in later childhood (Frisvold, 2007; Carneiro and Ginja, 2008), and being in poor health as a young adult (Deming, 2009). Building on this literature, in the next section we examine the influence of Head Start participation on risky behaviors of adolescents, particularly smoking, alcohol use, and drug use.

5. *An analysis of the influence of Head Start participation on risky behaviors in adolescence*

5.1. *Data*

The data we use to study the effect of Head Start participation on risky behaviors of adolescents come from the Panel Study of Income Dynamics (PSID) and its Child Development Supplement (CDS). The PSID is a longitudinal dataset that contains information about economic, health, and social behavior for approximately 9,000 families in the United States since 1968.[5] The CDS contains data on education, health, cognitive and behavioral development, as well as time use for children within the PSID families, with follow-ups every 5 years.[6]

Children and caregivers were first interviewed for the CDS in 1997 (CDS I). CDS I includes information about 3,563 children, aged 0–12 years, within 2,394 PSID families. The first follow-up of the CDS (CDS II) was done between 2002 and 2003, when 2,017 PSID families provided data on 2,908 children and adolescents aged 5–18 years. The second follow-up happened between 2007 and 2008 (CDS III), and it included information about 1,506 children and adolescents aged 10–19 years. The Transition to

---

[5] http://psidonline.isr.umich.edu/

[6] http://psidonline.isr.umich.edu/CDS/

Adulthood (TA) study collects data of CDS participant children after they turn 18 years.

For the purpose of this chapter, we use data from CDS II and CDS III. Our sample consists of adolescents aged 13–17 years who appear in either one of them, for whom we have Head Start participation information and information about at least one of the outcomes of interest, which leads us to 1,587 children from 905 PSID families.

The risky behaviors we are interested in are related to smoking, alcohol use, and drug use. In particular, we construct five different measures of these outcomes for our analysis. In order to capture the adolescent's smoking behavior, we use two binary variables. The first one considers if the adolescent has ever tried smoking, while the second one identifies whether the teenager is a current smoker. We classify an individual as a current smoker if she or he reports having smoked cigarettes at least 1 day during the past 30 days.[7] With respect to alcohol use, we use one binary variable that accounts for whether the individual incurs in binge drinking. We consider that an individual binge drinks if she or he reports having drunk five or more drinks in a row for at least 1 or 2 days over the past 12 months.[8] We use two binary variables to identify drug use. The first one accounts for whether the individual has ever tried marijuana, while the second one identifies if the teenager is a current consumer of marijuana. The adolescent is considered a current user if she or he reports having used marijuana at least 1 day during the past 30 days.[9]

The independent variables we use for this analysis include race/ethnicity, gender, age, a binary indicator for low birth weight, a binary variable indicating if the child is the oldest sibling, and a dichotomous variable that indicates whether the individual is disabled. We further include measures of residence (urban and rural) during ages 3 through 5, as well as family income (thousands in 2001 dollars), family size, and mother's education averaged over the years when the child was in ages 3 through 5. We also include a dichotomous variable indicating whether the father was not present during these ages. Finally, we control for whether the child is a participant of CDS II or CDS III.

Furthermore, in some of the regressions, we use an additional set of covariates that account for mother's participation in welfare programs when she was pregnant and the primary caregiver's behavior with respect to

[7] This definition was previously used by Carpenter and Cook (2008).

[8] The National Institute of Alcohol Abuse and Alcoholism defines binge drinking as a pattern of drinking that brings a person's blood alcohol concentration (BAC) to 0.08 percent or above. This typically happens when men (women) consume 5 (4) or more drinks on a single occasion, generally within about 2 hours (Centers for Disease Control and Prevention, 2010).

[9] Our results are robust to different definitions of the current smoker, binge drinks, and current marijuana user variables.

smoking, alcohol use, and drug use. We also incorporate a dummy variable that indicates whether the child's mother and/or father are/is dead and a dichotomous indicator that takes value 1 if the child has ever been spanked.

Table 1 presents descriptive statistics for the whole sample and for children whose family income was below twice the poverty line during ages 3, 4, and 5. We refer to the latter as the low-income sample. Restricting the sample to children in low-income households excludes many children who would not have been eligible to participate in Head Start. For each sample, Table 1 displays the differences between Head Start and non-Head Start participants and the p-value of a t-test that compares the means for these two groups. For the entire sample, the data show that Head Start participants are more likely to have ever smoked than non-Head Start participants. They are also more likely to currently smoke and to have ever used marijuana, although the difference in means for these two groups is not statistically significant in both cases. For the low-income sample, non-Head Start participants are more likely to present risky behaviors than Head Start participants, except in the case of having ever smoked, although the difference of the means for these two groups is not statistically significant.

Head Start participants are more likely to be black, to have had low birth weight, and to be disabled. Head Start participants are also more likely to have been raised in rural areas, in economically disadvantaged families, and without the presence of the father. In addition, they are more likely to have a deceased parent. Mothers of Head Start participants are less educated and more likely to have participated in welfare programs while pregnant. Primary caregivers of Head Start participants are more likely to present risky behaviors, especially smoking and alcohol use. The low-income sample reproduces the same pattern for most of the variables; however, the magnitudes of the differences in means are generally smaller. Thus, restricting the sample to children in low-income households improves the comparability of Head Start participants to non-Head Start participants, but does not eliminate the differences in observed family background characteristics.

5.2. *What are the determinants of Head Start participation?*

The first step in our analysis is to study the determinants of Head Start participation. Table 2 shows the results of linear probability models that predict participation in the Head Start program for the entire sample, as well as for the low-income sample. We also provide results using only the main set of covariates, using all covariates including the additional set of covariates as described in the "Data" section, and using all covariates except for the ones that account for mother's participation in other welfare programs when she was pregnant.

Results for the entire sample of children indicate that a variety of factors are important predictors of participation in Head Start. Black, oldest, and

Table 1. Means (and standard deviations)

	All children				Below twice poverty line			
	All	Head Start	No Head Start	*p*-value	All	Head Start	No Head Start	*p*-value
Ever Smoked	0.301	0.368	0.286	0.007	0.348	0.379	0.326	0.174
	(0.459)	(0.483)	(0.452)		(0.477)	(0.486)	(0.469)	
Currently Smokes	0.075	0.085	0.072	0.455	0.081	0.078	0.082	0.836
	(0.263)	(0.280)	(0.259)		(0.272)	(0.268)	(0.275)	
Binge Drinks	0.116	0.089	0.122	0.116	0.090	0.078	0.100	0.343
	(0.320)	(0.285)	(0.327)		(0.287)	(0.268)	(0.300)	
Ever Used Marijuana	0.179	0.183	0.178	0.836	0.192	0.185	0.197	0.721
	(0.384)	(0.388)	(0.383)		(0.394)	(0.389)	(0.398)	
Uses Marijuana	0.061	0.053	0.063	0.515	0.062	0.050	0.071	0.289
	(0.240)	(0.224)	(0.244)		(0.242)	(0.219)	(0.257)	
Head Start	0.180	1.000	0.000		0.413	1.000	0.000	
	(0.384)				(0.493)			
Black	0.429	0.768	0.355	0.000	0.647	0.784	0.551	0.000
	(0.495)	(0.422)	(0.478)		(0.477)	(0.412)	(0.497)	
White	0.458	0.119	0.532	0.000	0.232	0.104	0.322	0.000
	(0.498)	(0.325)	(0.499)		(0.421)	(0.306)	(0.467)	
Hispanic	0.071	0.084	0.068	0.320	0.088	0.089	0.087	0.940
	(0.256)	(0.278)	(0.251)		(0.283)	(0.284)	(0.282)	
Other Race	0.043	0.028	0.046	0.173	0.033	0.023	0.041	0.225
	(0.203)	(0.165)	(0.210)		(0.180)	(0.150)	(0.198)	
Female	0.490	0.505	0.487	0.576	0.491	0.515	0.474	0.310
	(0.500)	(0.501)	(0.500)		(0.500)	(0.501)	(0.500)	
Age	15.040	15.003	15.048	0.554	15.026	15.010	15.037	0.787
	(1.178)	(1.243)	(1.164)		(1.200)	(1.259)	(1.157)	
Low Birth Weight	0.092	0.148	0.080	0.000	0.113	0.147	0.089	0.020
	(0.284)	(0.351)	(0.266)		(0.310)	(0.349)	(0.277)	
Oldest	0.366	0.351	0.370	0.546	0.322	0.344	0.306	0.315
	(0.475)	(0.472)	(0.476)		(0.462)	(0.470)	(0.456)	
Disability	0.150	0.235	0.132	0.000	0.169	0.185	0.158	0.374
	(0.357)	(0.425)	(0.338)		(0.375)	(0.389)	(0.364)	
Urban	0.470	0.465	0.471	0.824	0.446	0.457	0.438	0.597
	(0.451)	(0.435)	(0.455)		(0.444)	(0.434)	(0.451)	
Rural	0.162	0.217	0.150	0.002	0.195	0.218	0.179	0.180
	(0.339)	(0.362)	(0.333)		(0.358)	(0.363)	(0.355)	
Family Income	51.066	20.492	57.759	0.000	19.915	17.960	21.293	0.000
	(43.854)	(13.520)	(45.332)		(10.436)	(9.745)	(10.696)	
Family Size	4.170	4.289	4.144	0.054	4.288	4.332	4.257	0.510
	(1.154)	(1.392)	(1.093)		(1.398)	(1.396)	(1.401)	
Mother is Head	0.309	0.603	0.245	0.000	0.552	0.638	0.491	0.000
	(0.452)	(0.469)	(0.422)		(0.488)	(0.462)	(0.497)	
Mother's Education	12.744	11.512	13.014	0.000	11.596	11.437	11.707	0.112
	(2.230)	(1.964)	(2.194)		(2.102)	(1.996)	(2.169)	
CDS III	0.494	0.544	0.483	0.063	0.545	0.550	0.542	0.843
	(0.500)	(0.499)	(0.500)		(0.498)	(0.498)	(0.499)	
Mother and/or Father Dead	0.021	0.041	0.017	0.013	0.030	0.041	0.023	0.184
	(0.143)	(0.193)	(0.129)		(0.167)	(0.193)	(0.146)	
WIC When Pregnant	0.440	0.811	0.359	0.000	0.742	0.838	0.675	0.000
	(0.485)	(0.383)	(0.466)		(0.423)	(0.362)	(0.449)	

Table 1. (Continued)

	All children				Below twice poverty line			
	All	Head Start	No Head Start	*p*-value	All	Head Start	No Head Start	*p*-value
Food Stamps When Pregnant	0.228 (0.409)	0.542 (0.485)	0.160 (0.356)	0.000	0.463 (0.483)	0.569 (0.483)	0.387 (0.469)	0.000
Other Food Program When Pregnant	0.028 (0.157)	0.052 (0.216)	0.022 (0.140)	0.003	0.051 (0.213)	0.049 (0.210)	0.053 (0.215)	0.835
AFDC When Pregnant	0.163 (0.360)	0.385 (0.475)	0.114 (0.309)	0.000	0.331 (0.457)	0.411 (0.481)	0.275 (0.430)	0.000
Other Assistance When Pregnant	0.024 (0.149)	0.045 (0.201)	0.020 (0.135)	0.010	0.044 (0.199)	0.045 (0.202)	0.044 (0.198)	0.970
Ever Spanked	0.879 (0.326)	0.909 (0.288)	0.872 (0.334)	0.086	0.898 (0.303)	0.904 (0.295)	0.894 (0.308)	0.682
Caregiver Uses Alcohol or Drugs	0.209 (0.325)	0.226 (0.325)	0.205 (0.325)	0.311	0.242 (0.336)	0.218 (0.315)	0.259 (0.349)	0.125
Primary Caregiver Smokes	0.210 (0.333)	0.309 (0.361)	0.188 (0.323)	0.000	0.272 (0.352)	0.304 (0.355)	0.250 (0.348)	0.057
Primary Caregiver Drinks Too Much	0.074 (0.210)	0.105 (0.234)	0.067 (0.204)	0.006	0.074 (0.192)	0.096 (0.216)	0.058 (0.171)	0.015
Negative Effect from Alcohol	0.057 (0.185)	0.055 (0.185)	0.058 (0.185)	0.843	0.047 (0.155)	0.051 (0.175)	0.043 (0.140)	0.526
Sample Size	1587	285	1302		629	260	369	

Note: Standard deviations in parentheses.
Source: Panel Study of Income Dynamics.

disabled children are more likely to participate in Head Start than white, not oldest, and not disabled children. Moreover, living in a rural area and not having a father present increase the chances that a child will participate in Head Start. Family characteristics, such as family income and family size, are also important determinants of Head Start participation as expected. The lower the child's family income and the larger the family size increases the probability of participation in Head Start. The mother's participation in other welfare programs, particularly the Special Supplemental Nutrition Program for Women, Infants, and Children (WIC) and Food Stamps, is also positively correlated with the probability of her child participating in Head Start. The main set of individual and family background covariates explain 24 percent of the variation in Head Start participation. The addition of other commonly unobserved family backgrounds that are often used by Head Start centers to determine which children are selected for admission explains only an additional 2 percent of the variation.

Table 2. The determinants of Head Start participation

	All children			Low-income children		
	(1)	(2)	(3)	(4)	(5)	(6)
Black	0.136	0.137	0.106	0.288	0.285	0.259
	(0.020)	(0.020)	(0.022)	(0.048)	(0.049)	(0.050)
Hispanic	0.055	0.069	0.072	0.233	0.246	0.252
	(0.039)	(0.040)	(0.041)	(0.083)	(0.083)	(0.085)
Other Race	0.013	0.010	0.012	0.123	0.096	0.113
	(0.036)	(0.035)	(0.035)	(0.100)	(0.101)	(0.099)
Female	0.015	0.016	0.020	0.026	0.030	0.035
	(0.017)	(0.017)	(0.017)	(0.038)	(0.038)	(0.038)
Age	−0.005	−0.006	−0.004	−0.006	−0.009	−0.005
	(0.007)	(0.007)	(0.007)	(0.016)	(0.016)	(0.016)
Low Birth Weight	0.047	0.043	0.043	0.089	0.077	0.081
	(0.034)	(0.035)	(0.034)	(0.064)	(0.065)	(0.064)
Oldest	0.039	0.042	0.047	0.050	0.055	0.068
	(0.020)	(0.020)	(0.020)	(0.043)	(0.043)	(0.043)
Disability	0.120	0.120	0.114	0.079	0.075	0.070
	(0.028)	(0.028)	(0.028)	(0.053)	(0.054)	(0.054)
Urban	0.016	0.012	0.008	−0.032	−0.050	−0.054
	(0.021)	(0.021)	(0.021)	(0.050)	(0.051)	(0.051)
Rural	0.078	0.077	0.072	0.115	0.097	0.087
	(0.028)	(0.028)	(0.028)	(0.059)	(0.061)	(0.061)
Family Income	−0.004	−0.004	−0.003	0.005	0.004	0.005
	(0.000)	(0.000)	(0.000)	(0.007)	(0.007)	(0.007)
Family Income^2	0.000	0.000	0.000	−0.000	−0.000	−0.000
	(0.000)	(0.000)	(0.000)	(0.000)	(0.000)	(0.000)
Family Size	0.035	0.037	0.032	0.030	0.032	0.029
	(0.010)	(0.010)	(0.010)	(0.018)	(0.018)	(0.018)
Mother is Head	0.104	0.096	0.073	0.076	0.066	0.060
	(0.027)	(0.027)	(0.028)	(0.048)	(0.048)	(0.049)
Mother's Education	−0.006	−0.005	0.001	−0.005	−0.004	0.000
	(0.005)	(0.005)	(0.005)	(0.010)	(0.010)	(0.010)
CDS III	0.040	0.045	0.034	0.028	0.038	0.027
	(0.017)	(0.017)	(0.017)	(0.039)	(0.039)	(0.039)
Mother and/or Father Dead		0.013	0.017		0.055	0.071
		(0.079)	(0.079)		(0.124)	(0.123)
Ever Spanked		0.004	0.008		−0.013	−0.012
		(0.024)	(0.023)		(0.060)	(0.060)
Caregiver Uses Alcohol or Drugs		−0.039	−0.042		−0.112	−0.103
		(0.029)	(0.029)		(0.063)	(0.063)
Primary Caregiver Smokes		0.052	0.054		0.097	0.103
		(0.029)	(0.029)		(0.060)	(0.059)
Primary Caregiver Drinks Too Much		0.067	0.053		0.090	0.062
		(0.043)	(0.041)		(0.107)	(0.105)
Negative Effect from Alcohol		0.032	0.030		0.137	0.107
		(0.045)	(0.045)		(0.130)	(0.139)
WIC When Pregnant			0.052			0.085
			(0.026)			(0.050)
Food Stamps When Pregnant			0.128			0.099
			(0.042)			(0.057)

Table 2. (Continued)

	All children			Low-income children		
	(1)	(2)	(3)	(4)	(5)	(6)
Other Food Program When Pregnant			−0.021 (0.075)			−0.073 (0.102)
AFDC When Pregnant			−0.008 (0.047)			−0.016 (0.060)
Other Assistance When Pregnant			−0.048 (0.083)			−0.059 (0.120)
Constant	0.171 (0.136)	0.142 (0.140)	0.018 (0.141)	0.095 (0.297)	0.136 (0.305)	−0.052 (0.311)
Observations	1,587	1,587	1,587	629	629	629
R-squared	0.238	0.243	0.260	0.107	0.119	0.134

Note: Heteroscedasticity-robust standard errors in parentheses.

For the low-income sample, the main set of individual and family background characteristics explains only 11 percent of the variation in Head Start participation and few of the covariates are statistically significant. Being black or Hispanic is the most important determinant of Head Start participation. Participation of the mother in the WIC and/or Food Stamps program when she was pregnant also significantly increases the probability of Head Start participation.

5.3. Selection on observables

In order to study the effect of Head Start participation on risky behaviors of adolescents, we first consider the case when there is only selection on observables. This assumes that, by controlling for a large enough set of independent variables, our model is not subject to unobserved heterogeneity. Table 3 shows our results from probit models for each of the dependent variables of interest, which account for selection on observables only.

Results for the full sample of children show that estimates for Head Start participation for all behaviors of interest are not statistically significant. For smoking and alcohol use variables, the sign of this effect is positive, but the effect with respect to drug use presents a negative sign. When the additional set of covariates is included in column 2, the effect of the Head Start program is still not statistically significant and the value of the estimate decreases for all outcomes.[10] As opposed to when the

[10] This result is consistent with the idea that the additional measures of growing up in a disadvantaged family are correlated with adolescent risky behaviors and with Head Start participation. However, these additional covariates are not strongly correlated with Head Start participation, as shown in Table 2, or with adolescent risky behaviors, which could explain why the results in Table 3 are hardly influenced by the addition of these covariates.

***Table 3.* Estimates of the influence of Head Start participation on adolescent health behaviors**

All children	All children (with additional covariates)	Low-income children	Low-income children (with additional covariates)
Outcome: Ever Smoked			
0.045	0.033	0.070	0.080
(0.034)	(0.034)	(0.039)	(0.038)
Outcome: Smoke			
0.015	0.013	0.005	0.002
(0.019)	(0.019)	(0.019)	(0.019)
Outcome: Binge Drink			
0.001	−0.007	−0.002	0.004
(0.020)	(0.020)	(0.019)	(0.019)
Outcome: Ever Used Marijuana			
−0.014	−0.025	−0.003	0.001
(0.028)	(0.029)	(0.032)	(0.032)
Outcome: Use Marijuana			
−0.008	−0.015	−0.014	−0.010
(0.017)	(0.018)	(0.018)	(0.017)

Note: Heteroscedasticity-robust standard errors in parentheses. Estimates are average partial effects for Head Start participation estimated from probit models. Covariates not shown include race/ethnicity, gender, age, a binary indicator for low birth weight, a binary variable indicating if the child is the oldest sibling, a dichotomous variable that indicates whether the individual is disabled, a binary variable indicating whether the child is a participant of CDS II or CDS III, measures of residence (urban and rural) during ages 3 through 5, as well as family income, family size, and mother's education averaged over the years when the child was aged 3 through 5 and whether the father was not present during these ages. Additional covariates included in columns 2 and 4 measure mother's participation in welfare programs when she was pregnant, primary caregiver's behavior with respect to smoking, alcohol use, and drug use, whether the child's mother and/or father are/is dead, and whether the child has ever been spanked.

additional set of covariates was not included, binge drinking now presents a negative sign.

Results for the low-income sample are very similar to the ones obtained for the full sample. The effect of Head Start participation is not significant for all dependent variables of interest. The signs obtained are the same as in the full sample case, except for the one on binge drinking, which is negative for the low-income sample. When we include the additional set of covariates, the effect of participation in the program becomes significant only in the case of having ever smoked, with a positive sign. Moreover, binge drinking and having ever used marijuana present opposite signs as compared to the case with only the main set of covariates.

5.4. Selection on unobservables

Comparisons between the estimates in Table 3 and the differences in means between the Head Start and non-Head Start groups in Table 1 suggest there is a reasonable degree of selection on observed characteristics associated with Head Start participation, which is consistent with the eligibility and admissions criteria of the program. Thus, there is likely to be selection on unobserved characteristics as well (Altonji *et al.*, 2005).

Head Start program administrators select the most disadvantaged of the eligible applicants to enroll in the program. Thus, it is likely that Head Start participants are disadvantaged across a variety of dimensions that are broader than the observable characteristics included in this analysis, which is a consistent finding in the Head Start literature described above. If these unobserved characteristics are related to future health behaviors, then estimates of the impact of Head Start participation will be biased against finding a beneficial impact of the program.

To assess the influence of observed and unobserved selection on the estimate of the average treatment effect on the treated, we follow the methodology of Altonji *et al.* (2005), which uses the extent of observed selection as a guide for the amount of unobserved selection.[11] The probability of Head Start attendance is specified as

$$\Pr(D = 1) = \Pr(Z\delta + \upsilon > 0)$$

and the probability of engaging in a risky behavior is specified as

$$\Pr(Y = 1) = \Pr(X\beta + D\alpha + \varepsilon > 0)$$

where Z and X represent observable characteristics that are independent of (υ, ε); δ, β, and α are parameters to be estimated; and υ and ε are random error terms. The assumption that υ and ε are distributed bivariate normal with $E(\upsilon) = 0$, $E(\varepsilon) = 0$, $Var(\upsilon) = 1$, $Var(\varepsilon) = 1$, and $Cov(\upsilon, \varepsilon) = \rho$ allows for the possibility that the unobserved determinants of Head Start participation are correlated with the unobserved determinants of risky behaviors.

We begin by estimating the bivariate probit model with Z equal to X and with a specified value for the correlation parameter to examine the sensitivity of the estimates in Table 3, which impose $\rho = 0$, to varying degrees of selection on unobservables. Based on the previous research and the admission criteria described above, we expect that the correlation between the unobserved determinants of Head Start participation and the unobserved determinants of risky behaviors is most likely positive. Thus, Table 4 displays estimates of the average partial effect of Head Start participation for each of the five outcomes for both samples for values of

---

[11] For additional examples of applications of this methodology, see Frisvold (2007) and Millimet *et al.* (2008).

Table 4. Bivariate probit estimates of the impact of Head Start participation for varying degrees of unobserved selection

	$\rho = -0.1$	$\rho = 0$	$\rho = 0.1$	$\rho = 0.2$	$\rho = 0.3$	$\rho = 0.4$	$\rho = 0.5$	Rho	Ratio
Outcome: Ever Smoked									
All Children									
ATT	0.099	0.045	−0.009	−0.061	−0.113	−0.165	−0.215	1.276	0.141
	(0.034)	(0.034)	(0.033)	(0.032)	(0.031)	(0.030)	(0.028)		
Low-Income Children									
ATT	0.124	0.070	0.015	−0.041	−0.097	−0.153	−0.210	−0.237	−0.364
	(0.039)	(0.039)	(0.039)	(0.039)	(0.038)	(0.037)	(0.036)		
Outcome: Smoke									
All Children									
ATT	0.036	0.015	−0.005	−0.024	−0.043	−0.063	−0.086	0.273	3.504
	(0.020)	(0.019)	(0.018)	(0.017)	(0.017)	(0.017)	(0.018)		
Low-Income Children									
ATT	0.025	0.005	−0.013	−0.032	−0.052	−0.075	−0.100	−0.221	−0.123
	(0.020)	(0.019)	(0.019)	(0.019)	(0.019)	(0.020)	(0.022)		
Outcome: Binge Drink									
All Children									
ATT	0.024	0.001	−0.020	−0.040	−0.059	−0.079	−0.101	−0.409	−0.011
	(0.021)	(0.020)	(0.018)	(0.018)	(0.017)	(0.017)	(0.018)		
Low Income Children									
ATT	0.017	−0.002	−0.020	−0.039	−0.058	−0.080	−0.105	−0.413	0.018
	(0.020)	(0.019)	(0.019)	(0.019)	(0.020)	(0.022)	(0.024)		
Outcome: Ever Used Marijuana									
All Children									
ATT	0.024	−0.014	−0.050	−0.084	−0.118	−0.152	−0.185	0.252	−0.223
	(0.029)	(0.028)	(0.027)	(0.026)	(0.025)	(0.024)	(0.024)		
Low-Income Children									
ATT	0.036	−0.003	−0.042	−0.081	−0.120	−0.160	−0.202	−0.229	0.035
	(0.033)	(0.032)	(0.032)	(0.031)	(0.031)	(0.031)	(0.031)		
Outcome: Use Marijuana									
All Children									
ATT	0.010	−0.008	−0.024	−0.040	−0.056	−0.073	−0.092	−0.054	0.463
	(0.018)	(0.017)	(0.016)	(0.016)	(0.016)	(0.016)	(0.017)		
Low-Income Children									
ATT	0.002	−0.014	−0.029	−0.045	−0.062	−0.082	−0.105	0.001	0.198
	(0.018)	(0.018)	(0.018)	(0.018)	(0.019)	(0.021)	(0.023)		

Note: Average partial effects for Head Start participation with heteroscedasticity-robust standard errors in parentheses are shown for estimates from a bivariate probit model with the specified correlation coefficient. The values in the column with the heading "Rho" are equal to the values of the correlation parameter when the amount of selection on observables equals the amount of selection on unobservables. The values in the column with the heading "Ratio" represent the ratio of the relative amount of selection on unobservables needed to fully account for the estimates with $\rho = 0$, under the null hypothesis that the true impact of Head Start participation is zero.

the correlation coefficient equal to −0.1, 0, 0.1, 0.2, 0.3, 0.4, and 0.5. The estimates shown in Table 4 demonstrate that the estimates of the impact of Head Start participation on risky behaviors are sensitive to assumptions about the degree of selection on unobservables. A modest amount of positive selection on unobservables ($\rho = 0.2$) yields statistically significant reductions in risky behaviors for nearly all outcomes and samples.

Next, we use the amount of selection on observables to guide the extent of the selection on unobservables. As suggested by Altonji *et al.* (2005), the correlation parameter, ρ, can be bounded between zero and $Cov(Z\delta, X\beta)/Var(Z\delta)$, where X = Z. When $\rho = 0$, there is no selection on unobservables and the bivariate probit model is equivalent to estimating two separate probit models; when $\rho = Cov(Z\delta, X\beta)/Var(Z\delta)$, the amount of selection on unobservables is equal to the amount of selection on observables.[12] As shown in Table 4, if the amount of selection on unobservables were equivalent to the extent of the selection on observables, Head Start participation would lead to a large, statistically significant reduction in having ever smoked, current smoking, and having ever used marijuana in the full sample. Interestingly, the estimates for rho are negative for binge drinking and marijuana use in the full sample and all outcomes in the low-income sample. These estimates suggest that there is no positive selection on unobservables for adolescent risky behaviors in the low-income sample and that Head Start participation is not likely to reduce smoking, binge drinking, or marijuana use.[13]

6. *Conclusion*

In this chapter, we discuss whether early childhood investments in low-income children could lead to a lasting impact on health outcomes. We note that such investments could improve adolescent and adult health by increasing child health, increasing educational attainment, or influencing parents' behaviors. Model preschool programs, such as the High/Scope

---

[12] For a discussion of the assumptions needed for this condition to hold, see Altonji *et al.* (2005). These assumptions include that the variables in X are a random subset of all characteristics that influence Y, that a large number of variables are included in X, and that the variables in X do not dominate the distribution of D or Y. As described before, a variety of individual and family background characteristics were selected that are related to Head Start participation and risky behaviors in adolescence from the PSID in this analysis.

[13] As an alternative method, Altonji *et al.* (2005) construct a ratio of the relative amount of selection on unobservables needed to fully account for the estimates with $\rho = 0$, under the null hypothesis that the true impact of Head Start participation is zero. The estimates of these ratios are shown in Table 4. Since these ratios are nearly uniformly very small, these results suggest that the estimates in Table 3 are sensitive to the possibility of selection on unobservables; however, the estimates in Table 3 were not statistically significantly different from zero.

Perry Preschool Program and the Carolina Abecedarian Program, have been successful in increasing the educational attainment and health behaviors of low-income children. The Head Start program, which is the largest public investment in low-income, preschool-aged children in the United States, has also improved child health and educational attainment.

Using PSID and CDS data on the health behaviors of 13- to 17-year-olds in 2002 and 2007, we examine whether Head Start participation influences adolescent risky behaviors. Our results suggest that Head Start participation does not reduce the likelihood of having ever smoked, current smoking, binge drinking, having ever used marijuana, or current marijuana use among low-income teens. These results contrast with the positive influences of Head Start participation on childhood and adult health outcomes and educational attainment described in the earlier literature. An important difference between these results and the previous literature is that many of the results from the previous literature are based on earlier years of the Head Start program.[14,15] Thus, changes to Head Start or changes to the child care experiences of children who did not attend Head Start may explain the differences in these results. An interesting possibility for future research will be to examine whether the recent expansions of public preschool programs have influenced who attends Head Start and the effects of attending Head Start.

Acknowledgment

This research was supported, in part, by the Robert Wood Johnson Foundation and the Emory Global Health Institute.

References

Almond, D. and J. Currie (2010), "Human capital development before age five", National Bureau of Economic Research Working Paper, No. 15827.

Altonji, J., T. Elder and C. Taber (2005), "Selection on observed and unobserved variables: assessing the effectiveness of catholic schools", *Journal of Political Economy*, Vol. 113(1), pp. 151–184.

---

[14] Exceptions to this statement are Frisvold and Lumeng (2009), Lumeng *et al.* (2010); and U.S. Department of Health and Human Services (2005, 2010).

[15] Consistent with the possibility that differences in the period of Head Start attendance explain the differences in results, sibling fixed effects estimates based on these data show no statistically significant impact on adolescent smoking. This finding contrasts with the results in Anderson *et al.* (2010) that show a sizable impact of Head Start participation on adult smoking using earlier cohorts and a sibling fixed effects methodology. Thus, differences in the methodology are not likely to explain the differences in the results.

Anderson, K., J. Foster and D. Frisvold (2010), "Investing in health: the long-term impact of Head Start on smoking", *Economic Inquiry*, Vol. 48(3), pp. 587–602.

Aughinbaugh, A. (2001), "Does Head Start yield long-term benefits?", *Journal of Human Resources*, Vol. 36(4), pp. 641–665.

Barnett, S.W. (1995), "Long-term effects of early childhood programs on cognitive and school outcomes", *The Future of Children*, Vol. 5(3), pp. 25–50.

Barnett, W.S. and L.N. Masse (2007), "Comparative benefit-cost analysis of the Abecedarian program and its policy implications", *Economics of Education Review*, Vol. 26(1), pp. 113–125.

Becker, G.S. and N. Tomes (1976), "Child endowments and the quantity and quality of children", *Journal of Political Economy*, Vol. 84(4), pp. S143–S162.

Behrman, J.R., Y. Cheng and P.E. Todd (2004), "Evaluating preschool programs when length of exposure to the program varies: a nonparametric approach", *Review of Economics and Statistics*, Vol. 86(1), pp. 108–132.

Blanc, D., C.L. Hart, G.D. Smith, C.R. Gillis, D.J. Hole and V.M. Hawthorne (1996), "Association of cardiovascular disease risk factors with socioeconomic position during childhood and during adulthood", *British Medical Journal*, Vol. 313, pp. 1434–1438.

Belfield, C.R., M. Nores, S. Barnett and L. Schweinhart (2006), "The High/Scope Perry Preschool Program: cost-benefit analysis using data from the age-40 followup", *Journal of Human Resources*, Vol. 41(1), pp. 162–190.

Carneiro, P. and R. Ginja (2008). *Preventing Behavior Problems in Childhood and Adolescence: Evidence from Head Start*, London: University College London.

Carpenter, C. and P.J. Cook (2008), "Cigarette taxes and youth smoking: new evidence from national, state, and local Youth Risk Behavior Surveys", *Journal of Health Economics*, Vol. 27, pp. 287–299.

Case, A., D. Lubotsky and C. Paxson (2002), "Economic status and health in childhood: the origins of the gradient", *American Economic Review*, Vol. 92(5), pp. 1308–1334.

Case, A., A. Fertig and C. Paxson (2005), "The lasting impact of childhood health and circumstance", *Journal of Health Economics*, Vol. 24, pp. 365–389.

Centers for Disease Control and Prevention (2010), *Fact Sheets: Binge Drinking*, Atlanta, GA: CDC, Available at http://www.cdc.gov/alcohol/fact-sheets/binge-drinking.htm. Accessed on August 3, 2010

Chou, S., J. Liu, M. Grossman and T. Joyce (2007), "Parental education and child health: evidence from a natural experiment in Taiwan", NBER Working Paper Series, No. 13466.

Clark, D. and H. Royer (2010), "The impact of education on mortality and health: evidence from UK compulsory schooling laws", National Bureau of Economic Research Working Paper 16013.

Currie, J. (2001), "Early childhood education programs", *Journal of Economic Perspectives*, Vol. 15(2), pp. 213–238.

Currie, J. and E. Moretti (2003), "Mother's education and the intergenerational transmission of human capital: evidence from college openings", *Quarterly Journal of Economics*, Vol. 118(4), pp. 1495–1532.

Currie, J. and D. Thomas (1995), "Does Head Start make a difference?", *American Economic Review*, Vol. 85(3), pp. 341–364.

Davey Smith, G., C. Hart, D. Blane and D. Hole (1998), "Adverse socioeconomic conditions in childhood and cause specific adult mortality: prospective observational study", *British Medical Journal*, Vol. 316, pp. 1631–1635.

de Walque, D. (2007), "Does education affect smoking behaviors? Evidence using the Vietnam draft as an instrument for college education", *Journal of Health Economics*, Vol. 26, pp. 877–895.

Deming, D. (2009), "Early childhood intervention and life-cycle skill development: evidence from Head Start", *American Economic Journal: Applied Economics*, Vol. 1(3), pp. 111–134.

Duncan, G.J., W.J. Yeung, J. Brooks-Gunn and J.R. Smith (1998), "How much does childhood poverty affect the life chances of children?", *American Sociological Review*, Vol. 63(3), pp. 406–423.

Fletcher, J. and D. Frisvold (2009a), "Higher education and health investments: does more schooling affect preventive health care use?", *Journal of Human Capital*, Vol. 3(2), pp. 144–176.

Fletcher, J. and D. Frisvold (2009b), *The Long Run Health Returns to College Quality*, Atlanta, GA: Emory University.

Frisvold, D. (2007), "Head Start participation and childhood obesity", Early Childhood Research Collaborative Discussion Paper 108.

Frisvold, D. and E. Golberstein (2010a), *The Effects of School Quality on Health*, Atlanta, GA: Emory University.

Frisvold, D. and E. Golberstein (2010b), *The Effects of School Quality on Black-White Health Differences: Evidence from Southern Segregated Schools*, Atlanta, GA: Emory University.

Frisvold, D. and J. Lumeng (2009), *Expanding Exposure: Can Increasing the Daily Duration of Head Start Reduce Childhood Obesity?* Atlanta, GA: Emory University.

Garces, E., D. Thomas and J. Currie (2002), "Longer-term effects of Head Start", *American Economic Review*, Vol. 9(4), pp. 999–1012.

Grimard, F. and D. Parent (2007), "Education and smoking: Were Vietnam War draft avoiders also more likely to avoid smoking?", *Journal of Health Economics*, Vol. 26(5), pp. 896–926.

Grossman, M. (1972), "On the concept of health capital and the demand for health", *Journal of Political Economy*, Vol. 80, pp. 223–255.

Grossman, M. and R. Kaestner (1997), "Effects of education on health", in: J. Behrman and N. Stacey, editors, *The Social Benefits of Education*, Ann Arbor, MI: The University of Michigan Press.

Hale, B., V. Seitz and E. Zigler (1990), "Health services and Head Start: a forgotten formula", *Journal of Applied Developmental Psychology*, Vol. 11, pp. 447–458.

Hayward, M.D. and B.K. Gorman (2004), "The long arm of childhood: the influence of early-life social conditions on men's mortality", *Demography*, Vol. 41(1), pp. 87–107.

Holzer, H.J., D.W. Schanzenbach, G.J. Duncan and J. Ludwig (2007). "The economic costs of poverty in the United States: subsequent effects of children growing up poor", Discussion Paper 1327-07, Institute for Research on Poverty.

Keane, M.J., R.W. O'Brien, D.C. Connell and N.C. Close (1996), *A Descriptive Study of the Head Start Health Component*, Washington, DC: U.S. Department of Health and Human Services.

Lee, V., J. Brooks-Gunn and E. Schnur (1988), "Does Head Start work? A 1-year follow-up comparison of disadvantaged children attending Head Start, no preschool, and other preschool programs", *Developmental Psychology*, Vol. 24(2), pp. 210–222.

Lee, V.E., J. Brooks-Gunn, E. Schnur and F. Liaw (1990), "Are Head Start effects sustained? A longitudinal follow-up comparison of disadvantaged children attending Head Start, no preschool, and other preschool programs", *Child Development*, Vol. 61, pp. 495–507.

Lleras-Muney, A. (2005), "The relationship between education and adult mortality in the United States", *Review of Economic Studies*, Vol. 72, pp. 189–221.

Ludwig, J. and D.L. Miller (2007), "Does Head Start improve children's life chances? Evidence from a regression discontinuity design", *Quarterly Journal of Economics*, Vol. 122(1), pp. 159–208.

Lumeng, J., N. Kaciroti and D. Frisvold (2010), "Changes in body mass index Z score over the course of the academic year among children attending Head Start", *Academic Pediatrics*, Vol. 10(3), pp. 179–186.

Maty, S.M., J.L. Lynch, J.L. Balfour, S.A. Everson, T.E. Raghunathan and G.A. Kaplan (2002), "Interaction between childhood socioeconomic position, adult body mass index and 34-year incidence of type 2 diabetes mellitus", *Annals of Epidemiology*, Vol. 12(7), p. 501.

Mazumder, B. (2007), "How did schooling laws improve long-term health and lower mortality?", Federal Reserve Bank of Chicago Working Paper, No. 2006-23.

McKey, R.H., L. Condelli, H. Ganson, B.J. Barrett, C. McConkey and M.C. Plantz (1985), *The Impact of Head Start on Children, Families and Communities: Final Report of the Head Start Evaluation, Synthesis and Utilization Project*, Washington, DC: CSR.

Millimet, D.L., R. Tchernis and M. Husain (2008). "School nutrition programs and the incidence of childhood obesity", National Bureau of Economic Research Working Paper, No. 14297.

Office of Head Start, S. (2010a), *2009 Head Start Program Fact Sheet*, Washington, DC: U.S. Department of Health and Human Services.

Office of Head Start, S. (2010b), *Head Start Program Performance Standards and Other Regulations*, Washington, DC: U.S. Department of Health and Human Services.

Schweinhart, L.J., J. Montie, Z. Xiang, W.S. Barnett, C.R. Belfield and M. Nores (2005), *Lifetime effects: The High/Scope Perry Preschool Study through Age 40*, Ypsilanti, MI: High/Scope Press.

U.S. Department of Health and Human Services, Administration for Children and Families (2005), *Head Start Impact Study: First Year Findings*. Washington, DC: U.S. Department of Health and Human Services, Administration for Children and Families.

U.S. Department of Health and Human Services, Administration for Children and Families (2010), *Head Start Impact Study: Final Report*. Washington, DC: U.S. Department of Health and Human Services, Administration for Children and Families.

CHAPTER 7

Universal Helmet Laws and Motorcycle Fatalities: A Longitudinal Analysis of Policy Changes[☆]

Michael T. French, Gulcin Gumus* and Jenny F. Homer

Abstract

Universal helmet laws (UHLs) are widely believed to be effective in reducing motorcycle fatalities. In this chapter, we further investigate the effectiveness of such policies by focusing on their long-term impact as well as their effect on motorcycle use. Using state-level longitudinal data from 1975 to 2005, we estimate how the adoption and repeal of UHLs influence motorcycle safety. Our results confirm earlier findings that adoption of UHLs prevents fatalities, whereas repeals lead to higher fatality rates. We provide evidence that UHLs operate as intended, decreasing fatalities mainly by improving safety rather than by reducing motorcycle riding. Finally, using dynamic specifications, we show that the long-term effects of both adoption and repeal persist in the years beyond the policy change.

Keywords: motorcycle safety, universal helmet laws, fatalities

JEL classifications: I18, K42

[☆] Authors of this chapter are listed alphabetically and do not reflect relative contributions.

* Corresponding author.

CONTRIBUTIONS TO ECONOMIC ANALYSIS
VOLUME 290 ISSN: 0573-8555
DOI:10.1108/S0573-8555(2010)0000290010

1. Introduction

In recent years, motorcycle riding in the United States has become increasingly popular among many groups of riders with different objectives. For some, motorcycles represent an economic form of daily transportation. Others own motorcycles purely for recreational purposes and mostly ride on weekends or holidays. Largely as a result of greater demand, motorcycle registrations and fatalities in the United States have been rising since the early 1990s in both simple counts and per capita figures (see Figure 1). More importantly, motorcycle fatalities account for a disproportionate share of all motor vehicle deaths. In 2007, motorcyclists were involved in 14 percent of all traffic fatalities even though motorcycles comprised only three percent of registered vehicles and 0.4 percent of all vehicle miles traveled (NHTSA, 2008a). The same data reveal that, per vehicle mile traveled, motorcyclists were about 37 times more likely to die and nine times more likely to be injured in a motor vehicle traffic crash than passenger car occupants (see Figure 2).

The trends in fatalities reflect changes in the demographic composition of motorcycle riders as well as characteristics of new motorcycles produced by manufacturers. According to Paulozzi (2005), motorcycles sold between 2000 and 2003 were involved in 52.5 percent of all motorcycle fatalities in 2003. Individuals may use newly purchased motorcycles more frequently, and drivers of new motorcycles may be less experienced operators or less familiar with the particular model (Paulozzi, 2005). Perhaps more importantly, in the late 1990s, manufacturers produced faster sport bikes

Figure 1. Motorcycle fatalities and registrations, 1975–2005

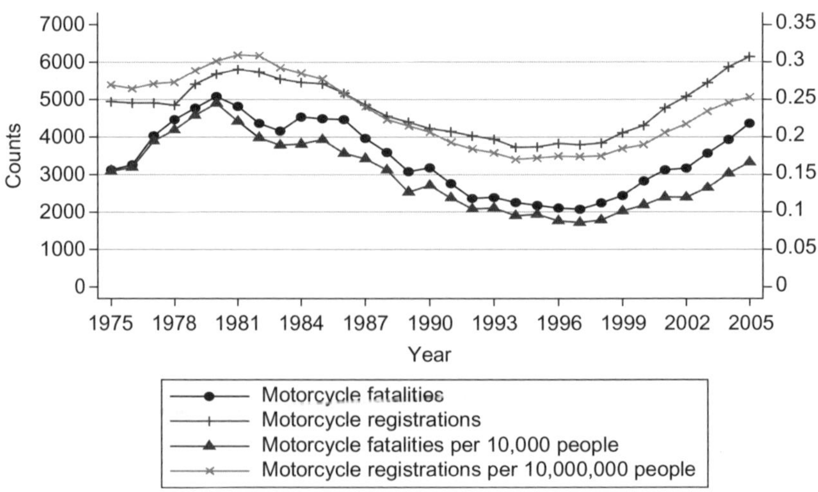

Figure 2. Motorcycle and passenger car fatality rates, 1975–2005

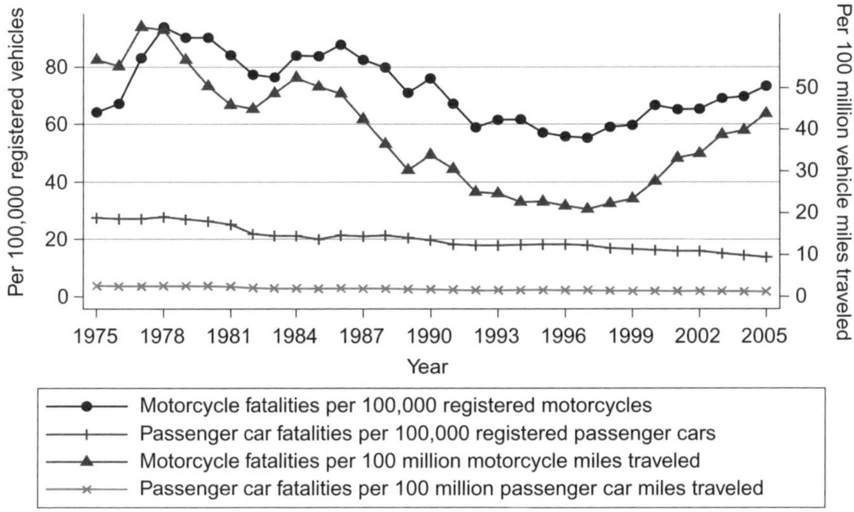

Source: NHTSA Safety Facts (2008c).

and marketed them to all age-groups, but particularly young male riders. All else being equal, riders of powerful bikes are more likely to drive at higher speeds and to have less control over their vehicles, increasing the risk of a crash (Welsh, 2007). These "superbikes" continue to represent an increasing segment of motorcycle sales and fatalities (Welsh, 2007). In 1996, 29.6 percent of all riders killed were age 40 or older, and 30.3 percent of all rider fatalities involved motorcycles with large engine sizes (i.e., between 1,001–1,500 cc). By 2006, 47.4 percent of rider fatalities were among those age 40 or older, and 38.6 percent involved large engine motorcycles (NHTSA, 2008b). In light of increases in both fatal and non-fatal motorcycle injuries, a Department of Transportation report (US DOT, 2007) recently referred to motorcycle fatalities as "our Nation's greatest highway safety challenge."

Previous studies have clearly demonstrated that well-constructed and properly used motorcycle helmets can reduce the likelihood of being killed or severely injured in a crash (Norvell and Cummings, 2002; Morrison *et al.*, 2003; Liu *et al.*, 2004). Helmet use and universal helmet laws (UHLs) have consistently been associated with lower injury severity (Rowland *et al.*, 1996; Dee, 2009) and lower medical costs (Max *et al.*, 1998; Bledsoe *et al.*, 2002). Nevertheless, in 2010, only 20 states and the District of Columbia have a UHL requiring all riders to wear a helmet (see Figure 3). Three states have no helmet laws, and the remaining 27 have partial helmet laws applying only to young riders. A review of legislative activity in 2009 revealed that among

Figure 3. Motorcycle helmet laws, 2010

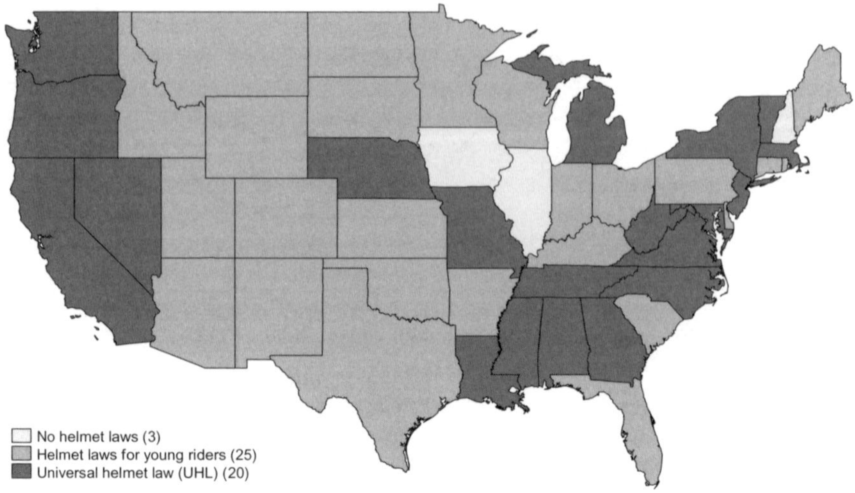

Source: Insurance Institute for Highway Safety (2010).

those 21 with a UHL, 19 of them unsuccessfully attempted to repeal their policies (Advocates for Highway and Auto Safety, 2010). During the period of our analysis, UHLs were adopted and repealed numerous times, with several states changing their UHLs more than once (see Figure 4).

Motorcyclists have shown two clear behavioral responses to changes in UHLs. First, adoption of a UHL promotes helmet use, mainly because enforcement is effective and certainly easier than it is for other traffic policies such as mandatory rider education programs or blood alcohol concentration (BAC) limits, violations of which may be harder to detect. Earlier research on changes in state helmet laws found that helmet use was close to 100 percent in states with a UHL (McSwain and Wiley, 1984; US GAO, 1991; NHTSA, 1992). These studies have also reported that repeals of UHLs reduced helmet use from almost 100 percent to about 50 percent (McSwain and Wiley, 1984). Recently, National Highway Traffic Safety Administration (NHTSA) estimated that helmet use among motorcyclists is about 86 percent in states with UHLs and about 55 percent in non-UHL states (NHTSA, 2009). Since helmets are strongly associated with a lower risk of head injuries, the primary cause of death in motorcycle crashes (Lin and Kraus, 2009), we expect policies that increase helmet use to reduce fatalities.

The second behavioral response to UHLs is unintended: a reduction in motorcycle ownership and riding. Carpenter and Stehr (2010) studied the effects of bicycle helmet laws and found that they lead to lower fatalities

Figure 4. Changes in motorcycle universal helmet laws, 1975–2005

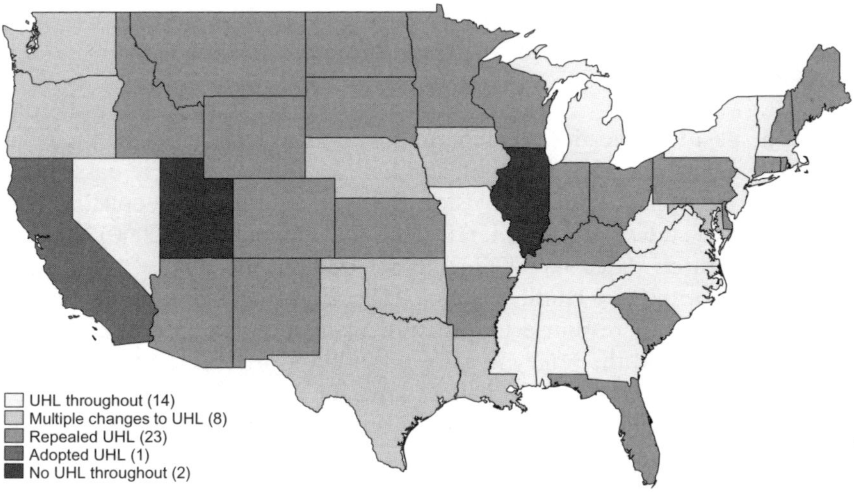

Source: Insurance Institute for Highway Safety (2010).

not only by encouraging helmet use but also by reducing bicycle riding among youth. Similarly, Dee (2009) and French *et al.* (2009) surmise that motorcycle helmet laws might be effective in decreasing fatalities partly because individuals are less likely to ride when UHLs are adopted. Thus, it is important to distinguish between the different mechanisms by which helmet laws might reduce fatalities (decreasing ridership versus improving safety through increased helmet use). From a policy perspective, UHLs are more palatable if they save lives and are technologically effective, not simply if they reduce riding.

In this study, we further investigate the long-term effectiveness of UHLs by focusing on their separate impacts on motorcycle fatalities and motorcycle use. For this purpose, we use state-specific longitudinal data for the United States from 1975 to 2005 to exploit variation in UHLs within states over time. Specifically, we estimate how the adoption and repeal of a UHL influence motorcycle use and safety. Our results confirm earlier findings that adoption of a UHL prevents fatalities, whereas repeals lead to increased fatality rates. We provide new evidence that UHLs operate as intended, decreasing fatalities mainly by improving safety rather than by reducing motorcycle riding. Finally, using dynamic specifications, we show that the effects of both adoption and repeal persist beyond the years the states enact or repeal helmet laws.

The rest of the chapter proceeds in the following manner: Section 2 provides a brief historical review of UHLs; Section 3 describes the data used in the analysis and outlines the empirical framework; Section 4 presents the results; and Section 5 offers conclusions.

2. Background

Over the past few decades, the federal government has varied the financial incentives available to states with UHLs.[1] In 1966, Congress passed the Highway Safety Act with a provision that withheld highway construction funding from states without a UHL (Sass and Zimmerman, 2000). At that time, only three states had helmet laws, but by mid 1970s, every state except California and Utah, passed UHLs requiring riders of all ages to wear a helmet. In response to pressure from motorcycle rights groups, Congress amended the policy in 1976 to withhold federal funds only from those states that did not have helmet laws for riders under age 18 (Jones and Bayer, 2007). Consequently, many states repealed their UHLs in the late 1970s, and most adopted partial helmet laws that required only young riders to wear helmets.

In subsequent years, Congress continued to institute and lift sanctions that induced many states to readopt or repeal their UHLs. In the early 1990s, California, Washington, and Maryland amended partial helmet laws and instituted UHLs. The most recent federal policy change occurred in 1995 when Congress repealed financial sanctions against states without a UHL. As a result, five states (Arkansas, Florida, Kentucky, Pennsylvania, and Texas) amended their UHLs to require only young riders to wear motorcycle helmets. Colorado instituted a helmet policy for young riders in 2007, 30 years after repealing its UHL. Louisiana instituted a partial helmet law in 1999 but reversed the policy and reinstated a UHL in 2004. As of June 2010, 20 states and the District of Columbia had UHLs (IIHS, 2010).

Part of the growing literature investigating the effectiveness of UHLs analyzed data from hospital records or trauma centers (Rowland *et al.*, 1996; Bledsoe *et al.*, 2002; Hotz *et al.*, 2002). Rowland and colleagues (1996) conducted a retrospective cohort study of injured motorcycle riders in Washington in 1989. They found that the risk of hospitalization was only slightly higher for unhelmeted riders than it was for helmeted riders, but unhelmeted riders had more severe injuries and were more likely to have a serious head injury. Readmission rates, length of stay, hospital costs, and fatality rates were also higher for unhelmeted riders. According to the University of Arkansas for Medical Sciences trauma registry, patients without motorcycle helmets had more severe head and neck

---

[1] Several papers provide a detailed historical overview of UHLs in the United States. See, for example, Sass and Zimmerman (2000) and Houston and Richardson (2008).

injuries and longer stays in the ICU than helmeted riders over a period of six years (Bledsoe *et al.*, 2002). In addition, unreimbursed hospital charges were higher for unhelmeted riders than for helmeted riders. Hotz and colleagues (2002) found that the number and severity of brain injuries for those admitted to a Miami-Dade trauma center increased following the repeal of Florida's UHL.

Other studies have focused on the adoption or repeal of a UHL within a given state, investigating the fatality or injury outcomes before and after the policy change.[2] For example, Bledsoe and Li (2005) examine the effect of Arkansas' 1997 UHL repeal on the number of motorcycle registrations, crashes, injuries, and fatalities. A comparison of the figures four years before and four years after the repeal suggests that each of these count measures increased. There was also an increase in alcohol-involved motorcycle crashes following the repeal. Registration-adjusted fatality and crash figures, however, decreased during the same time period. Bledsoe and Li (2005) attribute this decrease to a spike in the number of registrations following the UHL repeal as well as to the growing popularity of motorcycles nationwide. The use of data from a single state makes it difficult to account for time trends and contemporaneous changes in other traffic policies.

Given the shortcomings of analyzing state-level time series data, the majority of studies in this literature use variations in state-level panel data from the Fatality Analysis Reporting System (FARS), a surveillance system administered by the NHTSA. FARS contains detailed information from law enforcement reports on motor vehicle crashes that occurred on public roads in the United States and resulted in a fatality up to 30 days after the crash. Sass and Zimmerman (2000) investigated the association between UHLs and motorcycle fatalities using these panel data from 1976 to 1997. They control for demographic variables and other factors such as seat belt policies, speed limits, and alcohol consumption. Accounting for state and year fixed effects, they found that UHLs reduced annual motorcycle fatalities per capita by about 29–33 percent during this period.

Using a longer panel of FARS data from 1975 to 2004, Houston and Richardson (2008) found that fatality rates were about 22–33 percent lower in states with a UHL than in those without a UHL. In addition, partial helmet laws reduced fatality rates by about 7–10 percent. Partial helmet laws are associated with smaller effect sizes partly because such laws are much more difficult to enforce than UHLs. More recently, after assembling FARS data from 1988 to 2005, Dee (2009) analyzed the effectiveness of UHLs by providing within-vehicle comparisons of outcomes among

---

[2] A full review can be found in Table 2 of Lin and Kraus (2009).

"two-rider" motorcycles involved in fatal crashes. Using this innovative identification strategy to exploit within-vehicle variation, Dee estimated that helmets reduce fatality risk by 34 percent. He then compared this effect size to the estimated effect of UHLs on all motorcycle fatalities during the same period. Given the strong evidence supporting the technological effectiveness of motorcycle helmets, Dee concludes that neither risk-compensating behaviors nor reductions in riding appreciably attenuate the benefits of helmet laws.

Although non-fatal injuries far outnumber fatalities, a comparable reporting system for non-fatal injuries does not exist, and less is known about how UHLs influence them. French *et al.* (2009) address this gap in the literature by analyzing a unique, state-specific longitudinal dataset on non-fatal motorcycle injuries from 1990 to 2005. Controlling for traffic conditions, a series of traffic and alcohol policies, and a rich set of demographic, economic, and geographic characteristics, the authors found that UHLs lead to a 24 percent reduction in fatal motorcycle injuries and a 20 percent reduction in non-fatal injuries. In more recent research, French *et al.* (2010) found that UHLs are particularly effective in reducing both overall and alcohol-involved motorcycle fatalities among riders without a valid license (i.e., no license or revoked, suspended, canceled, or expired license).

The present study conducts a novel evaluation of UHLs by analyzing their long-term effects on fatality rates and motorcycle ridership as measured by registrations. States that adopt a UHL might reduce motorcycle-related fatalities by inadvertently reducing motorcycle use. From a policy perspective, it is important to isolate the effect of UHLs on motorcycle ridership from their effect on motorcycle safety. Ideally, helmet laws should prevent serious head injuries without discouraging motorcycle ridership, which is clearly a welfare-enhancing activity for many Americans. This study also offers a closer investigation of the long-term effects of adoptions and repeals of UHLs by exploiting 31 years of state-specific panel data. In the next section, we describe the data and econometric methods utilized in the analysis.

3. Data and methods

This study uses state-specific longitudinal data covering the continental United States from 1975 to 2005. Consistent with the previous literature, we exclude Alaska, Hawaii, and the District of Columbia.[3] Fatality figures

---

[3] The fatality data and several other variables are the same as reported in Houston and Richardson (2008). A data appendix A with variable definitions and sources appears at the end of this chapter.

in this dataset come from the FARS, the surveillance system administered by the NHTSA.[4] We evaluate the effects of UHLs on motorcycle rider fatalities, in which rider refers to both motorcycle drivers and passengers. Using an approach similar to that of the earlier literature on motor vehicle fatalities, we define the motorcycle fatality rate as motorcycle fatalities per 10,000 people (e.g., Ruhm, 1996; Dee, 1999, 2001; Sass and Zimmerman, 2000; Eisenberg, 2003; Freeman, 2007; Houston and Richardson, 2008).

Our analysis models fatality rates by state and year as a function of UHLs, traffic safety measures, and other observable variables. UHLs are the primary policy of interest in this chapter. Although BAC and speed limits apply to motorcycle riders as well as to operators of other types of motor vehicles, UHLs are intended to improve motorcycle safety by directly impacting the behavior of motorcycle riders. Between 1975 and 2005, these laws varied considerably (see Figure 4). One state (CA) adopted a UHL and kept it in place for the rest of the period, 23 states repealed UHLs (AR, AZ, CO, CT, DE, FL, ID, IN, KS, KY, ME, MN, MT, ND, NH, NM, OH, PA, RI, SC, SD, WI, WY), eight made multiple changes to their UHLs (IA, LA, MD, NE, OK, OR, TX, WA), and 14 had a UHL throughout the analysis period (AL, GA, MA, MI, MO, MS, NC, NJ, NV, NY, TN, VA, VT, WV). Only two states, IL and UT, never had a UHL between 1975 and 2005. In addition to a dummy variable indicating whether a state had a UHL, we also constructed continuous and binary variables measuring the number of years the state had a UHL and the number of years since the state repealed a UHL within our time period.

BAC limits are an important alcohol-related traffic safety policy that varies significantly both between and within states during this period. To account for this variation, the models include a dichotomous variable for a BAC limit of less than or equal to 0.08 g/dL. As an explanatory variable, we also added a dichotomous variable for a maximum speed limit greater than or equal to 65 mph. Traveling at higher speeds makes avoiding traffic crashes more difficult, so motor vehicle fatality rates may be positively related to speed limits (Grabowski and Morrisey, 2007). Areas with less vehicular traffic and its associated hazards may also be more likely to raise speed limits.

Motorcycle fatalities occur more frequently in states and years with greater motorcycle use (i.e., exposure). In our regression of motorcycle fatality rates, we control for motorcycle ridership using the number of motorcycle registrations per 10,000 people as a proxy for the intensity of motorcycle use. This variable is not an ideal measure of motorcycle ridership for at least two reasons. First, the number of motorcycle registrations does not necessarily have to coincide with the number of active motorcycle

---

[4] Further information on the FARS database is available on their Web site (http://www-fars.nhtsa.dot.gov).

riders in a given state and year. Second, and more importantly, motorcycle registrations do not fully reflect the frequency and intensity of riding. A better measure of frequency and intensity of use would be motorcycle vehicle miles traveled. These data, however, are unavailable for each state and year from 1975 to 2005. We use motorcycle registration rates (number of registrations per 10,000 people) as a second dependent variable to analyze how use varied in response to changes in UHLs and other factors.

In all our specifications, we control for average annual temperature and precipitation, real income per capita, and the inverse of population density. The inverse of population density is measured by the state area in square miles per 10,000 residents rather than by people per square mile to be consistent with the other per capita measures in the analysis. All these factors may significantly affect both motorcycle use and fatality rates.

In addition to the observable factors listed above, fatalities and registrations depend on unobserved state and year fixed effects (Baltagi, 2001; Wooldridge, 2002). Several previous studies examining how public policies affect motor vehicle fatalities have addressed unobserved heterogeneity by using panel data techniques and by modeling these state-specific factors as time-invariant fixed effects (Ruhm, 1996; Dee, 1999; Morrisey and Grabowski, 2005; Freeman, 2007). Hence, our initial specifications take the following basic form:

$$y_{st} = P_{st}\beta_1 + C_{st}\beta_2 + \mu_s + \delta_t + \varepsilon_{st} \quad (1)$$

where y_{st} denotes the fatality rate (or registration rate) in state s and year t, defined as the number of fatalities (registrations) per 10,000 people, P is a vector of state policies, and C is a vector of observable controls, as noted above.

We model unobserved heterogeneity as state fixed effects denoted by μ_s; these account for state characteristics that remain constant over time and are relevant to motorcycle riding and safety. δ_t denotes the unobserved year-specific determinants of motorcycle fatalities, which correct for secular nationwide trends in motorcycle riding intensity, driving patterns, vehicle characteristics, road conditions, and other characteristics. Finally, ε_{st} is a disturbance term.

The vector β_1 contains the coefficients of interest, which indicate the direction, magnitude, and significance of the effects of traffic policies on motorcycle riding and safety. The inclusion of state and time fixed effects cannot compensate for any important omitted variables that vary within states over time. The omission of these variables would bias the coefficient estimates if there were a systematic relationship between the trend in fatality or registration rates and the adoption of a UHL. For example, the influence of special interest groups such as the motorcycle industry and rider community (Homer and French, 2009) and advocacy groups such as Mothers Against Drunk Driving (Eisenberg, 2003) are time-varying unobserved factors related to motorcycle riding and fatalities.

In an effort to address this issue of unobserved trends, we also estimate models that include state-specific linear time trends.[5] Hence, we modify the specification in Eq. (1) as follows:

$$y_{st} = P_{st}\beta_1 + C_{st}\beta_2 + \mu_s + \delta_t + \mu_s \times T + \varepsilon_{st} \quad (2)$$

where $\mu_s \times T$ denotes the state-specific trends and controls for factors that change continuously over time within states. With this adjustment in our specification, we now identify the impact of the motorcycle safety measures by within-state variations in policies net of the time trends (e.g., Dee, 2009; Carpenter and Stehr, 2010).

Following Dee (1999) and Miron and Tetelbaum (2009), we also provide estimation results based on alternative definitions of the dependent variables in addition to the simple rates. Denoting fatality rates by F and registration rates by R, the dependent variables in Eqs. (1) and (2) can be transformed into the logarithm of the odds ratios as $\ln(F_{st}/1-F_{st})$ and $\ln(R_{st}/1-R_{st})$. Under this specification, a one-unit change in a particular explanatory variable leads to a corresponding percentage change in the log odds ratio. To account for potential heteroscedasticity, we employ weighted least squares estimation for all of our specifications in which the weights are the population figures in state s and year t. In addition, we adjust standard errors in all models for state-level clustering (Bertrand *et al.*, 2004).

4. Results

Table 1 contains descriptive statistics for the variables used in the analysis. The table reports summary figures for all observations ($N = 1{,}488$) and for the observations with a UHL (48 percent) and those without (52 percent). Next to each variable, we indicate statistically significant differences between these two groups of observations. The average number of motorcycle fatalities per 10,000 people is 0.150 for the entire sample, 0.123 for the observations with a UHL, and 0.174 for the observations without a UHL ($p < .01$). The average number of motorcycle registrations per 10,000 people also shows large variation between these two groups: approximately 174 registrations for observations with a UHL and 289 registrations for observations without these laws ($p < .01$). In terms of traffic policies, 20 percent of the state/year observations had a BAC limit of .08 or less during the period of analysis. Surprisingly, observations with a UHL are slightly less likely to have a BAC limit of .08, but this difference

---

[5] To conserve space in our tables, we do not report the estimated coefficients for the state and year fixed effects and the state-specific time trends. These results can be obtained from the authors upon request.

Table 1. Descriptive statistics by universal helmet law (UHL) status, 1975–2005[a]

	Full sample				No UHL (52%)		UHL (48%)	
	Mean	SD	Min	Max	Mean	SD	Mean	SD
Outcome measures								
Motorcycle fatalities	71.995	93.472	1.000	860.000	74.388	114.790	69.421	62.944
Motorcycle fatalities per 10,000 people (*F*)***	0.150	0.073	0.015	0.512	0.174	0.075	0.123	0.059
Odds ratio for motorcycle fatalities (*F*/1−*F*)***	0.186	0.117	0.016	1.048	0.222	0.125	0.147	0.094
Motorcycle registrations (1,000s)*	99.837	105.798	7.153	745.691	104.218	118.544	95.126	89.950
Motorcycle registrations per 10,000 people (*R*)***	233.345	128.556	56.572	935.793	288.961	134.611	173.540	89.015
Odds ratio for motorcycle registrations (*R*/1−*R*)***	0.371	0.552	0.060	14.575	0.504	0.725	0.228	0.170
Policies and controls								
BAC ≤ 0.08[b]	0.200	0.392	0.000	1.000	0.216	0.403	0.182	0.380
Maximum speed limits ≥ 65 mph[c]**	0.552	0.491	0.000	1.000	0.582	0.486	0.521	0.495
Ln(average annual temperature)***	3.983	0.140	3.721	4.407	3.950	0.138	4.019	0.133
Ln(average annual precipitation)***	3.429	0.538	1.952	4.302	3.263	0.544	3.607	0.471
Real income per capita ($1,000)[d]**	13.784	9.693	1.158	48.817	14.390	9.337	13.133	10.027
Inverse population density[e]***	0.030	0.044	0.001	0.257	0.039	0.050	0.020	0.035
Number of observations		1.488			771		717	

Note: *, **, *** denote the statistical significance of the difference in means between UHL and no UHL samples at 10, 5, and 1 percent levels, respectively.
[a]A universal helmet law requires motorcycle riders of all ages to wear a motorcycle helmet.
[b]Maximum allowable blood alcohol concentration (BAC) of driver ≤ 0.08 g/dL.
[c]Maximum legal speed limit on rural interstates (mph).
[d]Personal income per capita in constant 2005 dollars ($1,000).
[e]Inverse population density is defined as the state area in square miles per 10,000 people to be consistent with the rest of the per capita measures.

is not statistically significant. More than half of all observations had maximum speed limits above 65 mph during the analysis period.

We report the estimated coefficients and standard errors (in parentheses) of the effects of UHLs on motorcycle registrations and fatalities in Table 2. All specifications include state and year fixed effects. In the first four columns, we present the results of the model for registrations. The first two columns present the fixed effects estimation results with the number of motorcycle registrations per 10,000 people as the dependent variable. Model (1) reveals that UHLs significantly reduce registration rates while income per capita is positively associated with registrations. Quantitatively, UHLs reduce registration rates by about 41 units, corresponding to an 18 percent reduction (41.159 divided by the sample mean of 233.345 motorcycle registrations per 10,000 people).

The introduction of state-specific linear time trends in Column (2) significantly mitigates the effects of UHLs on registration rates (down to about seven percent) and eliminates the significant effect of income per capita. Thus, most of the observed decline in registrations in Column (1) can be explained by preexisting trends in the states rather than by a strong, unintended causal effect of UHLs. Columns (3) and (4) report the estimation results when the log odds ratio is regressed on the same set of variables as in Columns (1) and (2), respectively. The findings are quite similar with one notable exception: the estimated effect of the .08 BAC limit in Column (4) becomes positive and statistically significant ($p < .05$). This finding somewhat surprisingly suggests that stricter BAC laws are associated with greater intensity of motorcycle riding.

The models in Columns (5)–(8) correspond to the analysis of UHLs' effects on motorcycle fatalities. All of these specifications include motorcycle registration rates as an additional control variable to account for risk exposure. As with motorcycle registrations, once we add the state-specific time trends to the models, the effects of both the policy and control variables become smaller in magnitude and sometimes lose statistical significance. In all the models, UHLs have a highly significant effect ($p < .01$) on motorcycle fatalities. This corresponds to a reduction of about 27 percent in the fatality rate and 32 percent in the log odds ratio when we include state-specific time trends. These effect sizes are much larger than the impact of UHLs on registrations. Although UHLs might decrease motorcycle-related fatalities by inadvertently reducing motorcycle use, this is not the main mechanism by which they achieve the intended outcome of lower fatality rates. It is important to note that the findings for UHLs are consistent and robust to model specification.

The only other significant effects in the fatality specifications correspond to BAC limits and speed limits, in Column (6), as well as income per capita, in Columns (6) and (8). Motorcycle fatalities are positively related to income per capita in our regressions even after we control for state-specific registrations probably because our registration measure does not

Table 2. ***Effects of a UHL on motorcycle registrations and fatalities, 1975–2005 (N = 1,488)***

	Registrations				Fatalities			
	Per capita (*R*)		Ln(*R*/1−*R*)		Per capita (*F*)		Ln(*F*/1−*F*)	
	(1)	(2)	(3)	(4)	(5)	(6)	(7)	(8)
Universal helmet law (UHL)	−41.159***	−16.375***	−0.273***	−0.143***	−0.051***	−0.041***	−0.390***	−0.317***
	(9.594)	(5.904)	(0.043)	(0.032)	(0.009)	(0.004)	(0.058)	(0.045)
BAC ≤ .08	−4.846	9.749	0.002	0.111**	−0.024**	−0.012*	−0.094	−0.021
	(8.171)	(7.638)	(0.048)	(0.054)	(0.010)	(0.006)	(0.057)	(0.042)
Maximum speed limits ≥ 65 mph	−21.305	−19.022	−0.145	−0.125	−0.010**	−0.012***	−0.012	−0.026
	(17.277)	(17.103)	(0.149)	(0.150)	(0.005)	(0.004)	(0.033)	(0.030)
Ln(temperature)	−103.000	4.406	−0.507	0.025	−0.116***	0.001	−0.575***	−0.052
	(66.980)	(50.070)	(0.471)	(0.401)	(0.024)	(0.020)	(0.163)	(0.135)
Ln(precipitation)	−24.316	11.308	−0.164	0.068	−0.050**	−0.023	−0.268*	−0.201
	(34.258)	(22.953)	(0.239)	(0.193)	(0.022)	(0.018)	(0.149)	(0.128)
Real income per capita ($1,000)	4.863**	−1.927	0.031**	−0.029	−0.001	0.005*	−0.013	0.036**
	(1.964)	(2.788)	(0.012)	(0.019)	(0.001)	(0.003)	(0.009)	(0.018)
Inverse population density	1,511.298	−35.080	7.602	1.700	1.402**	0.493	5.775*	1.018
	(937.486)	(1,283.385)	(4.687)	(6.497)	(0.591)	(0.861)	(2.971)	(5.397)
Motorcycle registrations per 1,000,000 people					0.018***	0.010**	0.122***	0.053
					(0.005)	(0.004)	(0.035)	(0.035)
Year fixed effects	Yes	Yes	Yes	Yes	Yes	Yes	Yes	Yes
State fixed effects	Yes	Yes	Yes	Yes	Yes	Yes	Yes	Yes
State-specific time trends	No	Yes	No	Yes	No	Yes	No	Yes
R-squared	0.876	0.923	0.884	0.923	0.855	0.896	0.872	0.899

Note: For each explanatory variable, we report the estimated coefficient and the estimated standard errors in parentheses. *, **, *** denote the statistical significance at the 10, 5, and 1 percent levels, respectively.

sufficiently account for the intensity of motorcycle riding. Stricter BAC limits reduce fatality rates, but this effect is only marginally statistically significant ($p < .10$) and disappears in the log odds ratio specifications. Interestingly, higher speed limits seem to reduce fatality rates, but this effect does not persist in Columns (7) and (8). One possible explanation for this result could be that the adoption of higher speed limits reflects other factors that lower risks for motorcycle riders such as less traffic congestion and/or better driving conditions.

Table 3 presents specifications focusing on the dynamic effects of UHLs on motorcycle registrations and fatalities. Specifically, we include variables that indicate not only the presence or absence of a UHL but also the length of time a state has had or has been without a UHL throughout our analysis period. In each odd-numbered column, we include a variable to measure the number of years since a state has adopted a UHL, while we assign a zero to states without a UHL. The even-numbered columns include a variable measuring the number of years since a state has repealed its UHL, and we assign a zero to states with a UHL. All specifications include state and year fixed effects and state-specific time trends.

The results show that each additional year with a UHL reduces registration rates by about half a percent ($p < .01$), while repealing a UHL does not seem to lead to significant increases in motorcycle riding (Columns (1) and (2), respectively). The specifications using the log odds ratio (Columns (3) and (4)) suggest that both adoption and repeal of a UHL significantly influence motorcycle riding ($p < .01$). Each additional year with a UHL reduces the odds ratio by about 2.7 percent, whereas each additional year following the repeal boosts the odds ratio by about four percent. The only other relevant factor in these specifications is BAC laws, by which stricter BAC limits are once again associated with increased riding.

The last four columns of Table 3 use the same measures of years since the adoption and repeal of a UHL to identify the dynamic effects of policy changes on fatalities. Each additional year since adoption reduces fatality rates by an estimated 0.66 percent (Column (5)), whereas each additional year since repeal increases fatality rates by about 2.66 percent (Column (6)). These results correspond to a 5.4 percent decrease in the odds ratio of fatalities for every year since the adoption of a UHL and an 18 percent increase in the odds ratio of fatalities for every year since the repeal of a UHL. These findings, together with the estimates in Columns (3) and (4), suggest that the effects of repeals are larger and more enduring than the effects of adoptions. As in Table 2, the results in Table 3 show that UHL adoptions and repeals are far more effective in reducing fatalities than in reducing registrations.

In Tables 4 and 5, we use sets of binary variables measuring the time elapsed since the adoption or repeal of a UHL. These dynamic specifications allow us to consider the possibility that the long-term effects of UHLs are

Table 3. ***Dynamic effects of adopting and repealing a UHL on motorcycle registrations and fatalities, 1975–2005 (N = 1,488)***

	Registrations				Fatalities			
	Per capita (*R*)		Ln(*R*/1−*R*)		Per capita (*F*)		Ln(*F*/1−*F*)	
	(1)	(2)	(3)	(4)	(5)	(6)	(7)	(8)
Years since the adoption of a UHL	−1.069***		−0.010***		−0.001***		−0.010**	
	(0.266)		(0.003)		(0.000)		(0.004)	
Years since the repeal of a UHL		0.656		0.015***		0.004***		0.035***
		(0.934)		(0.005)		(0.001)		(0.007)
BAC ≤ .08	8.789	9.876	0.102**	0.109**	−0.014	−0.013*	−0.029	−0.028
	(6.890)	(7.579)	(0.049)	(0.054)	(0.008)	(0.008)	(0.059)	(0.053)
Maximum speed limits ≥ 65 mph	−20.548	−19.916	−0.138	−0.127	−0.016***	−0.013**	−0.050	−0.025
	(16.499)	(17.375)	(0.145)	(0.153)	(0.004)	(0.005)	(0.031)	(0.039)
Ln(temperature)	20.996	7.409	0.175	0.065	0.026	0.012	0.128	0.036
	(45.729)	(51.562)	(0.361)	(0.406)	(0.029)	(0.023)	(0.204)	(0.137)
Ln(precipitation)	13.456	12.667	0.088	0.107	−0.021	−0.014	−0.187	−0.115
	(23.451)	(24.261)	(0.204)	(0.183)	(0.024)	(0.018)	(0.186)	(0.115)
Real income per capita ($1,000)	−0.080	−1.070	−0.012	−0.020	0.008**	0.007*	0.062**	0.057**
	(2.615)	(2.650)	(0.019)	(0.018)	(0.004)	(0.004)	(0.025)	(0.026)
Inverse population density	−32.363	−125.217	1.760	1.178	0.379	0.336	0.031	−0.078
	(1,320.655)	(1,318.693)	(6.778)	(7.048)	(0.932)	(0.869)	(6.070)	(5.231)
Motorcycle registrations per 1,000,000 people					0.012**	0.013**	0.071*	0.079*
					(0.005)	(0.005)	(0.039)	(0.041)
Year fixed effects	Yes	Yes	Yes	Yes	Yes	Yes	Yes	Yes
State fixed effects	Yes	Yes	Yes	Yes	Yes	Yes	Yes	Yes
State-specific time trends	Yes	Yes	Yes	Yes	Yes	Yes	Yes	Yes
R-squared	0.923	0.922	0.923	0.922	0.883	0.885	0.887	0.891

Note: For each explanatory variable, we report the estimated coefficient and the estimated standard errors in parentheses. *, **, *** denote the statistical significance at the 10, 5, and 1 percent, respectively.

***Table 4.* Long-term effects of adopting a UHL on motorcycle registrations and fatalities, 1975–2005 (N = 1,488)**

	Registrations		Fatalities	
	Per capita (*R*)	Ln(*R*/1−*R*)	Per capita (*F*)	Ln(*F*/1−*F*)
	(1)	(2)	(3)	(4)
Year of the adoption of UHL	−13.133	−0.090	−0.028***	−0.151**
	(13.141)	(0.073)	(0.008)	(0.063)
1 year after the adoption of UHL	−1.175	−0.022	−0.048***	−0.394***
	(5.470)	(0.035)	(0.006)	(0.079)
2 years after the adoption of UHL	−6.044	−0.072	−0.044***	−0.321***
	(6.018)	(0.049)	(0.005)	(0.047)
3 years after the adoption of UHL	−8.578	−0.110**	−0.047***	−0.349***
	(6.425)	(0.055)	(0.005)	(0.036)
4+ years after the adoption of UHL	−19.741**	−0.170***	−0.041***	−0.328***
	(7.510)	(0.048)	(0.005)	(0.057)
BAC≤.08	8.569	0.101*	−0.013*	−0.026
	(7.331)	(0.054)	(0.006)	(0.046)
Maximum speed limits≥65 mph	−19.893	−0.132	−0.012***	−0.027
	(16.879)	(0.148)	(0.004)	(0.031)
Ln(temperature)	12.833	0.087	−0.000	−0.047
	(46.161)	(0.371)	(0.021)	(0.149)
Ln(precipitation)	13.215	0.084	−0.023	−0.193
	(23.056)	(0.194)	(0.018)	(0.130)
Real income per capita ($1,000)	−1.111	−0.022	0.005**	0.039**
	(2.480)	(0.017)	(0.002)	(0.016)
Inverse population density	−30.838	1.916	0.539	1.472
	(1,258.713)	(6.350)	(0.868)	(5.276)
Motorcycle registrations per 1,000,000 people			0.010**	0.054
			(0.004)	(0.033)
Year fixed effects	Yes	Yes	Yes	Yes
State fixed effects	Yes	Yes	Yes	Yes
State-specific time trends	Yes	Yes	Yes	Yes
R-squared	0.923	0.924	0.896	0.900

Note: For each explanatory variable, we report the estimated coefficient and the estimated standard errors in parentheses. *, **, *** denote the statistical significance at the 10, 5, and 1 percent, respectively.

different than their short-term impact. In fact, the estimated effects indicate that motorcycle fatality rates continue to decrease (increase) long after the adoption (repeal) of a UHL. With the exception of the first year of adoption and repeal, the effect sizes remain fairly stable over the few years following the UHL policy change. The effect sizes associated with the adoption of a UHL are somewhat larger when compared to those corresponding to the repeal of a UHL.

Table 5. ***Long-term effects of repealing a UHL on motorcycle registrations and fatalities, 1975–2005 (N = 1,488)***

	Registrations		Fatalities	
	Per capita (*R*)	Ln(*R*/1−*R*)	Per capita (*F*)	Ln(*F*/1−*F*)
	(1)	(2)	(3)	(4)
Year of the repeal of UHL	6.062	0.054	0.022***	0.177***
	(6.383)	(0.040)	(0.005)	(0.046)
1 year after the repeal of UHL	14.225**	0.110***	0.031***	0.238***
	(6.159)	(0.033)	(0.006)	(0.044)
2 years after the repeal of UHL	19.500**	0.136***	0.033***	0.249***
	(7.361)	(0.040)	(0.006)	(0.048)
3 years after the repeal of UHL	27.380***	0.179***	0.046***	0.299***
	(9.536)	(0.046)	(0.008)	(0.061)
4+ years after the repeal of UHL	23.632**	0.202***	0.037***	0.293***
	(10.643)	(0.058)	(0.008)	(0.069)
BAC≤.08	7.854	0.096*	−0.015*	−0.041
	(7.200)	(0.053)	(0.008)	(0.050)
Maximum speed limits≥65 mph	−18.728	−0.125	−0.013***	−0.031
	(17.308)	(0.152)	(0.004)	(0.031)
Ln(temperature)	12.245	0.077	0.016	0.052
	(52.067)	(0.412)	(0.020)	(0.129)
Ln(precipitation)	11.719	0.073	−0.024	−0.205
	(23.271)	(0.188)	(0.019)	(0.125)
Real income per capita ($1,000)	−1.262	−0.022	0.007*	0.050**
	(2.555)	(0.017)	(0.004)	(0.025)
Inverse population density	−3.945	1.834	0.462	0.720
	(1,311.512)	(6.674)	(0.862)	(5.326)
Motorcycle registrations per 1,000,000 people			0.010*	0.052
			(0.005)	(0.043)
Year fixed effects	Yes	Yes	Yes	Yes
State fixed effects	Yes	Yes	Yes	Yes
State-specific time trends	Yes	Yes	Yes	Yes
R-squared	0.924	0.924	0.890	0.894

Note: For each explanatory variable, we report the estimated coefficient and the estimated standard errors in parentheses. *, **, *** denote the statistical significance at the 10, 5, and 1 percent, respectively.

For registrations, the estimated coefficients on the UHL adoption variables in the first two columns of Table 4 jointly indicate that adoption of a UHL does not lead to a sharp decrease in motorcycle riding but rather gradually reduces ridership in the long-term. On the other hand, the results in the first two columns of Table 4 suggest that repeal of a UHL sparks a quick upsurge in motorcycle riding, which gradually increases in the long-term. Thus, the estimated short-term effects of adopting or repealing a UHL on motorcycle ridership differ from the long-term effects. Overall, the results in Tables 4 and 5 are consistent with those in Tables 2 and 3, which suggest much stronger effects of UHLs on motorcycle fatalities than on motorcycle registrations.

We performed robustness checks to investigate the stability of our findings. First, we regressed the logarithm of registrations and the logarithm of fatalities on the policy and control variables. Second, we estimated all specifications using a conditional fixed effects negative binomial model, a count data technique. Third, we extended the models for the long-term effects by including leads in addition to lags prior to adoption and repeal of a UHL (thus changing the omitted category) in order to test the sensitivity of our findings. All the robustness checks produced estimates that were very similar in sign, significance, and magnitude to the results presented in the tables. These results are available from the authors upon request.

5. *Conclusions*

In this study, we analyzed state-level longitudinal data from 1975 to 2005 to investigate how UHLs affect fatalities and motorcycle use over time. We formally address the possibility that helmet laws might reduce fatalities by influencing motorcycle ridership. We found that the effects of UHLs are far smaller on the intensity of motorcycle use – as proxied by motorcycle registrations – than they are on fatalities. Therefore, the effectiveness of UHLs is primarily attributable to the safety features of helmets per se, a conclusion that has been supported in earlier studies, rather than the unintended effects on ridership (Dee, 2009; Carpenter and Stehr, 2010).

We also show that, when analyzing the effects of UHLs on motorcycle registrations, the addition of state-specific time trends dramatically decreases the magnitude of the estimates. This suggests that much of the observed relationship between UHLs and motorcycle registrations is due to unobserved state-specific trends that change over time. However, even when we include state-specific time trends in the models, UHLs continue to have a highly significant negative effect on motorcycle fatalities. In quantitative terms, UHLs reduce fatality rates by about 27 percent, an estimate that is in line with earlier research (Sass and Zimmerman, 2000; Houston and Richardson, 2008; Dee, 2009; French *et al.*, 2009).

This study offers new information on the short- and long-term effects of UHL adoptions and repeals on motorcycle registrations and fatalities. Our results show that fatality rates continue to be affected long after the policy change occurs. In addition, repealing a UHL has a greater impact on increasing fatalities over time than adopting a UHL does on decreasing fatalities. We find that the adoption or repeal of a UHL has an immediate effect on fatalities that becomes stronger over time. In contrast, the adoption or repeal of a UHL does not have an immediate impact on registrations. Over time, however, adopting a UHL decreases registrations, whereas repealing a UHL has the opposite effect.

The current study has several limitations. First, motorcycle registrations are not an ideal measure of the intensity of motorcycle riding. Unfortunately, a better measure, annual motorcycle miles traveled, is unavailable at the state level. The inclusion of state-specific time trends might somewhat remedy this problem by picking up such differences in the preexisting trends across states. To the extent our models do not sufficiently capture the changes over time in terms of the intensity of motorcycle riding, our estimates could potentially be biased. However, the direction of the bias is unclear. States with increasing intensity of riding might experience higher fatalities, which in turn might lead to the adoption of safety measures such as a UHL. On the other hand, they might be less likely to adopt a UHL as more ridership means stronger motorcycle advocacy and lobbying (Homer and French, 2009).

Second, we were unable to control for other potentially important time-varying factors such as police enforcement, traffic conditions, and vehicle characteristics because these data are unavailable for the sample period. Our results could potentially be biased if there is a systematic relationship between either adoption or repeal of a UHL and some of these unobservable time-varying factors. Third, this analysis does not address the effectiveness of partial helmet laws, as there is limited variation in partial helmet laws during the period of our analysis. Finally, although non-fatal motorcycle injuries far outnumber fatal injuries, non-fatal injury data are only available for a few years. Analyzing non-fatal injury data could provide useful information about the extent UHLs can reduce an outcome that is much more common than fatal injuries. Despite these limitations, the present study contributes to a growing body of literature that consistently identifies UHLs as a highly effective policy for reducing motorcycle fatalities.

Even given this compelling evidence, less than half of all states currently have a UHL, and the policies remain controversial among certain rider groups and individual rights activists. More importantly, about 55 percent of motorcyclists in the United States voluntarily decide to forgo a helmet when riding (NHTSA, 2009). It is important for policymakers, riders, and public health groups concerned with the high number of motorcycle fatalities in the United States to understand the underlying mechanisms between helmet laws and fatality rates as well as whether the policies have indirect effects on ridership in the short- and long-term. Our study provides unique and policy-relevant evidence that UHLs' effects on motorcycle registrations are much less pronounced than their effects on motorcycle safety. The strong effects of UHLs on motorcycle fatalities persist long after a UHL has been instituted, even after controlling for observed characteristics, unobserved state and year fixed effects, and state-specific time trends. This result confirms the public health benefits of helmet use and demonstrates that UHLs do not appreciably impact the utility-enhancing practice of riding for thousands of motorcyclists.

Acknowledgments

We gratefully acknowledge David J. Houston and Lilliard E. Richardson Jr. for sharing their data with us. We thank Allison Johnson for editorial assistance.

References

Advocates for Highway and Auto Safety (2010), "The 2010 roadmap to State Highway Safety Laws" (http://www.saferoads.org/2010-roadmap-state-highway-safety-laws). Accessed on May 30, 2010.

Baltagi, B.H. (2001), *Econometric Analysis of Panel Data*, New York: Wiley.

Bertrand, M., E. Duflo and S. Mullainathan (2004), "How much should we trust difference-in-differences estimates?", *Quarterly Journal of Economics*, Vol. 119(1), pp. 249–275.

Bledsoe, G.H. and G. Li (2005), "Trends in Arkansas motorcycle trauma after helmet law repeal", *The Southern Medical Journal*, Vol. 98(4), pp. 436–440.

Bledsoe, G.H., S.M. Schexnayder, M.J. Carey, W.N. Dobbins, W.D. Gibson and J.W. Hindman (2002), "The negative impact of the repeal of the Arkansas motorcycle helmet law", *Journal of Trauma-Injury Infection and Critical Care*, Vol. 53(6), pp. 1078–1087.

Carpenter, C.S. and M. Stehr (2010). "Intended and unintended effects of youth bicycle helmet laws", NBER Working Paper Series, No. 15658.

Dee, T.S. (1999), "State alcohol policies, teen drinking and traffic fatalities", *Journal of Public Economics*, Vol. 72(2), pp. 289–315.

Dee, T.S. (2001), "Does setting limits save lives? the case of 0.08 BAC laws", *Journal of Policy Analysis and Management*, Vol. 20(1), pp. 111–128.

Dee, T.S. (2009), "Motorcycle helmets and traffic safety", *Journal of Health Economics*, Vol. 28(2), pp. 398–412.

Eisenberg, D. (2003), "Evaluating the effectiveness of policies related to drunk driving", *Journal of Policy Analysis and Management*, Vol. 22(2), pp. 249–274.

Freeman, D.G. (2007), "Drunk driving legislation and traffic fatalities: new evidence on BAC 08 laws", *Contemporary Economic Policy*, Vol. 25(3), pp. 293–308.

French, M.T., G. Gumus and J. Homer (2009), "Public policies and motorcycle safety", *Journal of Health Economics*, Vol. 28(4), pp. 831–838.

French, M.T., G. Gumus and J. Homer (2010). "Helmet laws, traffic policies, and motorcycle safety: an analysis by license state and status", Working Paper.

Grabowski, D.C. and M.A. Morrisey (2007), "System-wide implications of the repeal of the national maximum speed limit", *Accident Analysis and Prevention*, Vol. 39(1), pp. 180–189.

Homer, J.F. and M.T. French (2009), "Motorcycle helmet laws in the United States from 1990 to 2005: politics and public health", *American Journal of Public Health*, Vol. 99(3), pp. 415–423.

Hotz, G.A., S.M. Cohn, C. Popkin, P. Ekeh, R. Duncan, E.W. Johnson, F. Pernas and J. Selem (2002), "The impact of a repealed motorcycle helmet law in Miami-Dade County", *The Journal of TRAUMA Injury, Infection and Critical Care*, Vol. 52(3), pp. 469–474.

Houston, D.J. and L.E. Richardson (2008), "Motorcyclist fatality rates and mandatory helmet-use laws", *Accident Analysis and Prevention*, Vol. 40(1), pp. 200–208.

Insurance Institute for Highway Safety (2010), "Laws and regulations: helmet use laws" (http://www.iihs.org/laws/helmet_history.html). Retrieved on June 2010.

Jones, M.M. and R. Bayer (2007), "Paternalism and its discontents: motorcycle helmet laws, libertarian values, and public health", *American Journal of Public Health*, Vol. 97, pp. 2–11.

Lin, M. and J.F. Kraus (2009), "A review of risk factors and patterns of motorcycle injuries", *Accident Analysis and Prevention*, Vol. 41, pp. 710–722.

Liu, B., R. Ivers, R. Norton, S. Boufous, S. Blows and S.K. Lo (2004), "Helmets for preventing injury in motorcycle riders", *Cochrane Database of Systematic Reviews*, Vol. 2, p. CD004333.

Max, W., B. Stark and S. Root (1998), "Putting a lid on injury costs: the economic impact of the California motorcycle helmet law", *Journal of Trauma*, Vol. 45(3), pp. 550–556.

McSwain, N.E. and B. Wiley (1984), *Impact of the Re-enactment of the Motorcycle Helmet Law in Louisiana (DOT HS 806 760)*, Washington, DC: US Department of Transportation.

Miron, J.A. and E. Tetelbaum (2009), "Does the minimum legal drinking age save lives?", *Economic Inquiry*, Vol. 47(2), pp. 317–336.

Morrisey, M.A. and D.C. Grabowski (2005), "State motor vehicle laws and older drivers", *Health Economics*, Vol. 14(4), pp. 407–419.

Morrison, D.S., M. Petticrew and H. Thomson (2003), "What are the most effective ways of improving population health through transport interventions? Evidence from systematic reviews", *Journal of Epidemiology & Community Health*, Vol. 57, pp. 327–333.

National Highway Traffic Safety Administration (NHTSA). (1992), *Restraint System Use in 19 US Cities: 1991 Annual Report (DOT HS 808 148)*, Washington, DC: US Department of Transportation.

National Highway Traffic Safety Administration (NHTSA). (2008a), *Traffic Safety Facts – Motorcycles 2008 Data (DOT HS 811 159)*, Washington, DC: US Department of Transportation.

National Highway Traffic Safety Administration (NHTSA). (2008b), *Traffic Safety Facts – Motorcycles 2006 Data (DOT HS 810 806)*, Washington, DC: US Department of Transportation.

National Highway Traffic Safety Administration. (2008c), *Traffic Safety Facts 2008—A Compilation of Motor Vehicle Crash Data from the Fatality Analysis Reporting System and the General Estimates System (DOT HS 811 170)*, Washington, DC: NHTSA's National Center for Statistics and Analysis.

National Highway Traffic Safety Administration (NHTSA). (2009), *Motorcycle Helmet Use in 2009. Traffic Safety Facts: Research Note. (DOT HS 811 254)*, Washington, DC: US Department of Transportation.

Norvell, D.C. and P. Cummings (2002), "Association of helmet use with death in motorcycle crashes: a matched-pair cohort study", *American Journal of Epidemiology*, Vol. 156, pp. 483–487.

Paulozzi, L.J. (2005), "The role of sales of new motorcycles in a recent increase in motorcycle mortality rates", *Journal of Safety Research*, Vol. 36(October), pp. 361–364.

Rowland, J., F. Rivara, P. Salzberg, R. Soderberg, R. Maier and T. Koepsell (1996), "Motorcycle helmet use and injury outcome and hospitalization costs from crashes in Washington State", *American Journal of Public Health*, Vol. 86(1), pp. 41–45.

Ruhm, C.J. (1996), "Alcohol policies and highway vehicle fatalities", *Journal of Health Economics*, Vol. 15(4), pp. 435–454.

Sass, T.R. and P.R. Zimmerman (2000), "Motorcycle helmet laws and motorcyclist fatalities", *Journal of Regulatory Economics*, Vol. 18(3), pp. 195–215.

US Department of Transportation (DOT) (2007), *US Department of Transportation Action Plan to Reduce Motorcycle Fatalities (DOT HS 810 855)*, Washington, DC: US Department of Transportation (DOT).

US General Accounting Office (GAO). (1991), *Highway Safety: Motorcycle Helmet Laws Save Lives and Reduce Costs to Society (GAO/RCED-91-170)*, Washington, DC: US General Accounting Office.

Welsh, J. (2007). "The new motorcycles: bigger, faster, deadlier", *The Wall Street Journal*. September 18 (http://online.wsj.com/public/article_print/SB119006164438830162.html). Retrieved on May 2010.

Wooldridge, J.M. (2002), *Econometric Analysis of Cross Section and Panel Data*, Cambridge, MA: MIT Press.

Appendix A. Variable definitions and sources

Variable	Definition	Source
Motorcycle fatalities	Total motorcycle rider (driver or passenger) fatalities	NHTSA Fatality Analysis Reporting System (FARS) (http://www-fars.nhtsa.dot.gov).
Motorcycle registrations	Number of two-wheeled and three-wheeled motorcycles	H&R; Federal Highway Administration, Highway Statistics.
Universal helmet law (UHL)	A universal helmet law requires motorcycle riders of all ages to wear a motorcycle helmet	H&R; Insurance Institute for Highway Safety.
BAC limits	Maximum allowable blood alcohol concentration (BAC) of the driver	
	NHTSA Alcohol-Highway Safety Digest Topics and the Alcohol Policy Information System (http://www.alcoholpolicy.niaaa.nih.gov)	
Maximum speed limits	Maximum legal speed limit on rural interstates (mph)	H&R; Insurance Institute for Highway Safety.
Average temperature	Normal daily mean temperature, annual average (degrees F)	H&R; National Climatic Data Center.
Average precipitation	Normal annual precipitation (inches)	H&R; National Climatic Data Center.
Real income per capita ($1,000)	Personal income per capita in constant 2005 dollars	H&R; US Census Bureau, Statistical Abstract of the United States.
Inverse population density	State area in square miles per 10,000 people	H&R; US Census Bureau, Statistical Abstract of the United States; CDC, NCHS, Bridged-Race Population Estimates.

Note: H&R denotes Houston and Richardson (2008), the data source for the period from 1975 to 2004.

CHAPTER 8

Accounting for Racial/Ethnic Disparities in Children's Obesity Status at 2 Years of Age

Jason M. Fletcher

Abstract

Obesity in children in many developing countries has increased substantially over the last several decades. This change has implications for population health and human capital due to the strong persistence in weight through adulthood and the large social costs of a growing number of unhealthy individuals. As suggested by many educational interventions, targeting health status during early childhood may be more efficient and equitable due to accumulation of effects. Thus, examining the primary sources of obesity and obesity disparities is important, including focuses on school, family, and community factors, among others. Recent evidence has suggested that racial differences in obesity status occur before school age and are difficult to explain. However, this chapter shows that with nationally representative data, the differences can be explained and point to poverty, family structure, and home language rather than race as focal factors for future interventions. Suggestive evidence is also provided that parental investments in physical activities are associated with early-childhood weight status.

Keywords: early childhood health, racial/ethnic differences

JEL classification: I12

CONTRIBUTIONS TO ECONOMIC ANALYSIS
VOLUME 290 ISSN: 0573-8555
DOI:10.1108/S0573-8555(2010)0000290011

1. Introduction

Obesity has often been labeled as a current epidemic in the United States as well as many other developed countries (James, 2001). The *Healthy People 2010* initiative spotlights the current policy focus on the problem of obesity in the United States. The long-term consequences of adult obesity are relatively well established and include type 2 diabetes, coronary heart disease, stroke, cancer, and other health conditions (NTFPT, 2000). While documenting the determinants of *adult* obesity and providing policies that combat these determinants are important, a very large proportion of *children* who are overweight grow up to be overweight adults (Dietz, 1998; Freedman *et al.*, 2001), suggesting early interventions are necessary.

Even after shifting the focus from adults to children, it is often difficult to examine transitions into obesity because these transitions in many cases happen at a young age. This suggests that studies that examine young children are necessary to examine the determinants of first transitions into overweight.

One important research question in the area of early childhood overweight status is whether there are racial/ethnic differences that may require policy interventions. Kimbro *et al.* (2007) have recently examined the extent and possible determinants of racial/ethnic differences in a national sample of disadvantaged families (Fragile Families and Child Wellbeing Study). They find that Hispanic children are twice as likely as either black or white children to be overweight. Even after controlling for a wide variety of family characteristics, the authors were unable to explain either the white–Hispanic or black–Hispanic differences in overweight status. However, there are limitations with the sample used in this study, so that additional work is needed to examine the evidence of racial/ethnic differences in early childhood obesity.

This chapter contributes to knowledge of the determinants of early childhood obesity in three ways. First, similar to previous work, I show that there are differences in early overweight status at 2 years old across racial/ethnic groups in the nationally representative sample used in this chapter. Second, I provide evidence that marital status and whether English is the primary language spoken at home are two important predictors of childhood overweight status. In fact, controlling for these two family characteristics eliminates detectable differences in early-childhood overweight status across Hispanic, black, and white children. Finally, I provide an additional examination of the associations between some of the detailed family characteristics in the data set and early-childhood overweight status.

2. Literature review

There has been a tremendous amount of research detailing the potential causes and consequences of the rise in childhood and adult obesity in developed countries. For example, the effects of obesity on chronic health conditions have been compared with the biological process of aging in adults of 20 years, and the health costs associated with obesity are greater than two other behaviors widely recognized to cause significant harm: cigarette smoking and alcohol consumption (Sturm, 2002). Indeed, Finkelstein *et al.* (2009) estimate that the medical costs attributable to obesity were as high as $147 billion in 2008, which is nearly 10% of all medical spending nationally. The additional medical costs of obesity represent an externality because the obese do not fully pay for their higher costs within pooled health insurance and public health insurance programs and because being insured increases obesity (Bhattacharya *et al.*, 2009). Thus, government intervention may be needed to reduce externalities as well as potentially assist individuals (e.g., children) who may not take into account the future consequences of their activity and diet decisions.

Since childhood and adolescent obesity has been shown to increase the risk of adult obesity (Nader *et al.*, 2006), prevention, rather than treatment, of adult obesity may be a more effective tool in limiting lifetime health care costs. These prevention activities likely require a focus on very young children due to the growing prevalence of obesity in school-aged children and adolescents. For example, while the prevalence of overweight in children and adolescents has recently been reported to be 13% (Troiano and Flegal, 1998), researchers have found that almost 8% of 4- and 5-year-olds are overweight (Ogden *et al.*, 1997). More recently, researchers have documented that 18% of 3-year-olds are overweight in a national sample of disadvantaged families (Kimbro *et al.*, 2007).

As is well known, there have been many efforts aimed at reducing the burden of obesity, though few have shown great success. For example, Cawley *et al.* (2007) evaluate the effects of physical education requirement in schools and find little evidence of reductions in weight. Jacobson and Brownell (2000) have advocated soda taxation as a potential way to reduce obesity in adults and children, though Fletcher *et al.* (2010a, in press) find no effects on weight for the levels of taxation that are currently implemented. Fletcher *et al.* (2010b) also find no evidence that school vending machine restrictions have led to soda consumption or weight reductions in 5th and 8th graders.

The failure of many of these policies to produce weight loss in children could be explained in several ways. Several researchers suggest that many policies are neither large enough nor comprehensive enough to produce noticeable change (Fletcher *et al.*, 2010b). It could be the case that the other, earlier factors (e.g., preschool age) are "fundamental causes" of obesity and have not been the focus of these policy interventions.

Thus, one important research question in the area of early childhood overweight status is whether there are racial/ethnic differences that may require policy interventions. Racial differences could be caused by a number of factors, including cultural differences in eating and exercise practices as well as differences in social norms of weight status. For example, it has been shown that food consumption patterns vary across racial/ethnic groups (Haffner *et al.*, 1985; Frank *et al.*, 1991). Additionally, there is evidence that black mothers are less likely to identify their overweight children as overweight than mothers of other racial/ethnic groups (Jain *et al.*, 2001). More generally, Burke and Heiland (2008) have shown important racial differences in the social norms of "ideal" weight status between black and white individuals.

Recent research has focused specifically on attempting to explain race/ethnic differences in early childhood obesity. Kimbro *et al.* (2007) use national data to find that Hispanic 3-year-old children are twice as likely as either black or white children to be overweight. Even after controlling for a wide variety of family characteristics, the authors were unable to explain either the white–Hispanic or black–Hispanic differences in overweight status. Their evidence suggests that additional policies may need to focus on these differences that open up before school age by examining additional family and cultural predictors of weight gain in children.

However, a potential limitation of this chapter, acknowledged by the authors, is that their sample consists primarily of disadvantaged families, oversampling unmarried mothers (which also leads to an oversample of immigrant mothers). It could be the case that the characteristics that are used to select the Fragile Families sample are important characteristics in predicting early childhood obesity status and that using a nationally representative sample may produce different results.[1]

This chapter uses newer data that are nationally representative to examine the predictors of weight status in 2-year-old children. In particular, I follow work in the education literature by Fryer and Levitt (2006) that attempts to "explain" the sources of racial gaps in test performance in children. This chapter first presents evidence that a small number of family characteristics, such as marital status and home language status, can eliminate detectable racial differences in obesity, suggesting that policies should target these family-based pathways rather than strictly cultural-based mechanisms. This chapter then provides additional suggestive associations between other family practices and childhood weight. These relationships, including parental investments in physical activity with children, should then be the subject of ongoing empirical evaluation within experimental or quasi-experimental research designs.

---

[1] An appendix table (Table A.1) provides evidence of important differences between the Fragile Families sample used in Kimbro *et al.* (2007) and the nationally representative sample used in the current chapter.

3. Data and empirical methods

In this chapter, I use the restricted version of the Early Childhood Longitudinal Study-Birth Cohort (ECLS-B) data to examine the predictors of early childhood obesity status. The ECLS-B is a longitudinal nationally representative sample of over 10,000 children born in 2001 from diverse socioeconomic and racial/ethnic backgrounds.[2] The focus of the study is on the health, development, parental care, and education of these children. The sample was selected from birth certificate records received through the National Center for Health Statistics system from 46 states and the District of Columbia. Children ineligible to participate include those born to mothers under the age of 15 or children who died or were adopted before they were approximately 9 months of age. Information on a sample of eligible children was collected at birth and in several follow-up surveys at age 9 months and 2 years, and these children have since been interviewed again at 4 years and at kindergarten entry.[3] Parents completed an interview, direct child assessments were performed, and additional information was gathered from birth certificates, and child care providers or schools as the children aged.

Several aspects of the dataset make it valuable in research on overweight/obesity. First, the sampled population of the ECLS-B allows the opportunity to examine early transitions from normal weight into overweight status and obese status. In contrast to the ECLS-B, many datasets contain samples that are "too late" to capture many of these initial transitions into overweight status (adolescents in the National Education Longitudinal Study, school-aged children in the Early Childhood Longitudinal Study-Kindergarten Cohort). Additionally, many studies use datasets that are not nationally representative samples of children (Stettler *et al.*, 2002; Bergmann *et al.*, 2003), while the ELCS-B is representative of US children born in 2001. Importantly, the height and weight from each child are directly assessed rather than parent-reported. Finally, the many sources of information within the ECLS-B, including mother's reports, father's reports, teacher's reports, birth certificate information, etc., allow a particularly rich set of variables to be controlled when examining the determinants of early obesity.

While there are 10,700 children in the ECLS-B cohort, 8,500 children have valid height and weight information at age 2 and 8,250 children have

---

[2] Complete information about the data set can be found online: http://nces.ed.gov/ecls/birth.asp.

[3] Ongoing research will examine the longer term predictors of weight in children as well as predict the trajectories of early-life weight gain.

valid longitudinal sample weights.[4] Additional cases are removed from the analysis due to missing data from parental reports, county of residence, twin status, insurance status, and mother's body mass index (BMI), leaving an analysis sample of approximately 7,600 children.

The outcome of interest, labeled obese status, is whether a child's BMI measured at age 2 is greater than the Centers for Disease Control and Prevention (CDC) growth chart 95% cutoffs, which are reported by age and gender.[5] I include several types of child and family-level characteristics in the analysis. Child-level data include race/ethnicity, age, sex, and birth weight (from birth certificate records). Family-level information includes marital status, family income, maternal (and maternal grandmother's) education level, maternal BMI, language spoken at home, parental nativity, parental practices and behaviors (feeding practices, activities with the child such as television and playing games, maternal smoking), and social program participation (welfare, food stamps, women, infants and children (WIC)).[6] I also include neighborhood characteristics, such as perceived neighborhood safety, but use county fixed effects in some empirical results to control for all time-invariant community-level factors. Summary statistics are presented in Table 1.

Multivariate logistic regression is used to assess the relationship between children's obesity status and race/ethnicity, controlling for a parsimonious number of demographic characteristics such as child age and gender. Next, additional family-level characteristics were added to examine the robustness of the racial/ethnic differences in obesity status at age 2. Finally, an extended empirical model was estimated to examine additional determinants of early childhood obesity status. These analyses were weighted to account for the complex survey design in the data set.

4. Results

In Table 2, I present results from logistic regression analysis predicting obese status; odds ratios (robust *p*-values) are presented. I find that age

---

[4] These numbers are approximate. The restricted data agreement does not allow the reporting of specific unweighted Ns. Ns are rounded to the nearest 50. In order to account for the complex survey design, the cross-sectional weights for the 2-year-old wave of data provided in ECLS-B are used.

[5] As can be seen in the summary statistics in Table 1, the children in the sample are between the ages of 20 and 38 months at the time of the second wave of the survey, when BMI is calculated. This age range makes it more difficult to define whether each child is overweight (at the 95% cutoff by age/gender) because these cutoffs are not reported by age-month in the CDC growth charts. I checked the robustness of my results by dropping children who are younger than 20 months as well as coding overweight at ages 24 months, 30 months, and 36 months. Results did not substantially change and are available upon request from the author.

[6] I impute missing data for mother's weight for 1,400 individuals and for grandmother's education level for 300 individuals.

Table 1. Summary statistics

Variable	Mean	Std. Dev	Min	Max
Child Information				
Obesity (>95% of CDC growth charts)	0.15	0.36	0	1
Overweight (>85%, <95% of CDC growth charts)	0.13	0.34	0	1
BMI	17.34	2.22	10.3	36.3
Age (months)	24.42	1.19	20.9	38.2
Male	0.51	0.50	0	1
White	0.44	0.50	0	1
Black	0.16	0.37	0	1
Hispanic	0.20	0.40	0	1
Asian	0.10	0.30	0	1
Multirace	0.08	0.27	0	1
Other Race	0.03	0.16	0	1
Child Health (5 = excellent, 1 = poor)	4.42	0.80	1	5
Low Birth Weight Indicator	0.16	0.36	0	1
Very Low Birth Weight Indicator	0.10	0.30	0	1
Twin	0.16	0.37	0	1
Family Information				
Maternal Age	28.61	6.40	15	51
Maternal Years of Schooling	13.75	2.70	8	20
Married Household	0.67	0.47	0	1
Maternal Employment (Full time)	0.33	0.47	0	1
Maternal Employment (Part time)	0.19	0.39	0	1
Maternal Unemployment	0.08	0.27	0	1
English Is Not Primary Language Spoken in Home	0.20	0.40	0	1
Family Income	5.28	4.34	0.25	20
Parent Health (5 = excellent, 1 = poor)	3.93	0.96	1	5
SCHIP Status	0.09	0.28	0	1
Medicaid Status	0.40	0.49	0	1
Grandmother's Years of Schooling	11.61	3.80	0	21
Mother's Smoking Status	0.19	0.40	0	1
Mother's Alcohol Status	0.34	0.47	0	1
Mother's Religious Attendance	2.05	1.53	0	4
Rural Status	0.15	0.36	0	1
WIC	0.41	0.49	0	1
Food Stamps	0.21	0.41	0	1
Welfare	0.09	0.29	0	1
Access to Low-Cost Food	2.88	0.38	1	3
Move between Waves	0.34	0.47	0	1
Family Practices				
Breast-Fed	0.69	0.46	0	1
Age Started Solid Food (months)	4.68	1.68	1	13
Cries for Food/Toy	1.57	1.04	0	3
Used Baby Books	0.70	0.46	0	1
Read to Child	2.72	1.03	1	4
TV Hours/Week	1.61	1.34	0	14
Eat at Regular Time	5.49	2.14	0	7

Table 1. (Continued)

Variable	Mean	Std. Dev	Min	Max
Play Active Games	2.30	1.17	1	6
Play/Walk Outside Now	2.59	1.25	1	6
Play/Walk Outside	2.84	1.39	1	6
Feed When Hungry (vs. Schedule)	0.65	0.48	0	1
Number of Well-Baby Checkups	5.60	2.66	0	20
Ultrasound	0.90	0.30	0	1
Smoke in 3rd Trimester	0.73	3.19	0	100

Note: ECLS-Birth Cohort (Approximate Unweighted, $N = 7{,}600$).

Table 2. Determinants of obesity status for 2-Year-olds: examining racial/ethnic differences

Outcome Sample Column	Obesity Full 1	Obesity Full 2	Obesity Full 3
Age (months)	0.447	0.445	0.437
	(0.034)*	(0.033)*	(0.030)*
Age Squared	1.014	1.014	1.015
	(0.045)*	(0.046)*	(0.042)*
Male	1.075	1.071	1.071
	(0.390)	(0.415)	(0.417)
Black	1.243	1.083	1.064
	(0.049)*	(0.512)	(0.613)
Hispanic	1.452	1.365	1.122
	(0.000)**	(0.003)**	(0.378)
Asian	0.956	0.984	0.753
	(0.801)	(0.928)	(0.165)
Multiracial	0.671	0.627	0.625
	(0.039)*	(0.017)*	(0.016)*
Other Race	1.651	1.517	1.434
	(0.051)+	(0.101)	(0.163)
Married Household		0.769	0.755
		(0.006)**	(0.004)**
English is Not Primary Language Spoken in Home			1.440
			(0.009)**
Observations	7,600	7,600	7,600

Note: Logistic regression results, odds ratios (p-values).
**1%, *5%, +10%, Child Panel Weight (W1C0).

(in months) reduces the odds of being obese at an increasing rate. Like Kimbro *et al.* (2007), I find racial/ethnic differences in obesity status for these very young children: being black, Hispanic, or "other race" increases the odds of obesity status by 24%, 45%, and 65%, respectively. Children whose parents report as "multi-race" have over 30% reduced odds of being obese. In Column 2, I show that the black–white difference in early obesity status can be eliminated by controlling for marital status. The coefficient for black children decreases from 1.24 to 1.08 and becomes statistically insignificant. The coefficient for Hispanic children shrinks from 1.45 to 1.37 and is still statistically significant. Further, children with married mothers are at a lower risk of obesity status, decreasing the odds by nearly 25%.

In Column 3, I control for the language spoken at home, as reported by the respondent (usually the mother). The coefficient for Hispanic children (vs. white children) falls to 1.12 and is no longer statistically significant.[7] Additionally, households that report that English is not the primary language have an increased risk of having an obese child, increasing the odds by 44%. Taken together, these results are suggestive that racial and broad cultural factors may not be the most important focus for policies aimed at reducing obesity rates in young children. Rather, it could be the case that policies targeted at mechanisms emanating from marital status and language barriers may be more effective.

In Table 3, I present regression results showing the associations between obesity status and a variety of child and family-level characteristics; some associations have been reported in other literature (though not using nationally representative data) and other associations represent new findings. Several characteristics that have been shown to predict obesity status in young children using other datasets are shown to be significant predictors of obesity status, including whether the child was breast-fed, hours of television viewing, maternal smoking, and birth weight. Most of these traditional variables have the typical sign and are statistically significant. Also, I find that low and very low birth weight status significantly reduces the odds of obesity status for 2-year-olds. Parental practices, such as playing chasing games and walking/playing outside with their child, are associated with lower odds of obesity status. WIC status is associated with a reduction in the odds of childhood obesity status.[8]

5. *Discussion*

In this chapter, I use the nationally representative ECLS-B dataset to examine the predictors of early childhood (age 2) obesity status. This chapter has two primary goals. First, I show that racial/ethnic differences

---

[7] Results are similar if I control for mother's nativity rather than language spoken at home, although nativity status decreases the Hispanic coefficient to 1.20 (p-value <0.135).

[8] Other variables that were not statistically significant include whether the child cries for food/toys, whether the mother reported having an ultrasound, receipt of housing subsidies, access to low-cost food, alcohol consumption, age of child introduction to solid foods, and whether the parent used books/magazines on parenting.

***Table 3.* Determinants of obesity status for 2-year-olds: parental practices, child health, and county fixed effects**

Outcome Specification Column	Obesity 1	Obesity County FE 2
Age (months)	0.394 (0.002)**	0.462 (0.019)*
Age Squared	1.017 (0.002)**	1.014 (0.022)*
Male	1.181 (0.012)*	1.151 (0.036)*
Black	0.941 (0.604)	0.905 (0.403)
Hispanic	1.094 (0.405)	1.002 (0.985)
Asian	0.617 (0.003)**	0.596 (0.002)**
Multiracial	0.823 (0.153)	0.792 (0.097)+
Other Race	1.384 (0.071)+	1.258 (0.241)
Family Income	1.002 (0.877)	0.996 (0.717)
Maternal Education	1.006 (0.733)	1.007 (0.679)
Breast-fed	0.709 (0.000)**	0.697 (0.000)**
Smoked during Pregnancy	0.988 (0.328)	0.993 (0.571)
Maternal BMI	1.029 (0.000)**	1.027 (0.000)**
Very Low Birth Weight	0.470 (0.000)**	0.472 (0.000)**
Low Birth Weight	0.673 (0.000)**	0.681 (0.000)**
TV Hours/Week	1.054 (0.022)*	1.043 (0.087)+
ESL at Home	1.550 (0.000)**	1.471 (0.002)**
Married	0.859 (0.091)+	0.878 (0.150)
SCHIP Status	1.203 (0.101)	1.087 (0.482)
Medicaid Status	1.115 (0.238)	1.142 (0.166)
WIC Status	0.762 (0.006)**	0.807 (0.032)*
Parent Health	1.037 (0.313)	1.044 (0.240)
Parent Smokes	1.283 (0.009)**	1.266 (0.016)*

Table 3. (Continued)

Outcome Specification Column	Obesity 1	Obesity County FE 2
Grandmother's Education	0.986	0.987
	(0.200)	(0.220)
Eat at Regular Time	0.985	0.980
	(0.313)	(0.214)
Walk/Play Outside (age 9 months)	0.969	0.957
	(0.216)	(0.082)$^{+}$
Walk/Play Outside (age 2)	0.964	0.954
	(0.195)	(0.101)
Play Chasing Games	0.958	0.964
	(0.137)	(0.216)
Moved	1.027	1.043
	(0.708)	(0.565)
Drinks Sodas with Meals	0.785	0.767
	(0.089)$^{+}$	(0.073)$^{+}$
Observations	7,450	7,350
Number of Counties		89

Note: Logistic regression results, odds ratios (p-values).
**1%, *5%, $^{+}$10%, Child Panel Weight (W1C0)

in obesity status are found as early as 2 years of age, but these differences are largely eliminated with a small set of control variables. Overall, these results suggest that racial/ethnic differences in early childhood obesity are likely the result of other family characteristics rather than race/ethnicity per se. The results also suggest that the reason that Kimbro *et al.* (2007) were not able to eliminate the racial/ethnic differences in obesity status in their research was the design of their sample (oversampled unmarried mothers and disadvantaged families more generally).

Second, I corroborate and add to the list of early predictors of early childhood obesity using a national sample of children. Predictors of early childhood obesity include language spoken at home, parenting practices (eating at a regular time and playing outside), parental behaviors (e.g., smoking), and several measures of family resources, including family structure and social program participation. The follow-up surveys for these children, when the children are 4 years old and at kindergarten entry, will be useful both to examine additional transitions into obesity status and to study those children who are not obese. I also present several new associations between family characteristics and obesity status. Parental practices, such as playing chasing games and walking/playing outside with their child, are associated with lower odds of obesity status. WIC status is associated with a reduction in the odds of childhood obesity status. Additional research is necessary to determine whether these relationships are causal.

While this study makes progress in examining predictors of early childhood obesity status, there are several limitations that should be outlined. First, the study design was cross-sectional, making causal statements inappropriate. Second, while this study uses a representative sample of children born in the year 2001, it is unclear if the study's findings can be generalized to children born in other years. Finally, many of the measures used in the second set of analyses were self-reported and are thus not immune to recall bias and other biases from misreporting. These recall biases may be less problematic in the analysis that examines racial differences, as race, marital status, and language status are likely measured with little error and weight and height are measured rather than reported by parents. On the other hand, the analysis that examines the relationship between parental behaviors (e.g., smoking) and childhood weight status could be underestimated if some parents misreport their unhealthy behaviors.

With these limitations in mind, this study strongly suggests that family-level characteristics other than race/ethnicity are likely responsible for estimated racial/ethnic differences in previous work. Additionally, the use of a nationally representative dataset to examine other predictors of early childhood obesity status is an innovation of this study. Finally, this study corroborates and extends many of the parental and family-level characteristics associated with early childhood obesity that have been reported in small community, clinical, or convenience samples.

Overall, the findings of this study challenge previously reported associations and add to our knowledge of previously undocumented determinants of early childhood obesity status, although additional research examining early transitions into and out of obesity status is needed. In particular, family factors other than race/ethnicity may account for the large racial/ethnic differences in early childhood obesity status that have been found in previous research. Health investments in young children targeted to children from single-parent households and from households with low English language skills may be efficient. Additional research is required to examine the mechanisms that confer high obesity rates on children from single-family and non-native households.

Acknowledgments

The author thanks James Griffin, Jennifer Park, Andrew White, and participants of the ECLS-B First Release Conference for helpful comments.

References

Bergmann, K.E., R.L. Bergmann, R. von Kries, O. Bohm, R. Richter, J.W. Dudenhausen and U. Wahn (2003), "Early determinants of childhood overweight and adiposity in a birth cohort study: role of breast-feeding", *International Journal of Obesity*, Vol. 27, pp. 162–172.

Bhattacharya, J., K. Bundorf, N. Pace and N. Sood (2009), "Does health insurance make you fat?", NBER Working Paper Series, No. 15163.

Burke, M.A. and F. Heiland (2008), "Race, obesity, and the puzzle of gender specificity", Federal Reserve of Boston Working Paper No. 08-8.

Cawley, J., C. Meyerhoefer and J. Newhouse (2007), "The impact of state physical education requirements on youth physical activity and overweight", *Health Economics*, Vol. 16(12), pp. 1287–1301.

Dietz, W.H. (1998), "Childhood weight affects adult morbidity and mortality", *Journal of Nutrition*, Vol. 128, pp. 411S–414S.

Finkelstein, E.A., J.G. Trogdon, J.W. Cohen and W. Dietz (2009), "Annual medical spending attributable to obesity: payer- and service-specific estimates", *Health Affairs*, Vol. 28(5), pp. w822–w831.

Fletcher, J.M., D. Frisvold and N. Tefft (2010a), "Can soft drink taxes reduce population weight?", *Contemporary Economic Policy*, Vol. 28(1), pp. 23–35.

Fletcher, J.M., D. Frisvold and N. Tefft (2010b), "Taxing soft drinks and restricting access to vending machines to curb child obesity", *Health Affairs*, Vol. 29(5), pp. 1059–1066.

Fletcher, J.M., D. Frisvold and N. Tefft (in press), "The effects of soft drink taxation on soft drink consumption and weight for children and adolescents", *Journal of Public Economics*.

Frank, G.C., M. Zive, J. Nelson, S.L. Broyles and P.R. Nader (1991), "Fat and cholesterol avoidance among Mexican-American and Anglo preschool children and parents", *Journal of the American Diet Association*, Vol. 91, pp. 954–961.

Freedman, D.S., L.K. Khan, W.H. Dietz, S.R. Srinivasan and G.S. Berenson (2001), "Relationship of childhood obesity to coronary heart disease risk factors in adulthood: the Bogalusa heart study", *Pediatrics*, Vol. 108, pp. 712–718.

Fryer, R.G. and S.D. Levitt (2006), "The Black-White test score gap through third grade", *American Law and Economics Review*, Vol. 8(2), pp. 249–281.

Haffner, S.M., J.A. Knapp, H.P. Hazuda, M.P. Stern and E.A. Young (1985), "Dietary intakes of macronutrients among Mexican Americans and Anglo Americans: the San Antonio heart study", *American Journal of Clinical Nutrition*, Vol. 42, pp. 1266–1275.

Jacobson, M. and K. Brownell (2000), "Small taxes on soft drinks and snack foods to promote health", *American Journal of Public Health*, Vol. 90(6), pp. 854–857.

Jain, A., S.N. Sherman, L.A. Chamberlin, Y. Carter, S.W. Powers and R.C. Whitaker (2001), "Why don't low-income mothers worry about their preschoolers being overweight?", *Pediatrics*, Vol. 107, pp. 1138–1146.

James, P. (2001), "The worldwide obesity epidemic", *Obesity Research*, Vol. 9, pp. S228–S233.

Kimbro, R.T., J. Brooks-Gunn and S. McLanahan (2007), "Racial and ethnic differentials in children's overweight and obesity among 3-year-olds", *American Journal of Public Health*, Vol. 97, pp. 298–305.

Nader, P.R., M. O'Brien, R. Houts, R.H. Bradley, J. Belksy, R. Crosnoe, S. Friedman, Z. Mei, E.J. Susman and Development National Institute of Child Health and Human Development Study of Early Child Care and Youth (2006), "Identifying risk for obesity in early childhood", *Pediatrics*, Vol. 118, pp. e594–e601.

National Task Force on the Prevention and Treatment of Obesity (NTFPT) (2000), "Overweight, obesity, and health risk", *Archives of Internal Medicine*, Vol. 160, pp. 898–904.

Ogden, C.L., R.P. Troiano, R.R. Briefel, R.J. Kuczmarski, K.M. Flegal and C.L. Johnson (1997), "Prevalence of overweight among preschool children in the United States, 1971–1994", *Pediatrics*, Vol. 99, p. E1.

Stettler, N., B.S. Zemel, S. Kumanyika and V.A. Stallings (2002), "Infant weight gain and childhood overweight status in a mulitcenter, cohort study", *Pediatrics*, Vol. 109, pp. 194–199.

Sturm, R. (2002), "The effects of obesity, smoking, and drinking on medical problems and costs", *Health Affairs*, Vol. 21, p. 245.

Troiano, R.P. and K.M. Flegal (1998), "Overweight children and adolescents: description, epidemiology, and demographics", *Pediatrics*, Vol. 101, pp. 497–504.

Appendix A

Table A.1.* *Table comparison of ECLS-B and Fragile Families samples

Sample	Total	Total	White	White	Black	Black	Hispanic	Hispanic
	ECLS-B	Fragile Families	ECLS-B	Fragile Families	ECLS-B	Fragile Families	ECLS-B	Fragile Families
Sample Size	7,600	1,976	3,350	406	1,250	1,081	1,450	489
Weighted Sample	3,033,531		1,702,235		413,107		706,732	
Obesity (%)	18	18	16	18	19	17	21	24
Age (months)	24.37		24.33		24.38		24.45	
Male (%)	51	52	51	50	53	53	51	53
Married (%)	68	27	81	52	30	15	58	35
Non-English in Home (%)	16		2		4		52	
Immigrant (%)	18	11	4	4	9	3	50	34

Sources: Author's calculations for ECLS-B, and Table 1 in Kimbro *et al.* (2007) for Fragile Families.

CHAPTER 9

Effects of Education on Adult Health in Sweden: Results from a Natural Experiment

Jasmina Spasojević

Abstract

Understanding health determinants and exactly how they affect health is an important social policy question. Empirical tests in the health literature typically find that the number of years of formal schooling completed is the most important correlate of good health. However, there is less consensus as to whether this correlation reflects a causal relationship between more schooling and better health. This chapter capitalizes on a unique social experiment: the 1950 Swedish comprehensive school reform, which was implemented in stages and by municipal areas, through which people born between 1945 and 1955 went through two different school systems (one of which required at least one more year of schooling). It uses an instrumental variables technique to estimate formal schooling's causal effect on adult health in Sweden. The instrumental variable for degree of education (schooling) generated from compulsory school reform yields a consistent estimate of education's causal impact on health, as measured by an bad health index and of body mass index in the healthy range. The additional schooling generated by Sweden's compulsory school reform produces improved adult health (controlling for cohort and county effects, family background characteristics, and individual income).

Keywords: health, education, instrumental variables, compulsory school reform

JEL classifications: I1, C1, C2

CONTRIBUTIONS TO ECONOMIC ANALYSIS
VOLUME 290 ISSN: 0573-8555
DOI:10.1108/S0573-8555(2010)0000290012

1. Introduction

Traditionally, returns to education are viewed as private income returns (higher wages). More highly educated people can be expected to both produce more goods (market and nonmarket) and purchase more goods. However, returns to education may also manifest as social benefits. The income returns to education reflected in higher earnings may actually understate private returns – both in the labor market and in social benefits (Currie and Moretti, 2003). For example, one aspect of the nonmarket return to education is its impact on health. If more highly educated people are healthier, then they can be expected to produce more commodities (market and nonmarket). These people may live longer and contribute more to society. They may have more time available to produce wages and commodities, and to pursue other productive activities. Hence, the finding that investing in more years of formal schooling will produce healthier people and reduce morbidity has significant public policy implications.

In the health literature, many empirical tests show that the number of years of formal schooling completed is the major correlate of good health, irrespective of the measure of health employed: health status self-evaluation, mortality and morbidity rates, and psychological indicators of health. The results also hold whether the units of observation are individuals or groups (e.g., Auster *et al.*, 1969; Grossman, 1975; Leigh, 1983; Ross and Wu, 1995; Deaton and Paxson, 1999; Gerdtham and Johannesson, 1999; Gerdtham *et al.*, 1999; Goldman and Lakdawalla, 2001). Grossman and Kaestner (1997) provide an extensive review of the literature on education's effects on health.

There is less consensus, however, as to whether the health-and-schooling correlation reflects causality from more schooling to better health. Indeed, several alternative explanations may underlie the observed correlation between the degree of good health and the amount of schooling. One explanation claims that the health-and-schooling correlation does not reflect a *causal* relationship, but rather that this correlation is due to omitted "third variables" (such as future orientation) that affect both schooling and health (Farrell and Fuchs, 1982). It is commonly thought that individual preferences and decisions about investment in education and health are intertwined, because individuals who invest in education expect to live longer, and thus to collect greater educational returns over this extra time.

Initially, most studies of the education-and-health relationship used U.S. data. Recently, studies were conducted not only with U.S. data but also with data from European and other countries (e.g., Black *et al.*, 2004; Arendt, 2005; de Walque, 2007). This chapter uses the Swedish Level of Living Survey (SLLS) and complements recent research by using an instrumental variables (IV) technique to estimate the causal effect of the length of schooling on adult health outcomes in Sweden.

Here, I examine a unique social experiment – the 1950 Swedish comprehensive school reform – to uncover the causal effect of schooling on health. I use the Swedish compulsory school reform's characteristics to construct the instrumental variable for schooling. The school system created by the 1950 Act actually was implemented in stages and by municipal areas between 1949 and 1962. People born between 1945 and 1955 went through two different school systems, one of which required at least one further year of schooling (Meghir and Palme, 2005). I also investigate whether the increase in compulsory schooling is more closely linked to better adult health outcomes.

I discuss the conceptual framework in Section 2 and the empirical model in Section 3. Section 4 describes the Swedish compulsory schooling reform and Section 5 presents the data. The results are discussed in Section 6, and Section 7 concludes.

2. *Conceptual framework*

The correlation between schooling and health may be explained in several ways. One is the *productive efficiency* argument, which states that people with more education obtain better health outcomes from given quantities of health inputs (Grossman, 1972a, 1972b, 2000). If highly educated people do produce health more efficiently, then increases in the length of schooling will lead to improved health.

The *allocative efficiency* argument (Kenkel, 1991, 2000) explains the causal connection of schooling to health this way: because schooling improves an individual's knowledge about health, more highly educated people are better able to select the best health inputs. For instance, they are better informed about the harmful effects of smoking, so they are more likely to smoke less or to quit smoking. Greater education is expected to improve people's understanding of the relationship between health and lifestyles.

A third explanation argues that there is a causal relationship between health and schooling, but that the causality works in the opposite direction: from better health to more schooling. This *reverse causality* argument emphasizes the importance of *past* health, as reflected in the positive relationship between health and schooling: healthier people are more likely to attend school longer and to gain knowledge more efficiently.

Another argument states that the observed correlation between health and schooling does not reflect a causal relationship; instead, omitted third variables, such as an orientation toward the future, cause both the quality of health and the amount of schooling to change in the same direction. Future-oriented people value future benefits more highly; hence, they invest more in greater education levels and in better health practices. This is known as the *time preference* hypothesis (Farrell and Fuchs, 1982). While this is a valid explanation of the health-and-schooling correlation, time preference is difficult to measure.

An IV technique can be used to investigate whether the positive correlation between schooling and health indeed reflects better health being caused by lengthier schooling. The IV method predicts schooling using variables that are correlated with it but not likely to be correlated with any omitted determinants of either health or schooling. The predicted values of schooling replace the actual values in the health equation. Berger and Leigh (1989) and Sander (1995) are among the first studies to use the IV method to obtain consistent estimates of a causal relationship of schooling to health. However, in both studies, the fact that family background variables serve as instruments for schooling is problematic. These variables may be correlated with omitted variables, such as time preference.

Some instruments likely to be correlated with schooling but unlikely to be correlated with unobserved determinants of health and used in recent studies include compulsory schooling laws and reforms, teenage unemployment rates, and availability of college openings (e.g., Adams, 2002; Arkes, 2003; Currie and Moretti, 2003; Lleras-Muney, 2005; Arendt, 2005). All of these studies support a direct causal effect of formal schooling on such health measures as mortality, self-reported health, functional ability, body mass index (BMI), work-limiting health conditions, and child quality measured by birth weight. The IV coefficients are larger than the ordinary least-squares (OLS) coefficients in every study (Lleras-Muney, 2005; Arendt, 2005).

Using the school system's institutional characteristics as an exogenous factor of variation in the educational variable originates in the literature on the causal effect of education on earnings (e.g., Card, 1999; Acemoglu and Angrist, 1999). Variations in education across quarters of birth are used together with compulsory schooling attendance as an instrument for education (Angrist and Krueger, 1991); in Harmon and Walker (1995) changes in the minimum age for school-leaving serve as instruments for schooling.

The IV results are inconsistent with the time preference hypothesis: that both schooling and health are determined by omitted, unobserved common factors. This is because of the assumption that instruments are correlated with schooling but not likely to be correlated with unobserved variables represented by an error term in the health structural equation. In this chapter, I take advantage of the IV method used in recent studies of education's effect on health to investigate whether the increase in years of schooling (which resulted from the Swedish comprehensive school reform) causes improved adult health outcomes.

3. Model

The schooling and health relationship can be empirically investigated with the following two equations:

$$\text{Health} = \alpha_1 \text{Schooling} + \alpha_2 X + \varepsilon \quad (1)$$

$$\text{Schooling} = \beta_1 Z + \beta_2 X + \mu \quad (2)$$

The coefficient α_1 in Eq. (1) represents the causal relationship between schooling and health status. Any estimate of this effect must account for the potential correlation between the unobserved disturbance term (ε) in the health equation and the corresponding unobserved disturbance term (μ) in the schooling equation. If these terms are correlated, then schooling is correlated with ε, and the first equation cannot be estimated by using OLS because that would yield inconsistent estimates of all the model's coefficients.

Including variable Z in the schooling equation facilitates estimation of the health equation with the IV method. Z must be highly correlated with schooling and uncorrelated with ε, which in turn incorporates unobservable variables in the health equation. This means that the variable Z is excluded from the health equation and belongs only in the schooling equation (2).

The system is estimated using a two-stage least-squares (TSLS) method. The first stage is estimation of the schooling equation by OLS, the reduced-form equation for schooling. The second stage uses predicted schooling from the first stage instead of actual schooling in order to estimate health equation (1). The vector of variable X is the common determinant of both education and health, such as age or cohort effects, residential or county effects, and family background characteristics.

The time preference hypothesis is based on the premise that there are variables commonly assumed to be unobserved, such as an orientation toward the future, which create greater investment in both health and education. If health and education are affected by a common missing and important variable, then the estimates of education's effect on health will be not only biased but also, more importantly, inconsistent. The effect of the missing variable on health would be submerged under the total effect of education on health. Consequently, that effect would be overstated, because it would reflect not only education's direct effect on health but also the effect of that missing variable. The OLS estimate of education's effect on health is believed to be a priori inconsistent.

The close interdependence between time preference, schooling, and health makes it difficult to disentangle these effects. Separating education's effect on health from the time preference effect on health is difficult, because the available data lack time preference measurement. If time preference measurement were indeed available, then this problem might be resolved by including it in the health equation and estimating that equation with OLS. However, even with a time preference measurement, there may be complications. For example, time preference may depend on, or be caused by, changes in the level of schooling (Becker and Mulligan, 1997). A person who attends school longer may become more patient and future oriented. The inability to include time preference in the health structural equation leads us to the use of the IV method, which ensures consistent estimate of education's causal effect on health.

4. The Swedish natural experiment: compulsory schooling reform

Sweden's comprehensive schooling reform, which was in 1950, extended required schooling from seven or eight years, depending on the municipality, to nine years of basic education. This unique social experiment was implemented in stages and by municipal areas between 1949 and 1962. Meghir and Palme (2001) present overview of the 1950s' Swedish comprehensive school reform.

Actual implementation began in 1949 in 14 municipalities. The percentage of municipalities following the new system increased gradually, reaching 50 percent in 1961. Municipalities had the option to implement the new system from the first grade only, or for all grades up to fifth. In 1962, the remaining 50 percent of municipalities adopted the new nine-year comprehensive compulsory schooling program. Because of the 1950s' reform, a cohort of people went through two different school systems, one of which included at least one more year of compulsory schooling; this is a key feature of this chapter's analysis.

The cohort most affected by the compulsory schooling reform was born between 1945 and 1955. For people born in 1945, who were six or seven years old when the new system began, the majority were part of the old system unless they lived in one of the earliest municipalities to adopt the reform. However, for people born in 1955, who were six or seven years old by 1961 or 1962 when the reform was implemented nationwide, most attended the new postreform schools. It is worth noting that in any one year, the characteristics of municipalities that adopted reform were representative of Sweden as a whole (Meghir and Palme, 2001). This means that reform status should not be correlated with unobserved variables in the health status equation.

Other researchers have found that individuals completed more years of formal schooling if they were in the system requiring lengthier schooling. They have also shown that individuals who completed more years of formal schooling earned higher wages: for instance, Meghir and Palme (2005) show this for Sweden. Some studies show evidence of other benefits of extended compulsory schooling, including a lower incidence of teenage childbearing (Black *et al.*, 2004).

A number of recent studies that investigate the causal relationship between schooling and health use the characteristics of a compulsory schooling system as an instrument for education (e.g., Adams, 2002; Lleras-Muney, 2005; Arendt, 2005). These studies find that not only does the increase in compulsory schooling raise educational attainment, but it also improves health and life expectancies for individuals affected by the school reform.

This chapter investigates whether an increase in compulsory schooling could translate to better health, by asking whether individuals who complete more years of formal education (because of compulsory school requirements) indeed have better health. The assumption is that an individual is affected by the compulsory schooling reform if that person lived during childhood in a municipality that introduced the compulsory school reform. People are assumed to not move between municipalities during their childhood, or that any such migration was minimal. In econometric terminology, the compulsory schooling law (or the reform assignment) serves as an instrument for years of formal schooling completed in the health output equations.

5. *Data*

This chapter analyzes data from the 1981 and 1991 Swedish Level of Living Survey (SLLS) (Jonsson, 2003). The availability in the survey of health symptoms in both 1981 and 1991 prompted me to extend the analysis to a joint 1981-and-1991 set. Each survey represents a nationally representative random sample of 0.1 percent of the Swedish population between the ages of 15 and 75. The SLLS covers several dimensions of a person's lifestyle.

The SLLS data include end-result measures of health or health outputs, including health symptoms or conditions experienced in the previous year, self-rated health status, and BMI. Self-rated health status (first asked about in 1991) is used in constructing the bad health index, the primary health outcome of interest for this chapter, because health symptoms are the only health measures available in both the 1981 and 1991 surveys.

The health symptoms measure pertains to the presence of various illnesses and ailments (conditions) in the previous year. Information about approximately 50 symptoms is included, ranging from minor illnesses (such as a cough or cold) to chronic illnesses (such as back pain or fatigue) to major health conditions (such as heart attack, high blood pressure, diabetes, or cancer).

A continuous health symptoms measure can be developed using separate conditions as predictors in an ordered probit specification of self-rated health. The estimated coefficients serve as weights for constructing a linear latent health index, which is standardized with a mean of 0 and a standard deviation of 1, and which has no units. The standardized, weighted symptoms health index – based on whether people suffered from conditions in the previous year – actually represents a bad health index. Therefore, decreases in the bad health index are associated with better health outcomes. For instance, in analyzing the effect of income on health with the SLLS, Lindahl (2005) uses a standardized index of bad health as the dependent variable.

Although self-rated health status was asked only in 1991, a continuous linear health index can be created in the combined 1981-and-1991 set. Estimated health weights from the 1991 set, and symptom questions from both surveys, can be used to linearly predict the bad health index. One assumes that weights on health symptoms did not change significantly between the two surveys.

The bad health index includes measures of functional ability pertaining to difficulty in performing such activities as walking or running for 100 meters, and walking up and downstairs. In the 1991 survey, respondents were asked for the first time to self-report their height and weight. This information is used to create an additional health outcome, such as having BMI in the healthy range.[1]

The explanatory variables are indicators of an individual's characteristics, socioeconomic status, and family background. Individual characteristics include age (year of birth), gender, and marital status. Socioeconomic status includes information about a person's education (self-reported), employment, and earning potential (individual income measures). Real individual income is the individual's total annual income (in thousands of Swedish Kronor), taken from the tax registers and deflated by the CPI. Family background refers to a person's childhood living conditions, including parents' education level, whether the person lived with parents, whether there were siblings, characteristics of the residential area (rural, town, major town), a proxy for childhood economic situation (wealthy or poor), and a measure of the family's past health (whether anyone in the immediate, or extended, family suffered health problems).

6. *Empirical results*

In the SLLS, the cohort most affected by the compulsory schooling reform (and thus of particular interest) was born between 1945 and 1955 and was therefore between ages 36 and 46 in the 1991 survey. The combined 1981-and-1991 sample contains approximately twice the number of observations of the 1991-only set. There were 1,444 people born between 1945 and 1955 who responded in both years. There are 893 individuals

---

[1] Body mass index (BMI) is defined as weight in kilograms divided by height in meters squared. BMI in the healthy range is defined as greater than or equal to 18.5 and lower than 25.

left after accounting for the missing school reform measure. I present the results for both the 1991 and the combined sample, because self-rated health is available for 1991 but not for 1981 (Table 1).

The mean of years of formal education for the 1945–1955 male cohort in 1991 was 12.4 – about one year more than the average for the entire sample. The trend in education increases over time as younger cohorts attend school longer and receive more education than older cohorts. The 1991 dummy variable is included in the combined sample regressions to control for time trends. The education variable in the combined regressions is an auxiliary variable created from the 1981 and the 1991 self-reported education so as to account for misreported education in 1991. Respecifying education in the combined regressions did not affect the results. The 1991 self-reported education is retained as an educational variable in the 1991 regressions.

Simple correlations between differing measures of health and self-reported education indicate that more schooling is negatively associated with a bad health index, unhealthy BMI, smoking habits, and functional ability difficulties; it is positively associated with self-reported health status. People who report good health are more likely to have a BMI in the healthy range; they suffer fewer health symptoms in the previous year. On average, they also have completed more years of formal schooling and earn more.

6.1. Effect of the compulsory schooling reform on education

Exposure to the compulsory schooling reform is an instrumental variable for schooling. The predicted reform status is based on whether a person during childhood lived in a certain municipality when it implemented the new system of schooling; this instrument thus predicts a person's schooling reform status.

This chapter hypothesizes that people exposed to the school reform complete more years of formal schooling. Schooling is thus determined by a person's schooling reform status, after controlling for other common determinants of schooling, such as individual characteristics (cohort and county fixed effects) and family background.[2] The family background variables are parents' education levels (whether each parent completed elementary, vocational or professional, secondary, or university education, where the indicator for elementary is the omitted category); having lived with parents; the number of siblings; economic resources (a wealth proxy); family health during childhood; and whether resident in a rural, town, or major town area during childhood.

---

[2] A county represents a regional district; there are 25 counties.

Table 1. Summary statistics[a]

Variable	1991		1981 and 1991	
	Mean	Standard deviation	Mean	Standard deviation
Age	41.262	3.237	35.978	5.975
Father's education				
elementary	0.667	0.472	0.660	0.474
vocational	0.099	0.299	0.104	0.306
secondary	0.201	0.401	0.204	0.403
university	0.033	0.179	0.031	0.174
Mother's education				
elementary	0.755	0.431	0.750	0.433
vocational	0.085	0.279	0.086	0.281
secondary	0.146	0.354	0.152	0.359
university	0.014	0.118	0.011	0.105
Live with parents	0.856	0.351	0.849	0.358
Number of siblings	0.840	0.367	0.848	0.359
Economic resources	0.087	0.282	0.083	0.276
Family health	0.172	0.378	0.167	0.373
Type of residence at age 16				
rural area	0.396	0.490	0.391	0.488
town area	0.340	0.474	0.353	0.478
major town area	0.264	0.441	0.256	0.437
Education, self-reported	12.376	3.525	12.629	3.757
Ind. Income (ann, real in 000 Kr)	97.630	54.702	84.196	47.545
Married	0.762	0.426	0.740	0.439
Single	0.191	0.393	0.229	0.421
Self-reported health	0.882	0.323	only in '91	–
BMI in the healthy range	0.597	0.491	only in '91	–
Standardized bad health index	−0.213	0.659	−0.260	0.629
1991 dummy variable	–	–	0.475	0.500
Reform status	0.863	0.344	0.870	0.336
Reform exposure N	424		893	

Note: BMI in the healthy range variable is available in 1991 only because height and weight are reported for the first time in 1991. Self-reported health is available for 1991 only.
[a]Men born between 1945 and 1955.

The results in this chapter are for men only, because the reform does not predict schooling for the 1945–1955 female cohort and the preliminary results rejected pooling. The reform coefficient for females is significantly different from the corresponding coefficient for males. This may be because women interrupt their schooling and finish formal schooling only after having children, although the reform should affect them as well. Or, it may be because of the small sample, which makes detecting significant effects difficult.

Preliminary results reveal that standard errors clustered by county are almost identical to those not clustered. This holds for the 1991 regression and for the pooled regression and is attributed to the small number of observations per county. Given the small sample, standard errors are not clustered.

Groot and van den Brink (2007) use data from the Netherlands and also find the IV estimate of education insignificant for women. Indicators of a father's managerial job while an individual was at age 14, and of a mother's paid job, serve as instruments for education in an ordered probit model of health quality.

The base model of schooling with cohort and county effects, and when family background variables are omitted, shows that the exposure to school reform increases schooling by 1.7 years, which is significant at a 1 percent level. The coefficient on reform status decreases to 1.4 additional years of schooling after I control for a set of family background characteristics; it is significant at a 5 percent level (Table 2). In the first-stage equation with cohort and county effects, the F-statistic on the reform is 6.80 and the R^2 is 0.134. In the equation that controls for family background, those values are 5.55 and 0.292, respectively (Bound *et al.*, 1995). The coefficient on reform status is not sensitive to the exclusion of family background variables. Similar results also are obtained with the combined 1981-and-1991 sample. Men who lived in a municipality that enacted the new schooling system completed 1.4 additional years of schooling, after controlling for family background characteristics, as is shown by the coefficient on reform status, which is significant at a 1 percent level (Table 2).

As expected, parents' education levels significantly affect their children's education – this is especially true for fathers who completed secondary school and university education and for mothers who completed secondary school. For instance, having a father with a university education increases a person's schooling by 3.8 additional years in the combined set. Living with parents and not experiencing family economic hardship while growing up also significantly increases the individual years of formal schooling completed (see Table 2).

6.2. Treatment of education in the health structural equation

Here, I present the OLS and TSLS estimation results of the health structural equation, first discussing the model without income and married variables, and then including them. The OLS estimates show that more schooling implies a lower bad health index for the 1945–1955 male cohort. Schooling improves health significantly when education is treated as exogenous. The marginal effect of education on a standardized bad health index equals −0.022; this coefficient is significant at a 5 percent level (Table 3). In the bad health index regression, negative schooling coefficient

***Table 2.* *First-stage results model with cohort and county effects and family background*[a]**

	1991	1981 and 1991
Reform Status	1.447	1.452
	(2.22)**	(3.09)***
Father's Educ. Vocational	1.309	1.794
	(2.35)**	(4.61)***
Father's Educ. Secondary	1.636	1.825
	(3.55)***	(5.48)***
Father's Educ. University	3.295	3.805
	(3.25)***	(5.12)***
Mother's Educ. Vocational	0.879	0.736
	(1.50)	(1.78)*
Mother's Educ. Secondary	1.397	1.567
	(2.67)***	(4.22)***
Mother's Educ. University	0.283	1.039
	(0.19)	(0.88)
Live with parents	0.845	0.747
	(1.71)*	(2.17)**
Siblings	−0.050	−0.028
	(−0.11)	(−0.09)
Econ. Resources	−1.155	−1.078
	(−1.95)**	(−2.46)***
Family Health	−0.429	0.081
	(−1.02)	(0.26)
Rural area	−1.200	−0.567
	(−3.04)***	(−2.02)**
Town area	–	–
	–	–
Major town area	−0.392	−0.023
	(−0.58)	(−0.05)
Intercept	11.203	10.443
	(9.70)***	(12.11)***
1991dummy	–	0.494
	–	(2.22)**
N	422	890

Note: *t*-statistics are in the parentheses. Asterisks denote level of significance, respectively. * 10% ($p = 0.10$), ** 5% ($p = 0.05$), and *** 1% ($p = 0.01$) level of significance.
[a]Men born between 1945 and 1955.

represents better health; hence, one additional year of schooling reduces the standardized bad health index, or improves health as measured by health symptoms. I use one-tailed test because the alternative hypothesis is that the schooling coefficient is negative (the null hypothesis is that the schooling coefficient is zero). The other highly significant determinants of healthier men include such indicators as whether a mother completed secondary education and having siblings in the household.

Additional schooling also lowers the bad health index within the combined set. Therefore, the point estimate of schooling is lower than the

Table 3. Health outcomes in the model when married and income variables are excluded

	Bad health index, 1991		Bad health index, 1981 and 1991		BMI in the healthy range	
	OLS	TSLS	OLS	TSLS	OLS	TSLS
Education	−0.022	−0.185	−0.009	−0.126	0.014	0.118
	(−2.02)**	(−1.54)*	(−1.41)*	(−1.75)**	(1.86)**	(1.40)*
Father's Educ. Vocational	0.035	0.255	0.082	0.297	0.082	−0.067
	(0.30)	(1.16)	(1.10)	(1.88)**	(0.98)	(−0.43)
Father's Educ. Secondary	0.036	0.316	−0.048	0.173	0.037	−0.147
	(0.37)	(1.32)*	(−0.75)	(1.12)	(0.53)	(−0.86)
Father's Educ. University	0.153	0.705	0.126	0.580	−0.141	−0.487
	(0.71)	(1.44)*	(0.88)	(1.79)**	(−0.90)	(−1.44)*
Mother's Educ. Vocational	−0.055	0.091	−0.034	0.052	−0.098	−0.200
	(−0.44)	(0.48)	(−0.44)	(0.49)	(−1.09)	(−1.46)*
Mother's Educ. Secondary	−0.188	0.039	−0.122	0.062	0.0004	−0.156
	(−1.69)**	(0.18)	(−1.72)**	(0.44)	(0.01)	(−0.99)
Mother's Educ. University	0.012	0.063	−0.029	0.100	0.267	0.211
	(0.04)	(0.16)	(−0.13)	(0.37)	(1.19)	(0.77)
Live with parents	0.024	0.140	−0.043	0.033	0.131	0.040
	(0.23)	(0.90)	(−0.67)	(0.37)	(1.79)**	(0.35)
Siblings	−0.219	−0.223	−0.053	−0.056	0.015	0.013
	(−2.37)***	(−1.90)**	(−0.86)	(−0.78)	(0.23)	(0.16)
Econ. Resources	0.146	−0.041	0.132	0.007	−0.068	0.047
	(1.17)	(−0.20)	(1.59)*	(0.05)	(−0.76)	(0.33)
Family Health	0.058	−0.006	0.071	0.083	−0.092	−0.037
	(0.65)	(−0.05)	(1.22)	(1.20)	(−1.44)*	(−0.41)
Rural area	0.048	−0.153	−0.003	−0.073	−0.091	–
	(0.57)	(−0.84)	(−0.06)	(−0.96)	(−0.92)	–
Town area	–	–	–	–	−0.048	−0.089
	–	–	–	–	(−0.48)	(−0.69)
Major town area	0.057	−0.009	0.028	0.023	–	−0.014
	(0.40)	(−0.05)	(0.30)	(0.21)	–	(−0.09)
1991 dummy			0.090	0.146		
			(2.13)**	(2.42)***		
Intercept	0.146	2.112	−0.051	1.274	0.143	−0.998
	(0.55)	(1.43)*	(−0.30)	(1.52)*	(0.95)	(−1.14)
N	422	422	890	890	431	431

Note: *t*-statistics are in the parentheses. Asterisks denote level of significance, respectively. * 10% ($p = 0.10$), ** 5% ($p = 0.05$), and *** 1% ($p = 0.01$) level of significance.

corresponding point estimate in the 1991 set. Nevertheless, the educational coefficient is statistically significant at a 10 percent level. The mother's secondary education improves health significantly, while having family economic hardships during childhood decreases health. More years of schooling significantly increase health, as measured by BMI in the healthy range. Attending school for one additional year increases the probability of having a BMI in the healthy range. Living with parents significantly increases one's likelihood of having a healthy BMI. Having a family member, either immediate (parent or sibling) or extended family, with long-standing health problems negatively affects an individual's BMI.

Theoretically, if we believe that there are indeed unobserved variables that may determine both schooling and health levels, hence confounding the true effect of schooling on health, then education cannot be treated as exogenous in the structural equation of health. The health structural model, therefore, is estimated by the TSLS method, which takes into account the potential endogeneity of education.

In that analysis, one additional year of schooling reduces the standardized bad health index by −0.154 in a base model of health with cohort and county effects but when family background variables are omitted; this effect is significant at a 5 percent level (not presented). The educational coefficient equals −0.185 after controlling for a set of family background characteristics and is significant at a 10 percent level, while the educational coefficient in the same model with the combined sample is slightly lower (−0.126), but is significant at a 5 percent level (Table 3).

One year of additional schooling significantly increases the probability of having BMI in the healthy range. The educational coefficient equals 0.091 when family background variables are omitted (result not presented) and 0.118 when those variables are included; both are significant at a 10 percent level. Second-stage results are not sensitive to the exclusion of family background variables (as is the case in the first stage). Educational coefficients are significant even though the sample is small.

In the OLS model, after controlling for individual income and an indicator of being married, in addition to family background and cohort and county effects, the schooling coefficient equals −0.017; it is significant at a 10 percent level (Table 4). As expected, both marriage and higher income improve health significantly. Within the combined set, higher income improves health significantly, but the educational coefficient is not significant after controlling for income and marriage. The OLS point estimate in the healthy-range-BMI model is about the same (0.015) both before and after controlling for individual income and marriage.

The TSLS model of health with cohort and county effects, after controlling for family background, can be augmented by individual income and an indicator of being married. In that model, income and marriage are included in both TSLS estimation stages. The educational coefficient equals −0.210; it is significant at a 10 percent level in the 1991 model of bad health (Table 4). Having siblings reduces the bad health index, just as being married does, but being married turns insignificant. A person's income does not affect the bad health index. Some parental education indicators matter for a person's health, but they are of the incorrect sign.

In the same model of bad health with the combined set of years, the educational coefficient equals −0.134; it is significant at a 10 percent level

Table 4. Health outcomes in the model when married and income variables are included

	Bad health index, 1991		Bad health index, 1981 and 1991		BMI in the healthy range	
	OLS	TSLS	OLS	TSLS	OLS	TSLS
Education	−0.017	−0.210	−0.005	−0.134	0.015	0.145
	(−1.50)*	(−1.38)*	(−0.79)	(−1.58)*	(1.95)**	(1.33)*
Father's Educ.	0.020	0.278	0.077	0.309	0.081	−0.106
Vocational	(0.17)	(1.08)	(1.04)	(1.75)**	(0.96)	(−0.56)
Father's Educ.	0.043	0.348	−0.047	0.188	0.039	−0.168
Secondary	(0.44)	(1.28)*	(−0.74)	(1.09)	(0.55)	(−0.86)
Father's Educ.	0.218	0.727	0.186	0.605	−0.129	−0.464
University	(1.01)	(1.47)*	(1.30)*	(1.86)**	(−0.82)	(−1.34)*
Mother's Educ.	−0.058	0.119	−0.036	0.061	−0.101	−0.233
Vocational	(−0.48)	(0.55)	(−0.46)	(0.53)	(−1.11)	(−1.44)*
Mother's Educ.	−0.189	0.055	−0.122	0.072	0.001	−0.187
Secondary	(−1.71)**	(0.23)	(−1.72)**	(0.47)	(0.01)	(−1.00)
Mother's Educ.	−0.046	0.151	−0.029	0.104	0.249	0.084
University	(−0.15)	(0.34)	(−0.13)	(0.37)	(1.10)	(0.26)
Live with parents	0.037	0.150	−0.034	0.041	0.130	0.023
	(0.36)	(0.91)	(−0.53)	(0.44)	(1.78)**	(0.18)
Siblings	−0.209	−0.250	−0.047	−0.065	0.019	0.038
	(−2.26)***	(−1.94)**	(−0.76)	(−0.87)	(0.29)	(0.43)
Econ. Resources	0.117	−0.062	0.113	−0.005	−0.071	0.037
	(0.94)	(−0.28)	(1.36)*	(−0.04)	(−0.79)	(0.25)
Family Health	0.057	−0.026	0.071	0.080	−0.090	−0.015
	(0.65)	(−0.19)	(1.22)	(1.14)	(−1.40)*	(−0.15)
Rural area	0.043	−0.174	−0.011	−0.077	−0.090	0.044
	(0.52)	(−0.85)	(−0.21)	(−1.00)	(−0.91)	(0.26)
Town area	–	–	–	–	−0.046	−0.064
	–	–	–	–	(−0.45)	(−0.48)
Major town area	0.043	−0.027	0.015	0.018	–	–
	(0.31)	(−0.13)	(0.16)	(0.15)	–	–
Married	−0.108	−0.127	−0.038	−0.072	0.008	0.006
	(−1.30)*	(−1.13)	(−0.74)	(−1.08)	(0.13)	(0.07)
Income	−0.001	0.0015	−0.001	0.0004	−0.0003	−0.002
	(−1.83)**	(0.64)	(−3.01)***	(0.30)	(−0.65)	(−1.30)*
1991 dummy	–	–	0.128	0.142	–	–
	–	–	(2.93)***	(2.66)***	–	–
Intercept	0.309	2.362	0.061	1.397	0.159	−1.084
	(1.14)	(1.43)*	(0.34)	(1.55)*	(1.00)	(−1.02)
N	422	422	890	890	431	431

Note: *t*-statistics are in the parentheses. Asterisks denote level of significance, respectively. * 10% ($p = 0.10$), ** 5% ($p = 0.05$), and *** 1% ($p = 0.01$) level of significance.

and similar in magnitude to the schooling coefficient in the model without income. The 1991 year effect, a time indicator, has a positive, significant impact on bad health because it captures aging; this may indicate that people tend to suffer worse health as they get older. Additional schooling causes better health, as indicated by the healthy-range-BMI model. The educational coefficient is 0.145; it is significant at a 10 percent level, after accounting for the income effect on health.

Overall, the schooling coefficient ranges between −0.126 and −0.210; it is significant at least at the 10 percent level in the TSLS model on bad health, irrespective of income inclusion. Additional schooling reduces the bad health index significantly when education is treated as endogenous for the 1945–1955 male cohort. This result holds for both the 1991 and the combined samples. Additional schooling improves health significantly when BMI in the healthy range is used as another measure of health.

Notably, the TSLS educational coefficients are larger in comparison with the OLS counterparts, sometimes as much as 10 times larger, which is not an uncommon finding in similar research (Currie and Moretti, 2003; Arendt, 2005; Lleras-Muney, 2005). Larger IV than OLS coefficients are found in the monetary-returns-to-education literature and in the estimation of schooling's causal effect on health. Such results indicate that an extra year of schooling has a greater effect for a marginal person than for an average person (Imbens and Angrist, 1994).

Using the TSLS method and the schooling reform status as an instrument for schooling provides a consistent causal estimate of schooling's effect on health. The TSLS estimates show that additional schooling (induced by the compulsory school reform) causes significantly better health outcomes, both in terms of a lower bad health index or of a greater probability of having BMI in the healthy range. Indeed, the positive and significant effect of increased education on health remains whether schooling is treated as exogenous or endogenous. All of the results indicate that increased education causes better health.

6.3. Treatment of income

Including a person's current income in the first-stage equation may not be entirely adequate, because it may not reflect a contemporaneous income effect on education. In this chapter, the change in education analyzed is induced by the school reform, and it is assumed that a person's current health is also a function of current income. It is further assumed that the majority of people complete their formal education by age 25. Therefore, the model estimates income that is excluded from the first stage but included in the second stage (Table 5). The same applies to the indicator for being married: marital status is treated like income because, just like income, it may be determined after schooling or be caused by it.

The significant causal effect of education on health does not change once individual real income is included in the second stage. In the 1991 model of bad health, the educational coefficient equals −0.177. It is

***Table 5.* *TSLS model with income and married only in the second stage: selected variables*[a]**

	Bad health index, 1991	Bad health index, 1981 and 1991	BMI in the healthy range
Education	−0.177	−0.117	0.122
	(−1.47)*	(−1.64)*	(1.42)*
Married	−0.117	−0.043	0.017
	(−1.11)	(−0.72)	(0.23)
Income	−0.001	−0.0015	−0.0002
	(−1.63)*	(−2.64)***	(−0.32)
N	422	890	431

Note: *t*-statistics are in the parentheses. Asterisks denote level of significance, respectively. * 10% ($p = 0.10$), ** 5% ($p = 0.05$), and *** 1% ($p = 0.01$) level of significance.
[a]Men born between 1945 and 1955.

significant at a 10 percent level; and it is similar in magnitude to the educational coefficient in the TSLS model, which does not include individual characteristics (an income variable and a marriage indicator). Both measures of health share this finding. The effect of income on health in the TSLS model of bad health turns statistically significant when income is included only in the second stage. The income coefficient is also negative, meaning that higher income decreases bad health.

Using models that include an income variable, we can determine how much of the total effect of education on health is a direct effect of education on health and how much is an indirect effect (due to higher income). The indirect effect that comes through income is proportional to the difference between educational coefficient in the model without income (i.e., total effect) and coefficient in the model with income (i.e., direct effect). In the 1991 OLS model of bad health, about one-fifth of education's total effect on health is the indirect effect. This effect is much smaller (about 4 percent) in the IV model of bad health with income in the second stage. Hence, education has a substantially greater direct than indirect effect on health.

In addition, we could quantify the relative magnitudes of the schooling and income effects on health if the change in the stock of health were held constant. That is, how much can income fall when schooling rises by one year, without any changes in health? In the 1991 model of bad health, the OLS result suggests that a year of schooling nearly equals a $1,700 increase in income, holding health constant. The IV result suggests that a one-year increase in schooling nearly equals a $17,700 increase in income in terms of health. The IV result also indicates that less schooling will result in a better health outcome, because the IV result is up to 10 times larger than the OLS result.

7. Conclusion

The results in this chapter indicate that education has a direct and causal effect on health. One additional year of schooling generated by the compulsory schooling reform translates into better health status as shown by a lower value of the bad health index or by greater likelihood of having BMI in the healthy range. This result holds across various health measures, and for different samples and years.

In the 1991 bad health index regression, the educational coefficient equals: −0.185 after controlling for family background characteristics; −0.210 if individual real income is included in both stages of estimation; and −0.177 if income enters only in the second stage. In the TSLS health regressions, the educational coefficient is significant at a 10 percent level.

Similarly, using the combined 1981-and-1991 sample, an additional year of schooling significantly lowers the bad health index, therefore improving health. The educational coefficient equals approximately −0.13 in models with or without individual characteristics. One additional year of schooling significantly improves health, when health is measured as having a BMI in the healthy range.

There remains a positive, direct, and causal effect of education on health, even after controlling for income in the health structural equation. Additional schooling generated by the compulsory school reform in Sweden indeed produces better adult health outcomes (after controlling for cohort and county effects, family background, individual and childhood characteristics, and income).

Acknowledgments

The author thanks Michael Grossman for his support, help, and guidance. Thanks to Marten Palme, Janne Jonsson, and Robert Erikson for their kindness and help in making the Swedish Level of Living Surveys and the Swedish comprehensive school reform data and information available for this research. Thanks to Dhaval Dave for his helpful suggestions.

References

Acemoglu, D. and J. Angrist (1999), "How large are the social returns to education? evidence from compulsory schooling laws", NBER Working Paper Series, No. 7444.

Adams, S. (2002), "Educational attainment and health: evidence from a sample of older adults", *Education Economics*, Vol. 10, pp. 97–109.

Angrist, J. and A. Krueger (1991), "Does compulsory school attendance affect schooling and earnings?", *Quarterly Journal of Economics*, Vol. 106, pp. 979–1014.

Arendt, J.N. (2005), "Does education cause better health? A panel data analysis using school reforms for identification", *Economics of Education Review*, Vol. 24, pp. 149–160.

Arkes, J. (2003), "Does schooling improve adult health?", Working Paper no. DRU-3051, RAND, Santa Monica, CA.

Auster, R., I. Leveson and D. Sarachek (1969), "The production of health: an exploratory study", *Journal of Human Resources*, Vol. 4, pp. 411–436.

Becker, G.S. and C. Mulligan (1997), "The endogenous determination of time preference", *Quarterly Journal of Economics*, Vol. 112, pp. 729–758.

Berger, M. and P. Leigh (1989), "Schooling, self-selection, and health", *Journal of Human Resources*, Vol. 24, pp. 433–455.

Black, S., P. Devereux and K. Salvanes (2004), "Fast times at Ridgemont High? the effect of compulsory schooling laws on teenage births", NBER Working Paper Series, No. 10911.

Bound, J., D. Jaeger and R. Baker (1995), "Problems with instrumental variables estimation when the correlation between the instruments and the endogenous explanatory variable is weak", *Journal of the American Statistical Association*, Vol. 90, pp. 443–450.

Card, D. (1999), "The causal effect of education on earnings", pp. 1801–1863 in: O. Ashenfelter and D. Card, editors, *Handbook of Labor Economics*, Vol. 3, Amsterdam: Elsevier Science.

Currie, J. and E. Moretti (2003), "Mother's education and the intergenerational transmission of human capital: evidence from college openings", *Quarterly Journal of Economics*, Vol. 118, pp. 1495–1532.

Deaton, A. and C. Paxson (1999), "Mortality, education, income, and inequality among American cohorts", NBER Working Paper Series, No. 7140.

de Walque, D. (2007), "How does the impact of an HIV/AIDS information campaign vary with educational attainment? Evidence from rural Uganda", *Journal of Development Economics*, Vol. 84, pp. 686–714.

Farrell, P. and V.R. Fuchs (1982), "Schooling and health: the cigarette connection", *Journal of Health Economics*, Vol. 1, pp. 217–230.

Gerdtham, U.G. and M. Johannesson (1999), "New estimates of the demand for health: results based on a categorical health measure and Swedish micro data", *Social Science and Medicine*, Vol. 49, pp. 1325–1332.

Gerdtham, U.G., M. Johannesson, L. Lundberg and D. Isacson (1999), "The demand for health: results from new measures of health capital", *European Journal of Political Economy*, Vol. 15, pp. 501–521.

Goldman, D. and D. Lakdawalla (2001), "Understanding health disparities across education groups", NBER Working Paper Series, No. 8328.

Groot, W. and H.M. van den Brink (2007), "The health effects of education", *Economics of Education Review*, Vol. 26, pp. 186–200.

Grossman, M. (1972), "On the concept of health capital and the demand for health", *Journal of Political Economy*, Vol. 80, pp. 223–255.

Grossman, M. (1972), *The Demand for Health: A Theoretical and Empirical Investigation*, New York: National Bureau of Economic Research.

Grossman, M. (1975), "The correlation between health and schooling", pp. 147–211 in: N.R. Terleckyj, editor, *Conference on Research in Income and Wealth, Studies in Income and Wealth: Household Production and Consumption*, Vol. 40, New York: National Bureau of Economic Research.

Grossman, M. (2000), "The human capital model", pp. 348–408 in: A.J. Culyer and J.P. Newhouse, editors, *Handbook of Health Economics*, Vol. 1A, Amsterdam: North-Holland.

Grossman, M. and R. Kaestner (1997), "Effects of education on health", pp. 69–123 in: J.R. Behrman and N. Stacey, editors, *The Social Benefits of Education*, Ann Arbor, MI: University of Michigan Press.

Harmon, C. and I. Walker (1995), "Estimates of the economic return to schooling for the United Kingdom", *American Economic Review*, Vol. 85, pp. 1278–1286.

Imbens, G.W. and J. Angrist (1994), "Identification and estimation of local average treatment effects", *Econometrica*, Vol. 62, pp. 467–476.

Jonsson, J.O. (2003), "The Swedish Level-of-Living Surveys (LNU): history and current situation", Swedish Institute for Social Research, Stockholm University.

Kenkel, D.S. (1991), "Health behavior, health knowledge, and schooling", *Journal of Political Economy*, Vol. 99, pp. 287–305.

Kenkel, D.S. (2000), "Prevention", pp. 1675–1720 in: A.J. Culyer and J.P. Newhouse, editors, *Handbook of Health Economics*, Vol. 1B, Amsterdam: North-Holland.

Leigh, P.J. (1983), "Direct and indirect effects of education on health", *Social Science and Medicine*, Vol. 17, pp. 227–234.

Lindahl, M. (2005), "Estimating the effect of income on health and mortality using lottery prizes as an exogenous source of variation in income", *Journal of Human Resources*, Vol. 40, pp. 144–168.

Lleras-Muney, A. (2005), "The relationship between education and adult mortality in the United States", *Review of Economic Studies*, Vol. 72, pp. 189–221.

Meghir, C. and M. Palme (2001), "The effect of a social experiment in education", Working Papers Series in Economics and Finance, No. 451, Stockholm School of Economics.

Meghir, C. and M. Palme (2005), "Educational reform, ability and family background", *American Economic Review*, Vol. 95, pp. 414–424.

Ross, C.E. and C. Wu (1995), "The links between education and health", *American Sociological Review*, Vol. 60, pp. 719–745.

Sander, W. (1995), "Schooling and quitting smoking", *Review of Economics and Statistics*, Vol. 77, pp. 191–199.

CHAPTER 10

A Survey on the Economics of the U.S. Pharmaceutical Industry

Ian McCarthy

Abstract

With expenditures totaling $227 billion in 2007, prescription drug purchases are a growing portion of the total medical expenditure, and as this industry continues to grow, prescription drugs will continue to be a critical part of the larger health care industry. This chapter presents a survey on the economics of the US pharmaceutical industry, with a focus on the role of R&D and marketing, the determinants (and complications) of prescription drug pricing, and various aspects of consumer behavior specific to this industry, such as prescription drug regulation, the patient's interaction with the physician, and insurance coverage. This chapter also provides background in areas not often considered in the economics literature, such as the role of pharmacy benefit managers in prescription drug prices and the differentiation between alternative measures of prescription drug prices.

Keywords: Abbreviated New Drug Application (ANDA), Average Manufacturer Price (AMP), Average Wholesale Price (AWP), Bayh-Dole Act, Bioequivalence, Brand name drug, Center for Medicare and Medicaid Services (CMS), Chain pharmacy, Clinical trials, Closed formulary, Coinsurance, Compliance, Co-payment, Cost controls, Cost sharing, Detailing, Direct-to-consumer Advertising (DTC Advertising), Disease management, Drug manufacturers, Drug prices, Drug–product substitution, Experience goods, Fee-for-service (FFS), First-mover advantage, Food and Drug Administration (FDA), Formulary, Generic drug, Good Manufacturing Processes (GMP), Hatch-Waxman Act, Health plan,

CONTRIBUTIONS TO ECONOMIC ANALYSIS
VOLUME 290 ISSN: 0573-8555
DOI:10.1108/S0573-8555(2010)0000290013

Insurance, Investigational New Drug Application (IND), Mail-order pharmacy, Mail-order prescription drugs, Medicaid, Medicare, Medicare + Choice (M + C), Medicare Advantage, Medicare Modernization Act (MMA), Medicare Part D, Moral hazard, Negative goods, New Drug Application (NDA), Non-retail pharmacy, Original Medicare, Out-of-pocket, Paid search advertising, Patent, Patient, Pharmaceutical, Pharmacy, Pharmacy benefit manager (PBM), Physician, Prescription drugs, Product differentiation, Rebate, Reimbursement, Research and development (R&D), Retail pharmacy, Search costs, Switching costs, Therapeutic class, Third-party insurance, Tiered formulary, Wholesale Acquisition Price (WAC), Wholesaler

JEL classifications: I11, I18

1. Introduction

With approximately $227 billion in total expenditures in 2007, the prescription drug industry is one of the largest industries in the United States and functions substantially differently than many other markets. For example, at least some portion of the general public perceives prescription drugs as more of a right than a pure good. In a letter to the editor published in the *New York Times* in 2005, one reader writes: "You cannot simply tell a person in dire need, wait for the market to take care of you. That is a most callous thing to say, and only makes a person feel owned, and with no control over his life."[1] This type of public perception conflicts with the fundamental incentives of a profit-maximizing firm. Prescription drugs are also "negative goods" in that patients generally do not purchase prescription drugs out of want, but out of need. These points not only have textbook economic implications on, for example, demand elasticity, but can also have important regulatory effects. The operation of the prescription drug industry is made more complicated by the sheer multitude of economic agents involved, which includes physicians, pharmacists, patients, insurance companies, drug manufacturers, wholesalers, pharmacy benefit managers (PBMs), government regulatory agencies such as the Food and Drug Administration ("FDA"), and others. Many of these agents have different, sometimes conflicting, incentives.

This chapter presents a survey of the economics of the pharmaceutical industry, with a general focus on the role of R&D and marketing, the determinants (and complications) of prescription drug pricing, and various

[1] See also McFadden (2006).

aspects of consumer behavior specific to the pharmaceutical industry (such as prescription drug regulation, the patient's interaction with the physician, and insurance coverage). This chapter also provides background in areas not often considered in the economics literature, such as the role of PBMs in prescription drug prices and the differentiation between alternative measures of prescription drug prices. The goal of this chapter is not to focus on any specific element in the prescription drug market but rather to present an overview and introduce many complex economic issues relevant to the prescription drug industry. As is evident from the remaining sections, the prescription drug industry is complex and much of the research in this industry remains inconclusive.

This chapter begins with a discussion of the standard product life cycle for a prescription drug, including the stages of R&D and the role of marketing. Next, I discuss prescription drug prices and various pricing considerations, including the role of generic drugs versus brand name drugs, product differentiation, and regulation. I then broadly analyze consumer behavior in this market with regard to demand elasticity, insurance coverage, physician interaction, and various informational considerations. Unless otherwise mentioned, the discussion in this chapter generally applies to brand name prescription drugs sold at retail pharmacies.

2. *Product life cycle*

2.1. *Research and development*

The pharmaceutical industry is one of the most research-intensive industries in the United States. In 2006 and 2007, the Pharmaceutical Research and Manufacturers of America ("PhRMA") estimated total pharmaceutical R&D expenditures at just over $56 billion and $63.2 billion, respectively (PhRMA, 2008). According to Congressional Budget Office estimates, the 2006 investment accounted for as much as five times more as a percentage of sales than the average U.S. manufacturing firm (United States Congressional Budget Office, 2006). As illustrated in Table 1, total R&D expenditures for PhRMA member companies have increased steadily over the past 10 years. Since 2004, this increase has been driven largely by the development of biopharmaceutical drugs (PhRMA, 2009).

According to PhRMA estimates, a prescription drug costs approximately $1.3 billion to develop, and only approximately 20% of marketed drugs generate revenues in excess of their R&D expenditures (PhRMA, 2008). These expenditures (or costs) are spread over approximately 10–15 years and span three general phases: (1) discovery, (2) development, and (3) manufacturing.

During the discovery period, drug manufacturers screen thousands of compounds, including newly developed compounds, where the most promising compounds undergo various chemical modifications to improve

***Table 1.* R&D expenditures for PhRMA member companies (millions of dollars)**

Year	Domestic	International	Total
2007			$47,900
2006	$34,468	$8,971	$43,439
2005	30,969	8,889	39,858
2004	29,556	7,463	37,018
2003	27,065	7,388	34,453
2002	25,655	5,357	31,012
2001	23,502	6,221	29,723
2000	21,364	4,667	26,031
1999	18,471	4,220	22,691
1998	17,128	3,839	20,967
1997	15,446	3,492	18,938
1996	13,627	3,279	16,906
1995	11,874	3,334	15,208

Source: PhRMA, 2008 and 2009 Industry Profiles.

safety and effectiveness. After a compound has been preliminarily developed, only approximately 250 compounds (2.5–5% of the initial compounds considered) move on to the preclinical discovery phase, where the drugs are initially tested and where researchers first consider the manufacturability, dosing, and delivery of the drug in question (PhRMA, 2008, 2009).

When developing a new compound, pharmaceutical companies usually apply for patent protection after the discovery phase. Patents therefore play an important role at this point in the R&D process, which is discussed in more detail throughout this chapter. Note here, however, that until 1980, private industry bore the larger burden of the discovery of new prescription drugs. But after the Bayh-Dole Act of 1980, institutions could obtain ownership of an invention discovered though government-funded research. This allowed universities, small businesses, and public research institutions the ability to profit from their research endeavors and incentivized universities and other public institutions to invest in developing, among other things, new pharmaceutical compounds.

Approximately 20% of the drugs in preclinical discovery move on to the development phase. In this phase, researchers submit a formal Investigational New Drug ("IND") application to the FDA, presenting the results of the preclinical stage and a comprehensive plan for clinical trials (PhRMA, 2008, 2009). Upon FDA approval of the plan, drugs can formally begin clinical trials. These trials are essentially a rigorous evaluation process by the FDA and are required in order for pharmaceutical companies to legally market a drug for use in the United States. This process takes up to nine years and consists of four primary phases: (1) Phase I clinical trial, where the drug is tested on healthy human volunteers, the focus of which is on the drug's common side effects and how quickly the drug leaves the body;

(2) Phase II clinical trial, where people with relevant diseases or conditions take part in controlled studies to measure the drug's effectiveness; (3) Phase III clinical trial, essentially a larger scale of Phase II, with a focus both on safety and effectiveness, as well as the effects of different dosages, different populations, combination therapy with other drugs, etc.; and (4) New Drug Application ("NDA"), where companies formally request FDA approval of a new drug for marketing in the United States and where the FDA thoroughly analyzes all of the data from the drug's clinical trials.[2] The FDA analyzes the results at each stage, and a drug can only move on to the next phase upon successful completion of all previous phases.[3] Note that FDA approval is not technically required for a physician to prescribe a particular treatment but is required only for a drug company to market the drug in the United States.

The FDA drug review process is not without its own controversy. Carpenter (2004), for example, discusses the incentives behind the FDA process, arguing that the review process is largely political and that the FDA may have reputational concerns beyond safety and efficacy. Carpenter also discusses the large and growing role of patient advocacy groups and lobbyists in the FDA's approval process.

FDA approval generally does not encompass all symptoms and all stages of a given condition. Rather, the FDA often approves drugs only for specific stages of a disease or to assist in specific functions for those diagnosed with a given disease. This specificity of FDA approval constricts the role of a given drug to a narrower patient base, even among patients with the same disease. After a drug has received marketing approval by the FDA, companies move to large-scale manufacturing of the drug. These manufacturing processes are regulated by the FDA's guidelines for Good Manufacturing Processes ("GMP") and periodically inspected by the FDA.

Various authors have analyzed R&D expenditures in the pharmaceutical industry, the returns to such expenditures, and the effect of more stringent price regulations on the willingness and ability of firms to appropriately invest in R&D. For example, Scherer (2001) and Giaccotto *et al.* (2003), among others, estimate the link between R&D and prescription drug prices. Both find strong positive correlation between drug prices and R&D expenditures and find that the expectation of future

---

[2] In the case of biopharmaceutical drugs, manufacturers submit a Biologic License Application ("BLA") rather than an NDA. For more detail, see "The FDA's drug review process: ensuring drugs are safe and effective", *FDA Consumer Magazine*, September 2005 (http://www.fda.gov/fdac/features/2002/402_drug.html).

[3] According to the FDA's Web site, in cases involving "new drugs for serious and life-threatening illnesses that lack satisfactory treatments," companies may ask for consideration of accelerated approval.

profits for a particular drug generally spurs increased R&D outlays. Giaccotto *et al.* estimate that R&D spending would have been reduced by approximately 30% if the government restricted price growth to be no higher than the overall growth of the consumer price index. The authors estimate that this reduction in R&D would have led to as many as 365 fewer new drugs produced between 1980 and 2001. Danzon (1997) also finds evidence that drug manufacturers may subsidize their high R&D expenditures by charging higher prices in the United States while still maintaining some market position throughout the world in more price-regulated countries with perhaps more price-sensitive consumers, although the empirical evidence regarding U.S. and rest-of-world price differentials is somewhat unclear (Danzon, 1997, 2000).

2.2. Marketing

Once a drug receives FDA approval, pharmaceutical firms can begin marketing the drug to patients and physicians. Donahue *et al.* (2007) describes the following channels by which pharmaceutical companies generally market or otherwise promote prescription drugs: (1) in-office visits from pharmaceutical sales representatives to physicians (also termed "detailing"); (2) free samples provided to physicians; (3) advertising in professional journals; (4) meetings, conferences, and educational events for physicians; (5) online promotion to physicians; and (6) direct-to-consumer ("DTC") advertising through magazines, radio, newspapers, Web/Internet, and television. Table 2 summarizes promotional spending from 1996 through 2005.

As illustrated in Table 2, total promotional spending in the pharmaceutical industry has increased steadily over the past several years, with free samples and detailing consistently the top one and two promotional expenditure categories, respectively. The level of advertising, as well as the specific form of advertising, can have important effects on a drug's success and adoption in the market. I discuss each of these issues below in more detail, as well as the specific growth and role of DTC advertising in the prescription drug market.

2.2.1. Level of promotional activity

At a high level, evidence generally suggests that increases in promotions can also increase sales.[4] But there are several more granular explanations for why advertising can be a successful strategy in the prescription drug market. One driver of this success is an increased diffusion into the market. Azoulay (2002), for example, finds that promotional activities may play a

---

[4] See, for example, Donahue *et al.* (2007).

***Table 2.* Promotional expenditure from 1996 through 2005 (millions of dollars – adjusted to 2005 dollars)**

	1996	1997	1998	1999	2000	2001	2002	2003	2004	2005
DTC advertising	$985	$1,301	$1,578	$2,166	$2,798	$2,954	$2,864	$3,478	$4,160	$4,237
Detailing	3,747	4,093	4,861	5,064	5,447	6,055	6,731	7,364	7,585	6,777
Journal advertising	571	621	597	551	549	469	474	476	516	429
Free sample	6,104	7,358	7,910	8,476	9,021	11,539	12,928	14,362	16,404	18,438
Total promotional spending	$11,407	$13,373	$14,946	$16,257	$17,815	$21,018	$22,997	$25,680	$28,664	$29,881

Source: Donahue *et al.* (2007).

large role in a drug's acceptance into the antiulcer drug market. King (2000) established similar results, finding specifically that marketing can increase the perceived degree of differentiation for a given antiulcer drug. This coincides with established results in the economic literature that advertising can signal a higher quality product, thereby generating a perception of product differentiation.[5] These results are particularly applicable in the prescription drug market, where the FDA maintains strict regulations on advertising content and where drugs are, at least to some extent, experience goods.[6]

Through surveys and empirical studies, advertising (particularly DTC advertising) has also been found to improve a patient's overall health by increasing compliance.[7] This is an important potential benefit of prescription drug advertising, as it offers somewhat of a market solution to an expensive problem that has been previously addressed with little success by several government programs and regulatory policies.

Advertising expenditures may also have negative consequences on the prescription drug market. For example, additional advertising expenditures may lead to higher prescription drug prices. Brekke and Kuhn (2005) develop a theoretical model in which pharmaceutical firm pricing and advertising are strategic complements from the firm perspective, meaning that drug manufacturers find it profitable to increase price as they increase promotional expenditures. Increases in price have obvious welfare implications, particularly if demand elasticity is arbitrarily low due to high co-payments or coinsurance rates, in which case price increases intuitively decrease welfare.[8] Advertising might also decrease demand elasticity, thereby generating an opportunity for drug manufacturers to increase price. Rizzo (1999) finds evidence of such a decrease in elasticity on behalf of patients, while Gonul *et al.* (2001) demonstrate that advertising has more of an informative effect on physicians.

Increased advertising expenditures may also lead to drug overuse or inefficient prescribing behaviors on behalf of physicians.[9] These claims are inconsistent, however, with the survey evidence regarding improved patient compliance discussed above. Calfee (2003) also discusses a general lack of empirical evidence that advertising may negatively impact a physician's prescribing behavior.

---

[5] See Grossman and Shapiro (1984), Spence (1980), Schmalensee (1986), and Hertzendorf (1993), among others, for more detail.

[6] Tirole (2003, pp. 289–290) briefly discusses the theoretical role of advertising for experience goods.

[7] See Calfee (2003) for a summary and discussion of these surveys and some supporting empirical results.

[8] Brekke and Kuhn (2005) analyze this point in more detail.

[9] See, for example, Brekke and Kuhn (2005).

2.2.2. Type of promotional activity

In addition to the level of promotional expenditure, the specific type of promotional activity utilized for a particular prescription drug can also have important effects on the drug's success in the market. For example, Coscelli and Shum (2004) argue that, because a physician's first-hand experience in prescribing a drug is a large determinant of a drug's market share, new drug manufactures may overcome any first-mover advantages of their competitors' drugs by issuing free samples to physicians. Bhattacharyya (2005) also finds empirical evidence that, under certain circumstances, DTC advertising is not a substitute for physician-directed advertising (e.g., detailing and free samples). This latter result implies that both forms of advertising may have non-overlapping yet complementary roles from the drug manufacturer's perspective, in which case the drug manufacturer's choice of one mode of advertising over the other may have important effects on the drug's success.

From an economic perspective, the choice of DTC or physician-directed advertising has important consequences because of the role of each agent in the final prescription decision. In particular, since patients do not fully control their "purchase" decisions, pundits often question the role of DTC advertising. For this and other reasons, many countries explicitly forbid DTC advertising.

2.2.3. DTC advertising

When the first DTC advertisement appeared in print in 1981, and shortly after in 1982, the FDA requested that pharmaceutical companies voluntarily restrict DTC advertising so that the FDA could research the issue. In 1985, the FDA officially withdrew its requested stoppage of DTC advertising and determined that DTC advertisements should be held to the same standard as advertisements geared toward physicians. The FDA's stance on DTC advertising essentially remained the same until 1997, when the FDA issued the "Draft Guidance for Industry, Consumer-Directed Broadcast Advertisements." The guidance was formally released in 1999, in which the FDA relaxed the requirements for commercial advertisements relative to print advertisements.

DTC advertising expenditures have increased rapidly since 1997. From Table 2, industry-wide DTC advertising expenditures increased 32% from $985 million in 1996 to $1.3 billion in 1997. By 2005, DTC advertising expenditures increased another 236%, totaling approximately $4.3 billion. This increase in spending has spurred calls for more stringent government regulation and has been blamed, at least in part, for the steady increase in pharmaceutical drug costs in recent years.

In addition to cost concerns, many regulatory agencies and consumer groups are concerned that DTC advertising may mislead patients simply because patients may not have the full capacity to understand their disease and potential treatments. DTC advertising, as some argue, instills an inflated positive belief as to the efficacy of a given treatment for a patient with certain symptoms. DTC advertising may therefore lead to drug misuse, less effective prescription behaviors on behalf of physicians, or more inelastic demand.

Contrary to these negative claims, there is evidence that DTC advertising can improve a patient's compliance and lead to more appropriate care (Masson and Rubin, 1985; Keith, 1995). Consistent with Masson and Rubin (1985) and Keith (1995), Bradford *et al.* (2010) find evidence that DTC advertising improves the matching process between the patient and the appropriate class of treatment. DTC advertising has also been found to significantly increase the sales for the relevant therapeutic ***class*** of drugs while potentially generating little noticeable increase in sales for a given drug (Berndt *et al.*, 1995; Rosenthal *et al.*, 2003). Bradford *et al.* (2006) find similar cross-price effects in their analysis of DTC advertising of Vioxx and Celebrex.

DTC may still have negative consequences. For example, the results from Rosenthal *et al.* (2003) and Berndt *et al.* (1995) imply that an entire therapeutic class of drugs for relatively ***unfamiliar*** symptoms and diseases may benefit from the advertising of just one firm. And depending on the welfare costs of the disease in question, improved awareness may substantially improve a patient's quality of life and unambiguously improve welfare. However, if a disease and its symptoms are well known, such that the market for the relevant therapeutic class of drugs is relatively mature, DTC may simply shift market share without any noticeable improvement in patient health. Assuming that the company receiving the higher share has a comparable cost structure and margin as the company (or companies) losing share, this is an unambiguous welfare loss.

A specific form of online DTC advertising, known as paid search advertising, has also come under question recently. This type of advertising is where drug manufacturers pay for certain key word searches on search engines such as Google. On entering a particular search phrase into the search engine, the user may see sponsored links for a certain prescription drug, whereby clicking on this link can take the user to the drug's Web site. This type of media is currently not explicitly regulated by the FDA, whose DTC advertising requirements generally pertain only to print and broadcast mediums and not online or social mediums. However, the FDA issued 14 different warning letters to various drug manufacturers in March 2009 notifying them of potential violations. Several drug manufacturers abandoned this form of drug marketing soon after the FDA issued these letters.[10]

---

[10] See Thomaselli (2009) for more detail.

Although new studies appear regularly, DTC advertising has so far been well received by patients in the prescription drug market, and the potential benefits of DTC advertising have been well documented. This is not to say that enhanced regulation, particularly for certain therapeutic classes of drugs, may not improve welfare; however, the theoretical and empirical evidence generally points to important potential benefits of DTC that policy makers should also consider.

2.3. Supply chain

Once a drug is manufactured, the drug is sold to wholesalers, retail and non-retail pharmacies,[11] and finally to the patient. For the most part, pharmacies and other providers purchase prescription drugs from wholesalers, although some large retail pharmacies, mail-order pharmacies, and non-retail pharmacies may internalize the role of the wholesaler and purchase directly from drug manufacturers. Wholesalers are essentially the middlemen of the pharmaceutical industry. By purchasing drugs for a large number of pharmacies and alternative sites, wholesalers decrease the number of transactions that would be required if pharmacies purchased directly from the manufacturers. Wholesalers then sell these drugs to pharmacies and other providers such as hospitals and clinics, who then sell to patients.

In 2005, the Congressional Budget Office estimated that wholesalers accounted for approximately 64% of all drugs sold by manufacturers. The remaining 36% of sales went directly from the manufacturer to pharmacies or alternative suppliers. Chain pharmacies and food stores with pharmacies accounted for the majority of the remaining 36%, and mail-order pharmacies and other providers accounted for the remaining sales (United States Congressional Budget Office, 2007).

As mentioned above, 64% of drugs are sold first to wholesalers before passing to pharmacies or other providers. The Congressional Budget Office estimates that independent pharmacies rely heavily on wholesalers for approximately 98% of all drug purchases. Non-retail providers purchase approximately 90% of their drugs from wholesalers, while mail-order pharmacies and food stores with pharmacies purchase approximately 85% and 53%, respectively, of their drugs from wholesalers. Chain pharmacies purchase only 25% of their drugs from wholesalers (United States Congressional Budget Office, 2007).

Once drugs are in the pharmacy, clinic, hospital, etc., they are ready for purchase from the patient. In 2005, consumers purchased approximately 43% of all prescription drugs from chain pharmacies and food stores with

---

[11] Examples of non-retail pharmacies include hospitals, nursing homes, and home health care providers.

in-house pharmacies, 14% from independent pharmacies, 15% from mail-order pharmacies, and 28% from other non-retail providers including hospitals and clinics (United States Congressional Budget Office, 2007). In total, consumers purchased approximately 72% of all prescription drugs from retail pharmacies and 28% from non-retail providers.

The location of a patient's prescription drug purchase can have important economic implications. For one, prices and reimbursement policies may differ from one location to the next. Certain pharmacies may be part of a PBM network and may therefore benefit from a higher negotiated reimbursement rate (and thus a lower price). Health care plans might also offer higher reimbursement amounts for mail-order prescription drugs. Therefore, depending on the location of the prescription drug purchase, different economic agents are involved in the transaction and potentially different prices are charged. Another important implication related to the location of a patient's prescription drug purchase involves the role of the physician in a patient's final prescription drug choice. Relative to a non-retail purchase, a retail purchase more likely results from a patient/physician interaction where the patient has had a chance to research treatment options and perhaps view drug advertisements. The location of a patient's prescription drug purchase may therefore provide a signal of various information asymmetries in the underlying decisions made at the retail or non-retail level.

2.4. *Prescription drug sales and profitability*

Total U.S. prescription drug expenditures have increased steadily over the past several years. In 2000, prescription drug expenditures totaled approximately $120 billion, and by 2007, this figure increased over 88% to approximately $227 billion. Figure 1 presents graphically this growth in U.S. prescription drug expenditures from 1995 through 2007.

Regarding profitability, the public generally considers the prescription drug industry as one of the most profitable U.S. industries. Common profitability measures generally support this perception. Several authors have commented, however, that the standard measures of accounting profitability (e.g., the ratio of accounting profits to total sales) may not appropriately assess profitability in the U.S. prescription drug market. For example, a 1993 study found that the U.S. pharmaceutical industry's profitability exceeded the all-industry average by just 2–3 percentage points after appropriately amortizing R&D outlays, rather than simply writing all R&D expenses off in the year they occur (United States Office of Technology Assessment, 1993). These results have been supported in more recent research as well.[12]

---

[12] See Berndt (2002) for more detail.

Figure 1. U.S. prescription drug expenditures (billions of dollars)

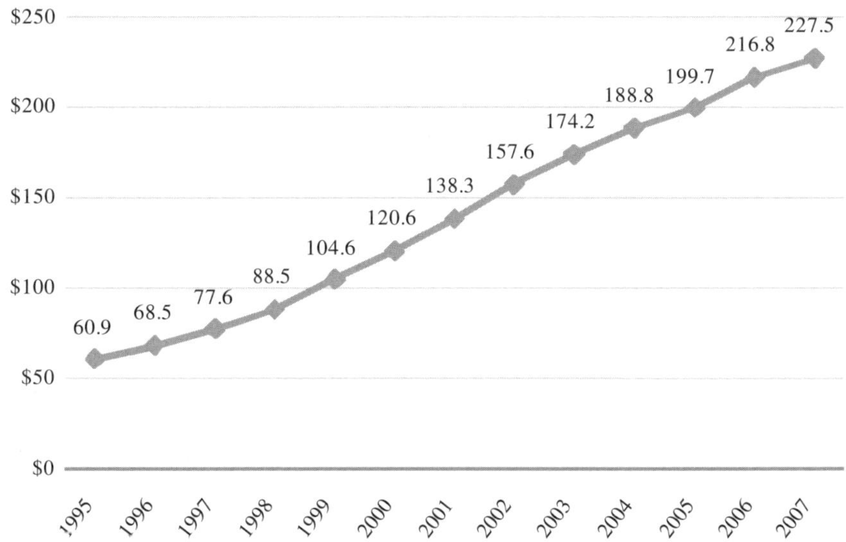

Source: National Health Expenditure Accounts, U.S. Department of Health and Human Services, CMS, 2009.

3. Prescription drug prices

3.1. Defining price

Several authors have analyzed the determinants of price in the pharmaceutical industry;[13] however, many of these studies do not explicitly define the measure of price under consideration. This is an important point because the price paid by the patient, which itself can vary from one patient to the next depending on insurance coverage, the location of the purchase, etc., is just one of a series of transactions in the supply chain. Throughout this supply chain, the concept of price becomes less and less transparent. Essentially, three common measures of prescription drug prices exist between the manufacturer, wholesaler, and pharmacy: (1) average wholesale price ("AWP"), (2) average manufacturer price ("AMP"), and (3) wholesale acquisition price ("WAC").[14]

[13] See, for example, Berndt (2002), Danzon (1997, 2000), and Kolassa (1997), among others.
[14] See Causey (2009) and United States Congressional Budget Office (2007) for more detail.

AWP can be thought of as an approximation of the price paid by retail pharmacies and non-retail providers to wholesalers and is publicly available through several sources, including Red Book, First Databank, and Medispan. AWP is not an actual purchase price but more of a suggested purchase price similar to a vehicle's sticker price. AMP is the average price paid by wholesalers or retail pharmacies to manufacturers. It includes rebates paid by manufacturers to wholesalers and pharmacies but not rebates paid to other negotiating parties such as PBMs and Medicaid. The United States requires manufacturers to report the AMP to the Center for Medicare and Medicaid Studies ("CMS") for reimbursement, but AMPs were not publicly available as of September 2009. Finally, WAC is the list price paid by wholesalers to manufacturers. Again, the WAC is often not what wholesalers actually pay for drugs; however, for brand name drugs, the WAC may approximate prices paid by retail pharmacies to wholesalers.

Accurately measuring prescription drug prices throughout the supply chain is made more difficult by various rebates between the manufacturer, wholesaler, PBM, and other entities such as purchasing organizations. These rebates result from, among other things, three general types of negotiations: (1) pharmacies and other providers negotiate prices with wholesalers or directly with drug manufacturers; (2) PBMs, on behalf of health care plans, or health care plans themselves negotiate prices with manufacturers in the retail prescription drug market; and (3) PBMs and health plans negotiate reimbursement rates directly with retail pharmacies.

A somewhat simplified flow of funds (including rebates) for a brand name prescription drug is as follows. The wholesaler purchases drugs from the manufacturer, where the average price for all such transactions becomes the AMP. The pharmacy then purchases drugs from the wholesaler at some price roughly approximated by the WAC (at least for brand name drugs). For patients without prescription drug coverage, or for a patient purchasing a drug that their insurance does not cover, the pharmacy receives the full payment from the patient. For a covered drug, the pharmacy receives payment from two sources: (1) the patient pays some co-payment directly to the pharmacy; and (2) the health plan, using funds collected from patient premiums and employers, pays the pharmacy, usually indirectly through a PBM. The PBM then transfers a portion of these payments to the pharmacy. Within this flow of payments, the drug manufacturer sends rebates to the PBMs who then pass through some portion of these rebates to the health plan.

Prescription drug coverage through Medicaid provides another source of rebates. By law, drug manufacturers are required to enter into rebate agreements to distribute rebates to state Medicaid agencies in order to be covered under the Medicaid program. These rebate agreements also require that drug manufacturers submit AMPs to the CMS. The amount of the rebate differs by drug but is generally higher for brand name drugs than for generic drugs.

In many ways, this complicated pricing scheme is the result of general attempts to regulate or otherwise control costs in the prescription drug market while still maintaining some sort of free market mechanism. There are essentially two economic issues that complicate prices in the prescription drug market: (1) how prices are actually determined and (2) how prices are reported.

First, prices are largely determined by an outside agent not directly involved in the purchase decision. For example, insurance coverage introduces a clear moral hazard problem in the prescription drug market, whereby patients and physicians are essentially distanced from the full costs of their decisions and therefore more likely to overconsume or otherwise make inefficient prescription drug decisions. This introduces a role for some outside agent (e.g., the PBM) to help curb these moral hazard effects. But rather than rigidly enforcing strict prescription drug choices and options, PBMs have adopted more subtle mechanisms aimed to control costs, adjust consumption decisions, and somewhat constrain physician and patient choice sets. These processes help adjust final prescription and purchasing decisions while still maintaining some form of free market mechanism. However, these processes also shift pricing considerations largely from the patient and physician to the PBM, which is not directly involved in the purchase decision. The resulting negotiated prices (i.e., resulting from formulary considerations, pharmacy networks, etc.) therefore may not fully represent true patient and physician preferences.

Second, because prices can differ at the patient level, prescription drug manufacturers can only report either *ex ante* price estimates, such as the AWP, or *ex post* aggregate prices, such as the AMP.[15] Pharmacies and drug manufacturers therefore have little incentive to publish prices since any reported price may not accurately depict the actual price paid by a given patient. This disincentive to accurately report individual prices implies that there will be little transparency regarding prices in the prescription drug market, where reported prices serve only as an approximation to an individual purchase price.

3.2. Trends in prescription drug prices

One measure of price devoid of many of the issues discussed above is simply the average sales price calculated as total prescription drug sales over the number of prescriptions. Using this measure, prescription drug prices have increased steadily in recent years. The National Association of

---

[15] Pharmacies can and do publish certain prices, but these prices generally represent the price paid by an uninsured patient with no discounts and therefore may be much higher than the actual price charged to a majority of patients.

Table 3. ***Average retail prescription drug prices for brand name and generic drugs (prices per prescription)***

	1995	2000	2005	2006	2007
Brand name drugs	$40.22	$65.29	$97.65	$107.48	$119.51
Generic drugs	14.84	19.33	29.21	31.39	34.34
All prescriptions	30.01	45.79	63.87	66.97	69.91

Source: NACDS Foundation Chain Industry Profile, 2007.

Chain Drug Stores ("NACDS") estimates that average retail prescription drug prices increased from $45.79 to $69.91 in 2000 and 2007, respectively – an increase of 53% (National Association of Chain Drug Stores, 2007).

Price trends also differ sizably between brand name and generic drugs. From the NACDS, the average retail price for brand name prescription drugs in 2000 was $65.29 per prescription, nearly $50 higher than the average retail price of generic drugs at $19.33 per prescription in the same year. By 2007, this premium increased to approximately $85, with brand name retail prices of $119.51 per prescription and generic retail prescription drug prices of $34.34 per prescription (National Association of Chain Drug Stores, 2007). Table 3 summarizes brand name and generic prescription drug prices for 1995, 2000, 2005, 2006, and 2007.

Prices also differ among groups of consumers, due in part to heterogeneities across consumers' health care plans (or, more specifically, heterogeneous negotiating power across PBMs and health care plans). For example, Frank (2001) reports that the lowest prescription drug prices are negotiated by the Department of Veteran Affairs and the Department of Defense, followed by hospitals and clinics. Uninsured patients (i.e., cash patients) purchasing from a retail pharmacy generally pay the highest prices, and insured patients pay somewhere in between.

There are some clear economic justifications for these types of differentiated pricing schemes. For example, PBMs derive negotiating power partly from contracting with various health care plans, which serves as an indication of the base of patients available to the PBM's network of pharmacies and to a prescription drug manufacturer. Manufacturers and pharmacies are then willing to accept a slightly lower price in exchange for a higher base of patients. Health plans also have an incentive to contract with the PBM because the PBM can impose a variety of mechanisms intended to adjust patient and physician incentives away from more costly treatments, thereby lowering the expected cost of insuring a given patient. The remaining uninsured patients are left in a higher-priced, largely uncompetitive residual market (uncompetitive due to incomplete information, market size, and other factors).

Recently, price differentials in the United States and the rest of the world have received more attention in the literature and media, with many authors citing higher U.S. prices relative to the rest of the world to illustrate a need for more intense price controls in the United States. Using 2008 data, Canada's Patented Medicine Prices Review Board ("PMPRB") estimates U.S. prices for brand name drugs to be the highest among eight countries considered and 63% higher than brand name drug prices in Canada (Patented Medicine Prices Review Board, 2008). Previously, a 2004 study by the U.S. Department of Commerce also found that, among best-selling U.S. brand name prescription drugs, U.S. prices were at least 18% higher and as much as 67% higher than prices in other OECD countries (United States Department of Commerce, 2004).

Although brand name prescription drug prices are generally higher in the United States, Danzon (1997) and Berndt (2002) note that generic drugs in the United States are generally lower priced relative to the rest of the world. Moreover, comparisons in brand name prescription drug prices are somewhat unclear due in part to molecular heterogeneity across countries, even for similar drugs. For example, Danzon and Chao (2000) find that in only 40% of bilateral country comparisons did the same molecule actually exist in both countries. Other difficulties in cross-country brand name drug price comparisons stem from understanding exactly which prices are compared (e.g., list prices, prices paid by patients, prices paid by pharmacies, etc.) and which patient groups are being considered. When correcting for these and other methodological problems, Danzon (2000) argues that differences in U.S. prescription drug prices compared to other industrialized nations are smaller than what are often reported in the literature.

3.3. Determinants of price

As first mentioned in the introduction, the prescription drug market involves several economic agents, each with its own interests and each playing an important role in determining the final prices paid at the pharmacy. In this section, I discuss just a few of these determinants – including patents, selected regulatory policies, product differentiation, and price controls. Next, in Section 4, I discuss in more detail some specific consumer-oriented aspects of the prescription drug market that may also have important effects on price, such as the extent of insurance coverage and the interaction between patients and physicians.

3.3.1. Patents

By definition, a generic drug does not have patent protection, whereas a brand name drug does have patent protection. Since generic drugs are often cheaper than brand name drugs, patents play a large role in the pharmaceutical industry, particularly as consumer expenditures on prescription drugs (and health care in general) escalate. When developing a new compound, pharmaceutical companies usually apply for patent protection after the discovery phase but before human trials. If issued, the patent generally lasts 20 years, which leaves approximately 11–14 years of patent protection after receiving FDA approval. During this time period, the producer of the patented drug maintains a degree of monopoly pricing power throughout the life of the patent, as well as through the extension period should such an extension be granted. However, most drugs are subject to some degree of substitutability with other drugs in the same therapeutic class, thereby prohibiting complete monopoly pricing power in the standard economic definition.

Several authors have studied the effect of patents on pharmaceutical drug prices.[16] As illustrated in Table 3, brand name prescription drugs carry a premium over generic drugs, and this, in itself, evidences the impact of patents on prescription drug prices. By some estimates, patent protection or exclusivity increases the drug's price by as much as 18% (Kolassa, 1997).

As discussed above, prescription drug prices have increased over the past several years. However, price increases have been somewhat offset by an increasing share of generic drug sales relative to brand name drugs. In 2000, generic drugs accounted for approximately 42% of all retail prescription drug sales, with brand name drugs accounting for the remaining 58%. By 2007, these figures switched, with generic drugs accounting for 58% of total retail sales and brand name drugs accounting for 42% (National Association of Chain Drug Stores, 2007). This increase in generic drugs relative to brand name drugs has resulted from a variety of factors, including regulatory policies such as the Hatch-Waxman Act of 1984 and various drug-product substitution laws enacted at the state level, as well as a stronger push by health care plans and PBMs to use generic drugs when possible.

The Hatch-Waxman Act, or formally the Drug Price Competition and Patent Term Restoration Act, essentially did two things:[17] (1) pharmaceutical firms could now effectively extend the term of patent protection for a short period after the patent expired and (2) generic drugs could enter the market more easily once a brand name drug's patent protection ended. The first condition was designed to compensate for a drug patent's lost time during the regulatory process by allowing an additional exclusivity period of up to five years for new molecule entities ("NMEs"). The second condition shortened the regulatory process for generic drugs, requiring an

---

[16] See, for example, Grabowski and Vernon (1986), Grabowski and Vernon (1992), Kolassa (1997), and Giaccotto *et al.* (2003).

[17] Biologic drugs are not explicitly covered under the Hatch-Waxman Act; however, an intuitively similar process (the Biosimilars Pathway) was recently signed into law on March 23, 2010 that applies explicitly to Biologic drugs. See Simmons (2010) for more detail.

abbreviated new drug application ("ANDA") in lieu of a full IND for generic drugs.[18]

The second condition has played a particularly important role for generic drugs in the pharmaceutical industry. Generic drugs wishing to enter the market, once the patent has expired and exclusivity period ended for the original drug, now need only to show bioequivalence. In other words, a generic drug must show that it is essentially the same compound as the original, patented compound. Rather than going through various trials, illustrating safety and efficacy, generic drugs can now enter the market relatively quickly based on purely lab-based test results. In fact, the Hatch-Waxman Act explicitly mandated that the FDA not require any additional studies for ANDAs beyond bioequivalence.

Drug-product substitution laws have also increased the use of generic drugs. The term "drug-product substitution law" pertains to various laws passed at the state level regarding the pharmacist's ability to dispense generic drugs even when the prescription calls for a brand name drug, although physicians can still restrict the pharmacist from making any substitutions by indicating, for example, "dispense as written." All states currently have some form of substitution laws in place. At a minimum, the replacement drug must be therapeutically equivalent to the drug originally prescribed, but there may be additional state-specific requirements. For example, Oklahoma requires the pharmacist to have physician or patient approval before making any substitutions. Some states also maintain lists of drugs that cannot be substituted.

Finally, health care plans and PBMs also encourage generic drug use when possible. Particularly, as prescription drug expenditures increase, the pressure that health care plans and PBMs exude on patients and physicians to utilize and prescribe generic drugs plays an important role on the extent of generic drugs used in the pharmaceutical market. As discussed in more detail in Section 4.5.1, methods by which health care plans and PBMs encourage generic drug use include reimbursement restrictions, formulary restrictions, additional cost-sharing provisions, and other services offered by PBMs such as drug utilization review and disease management.

3.3.2. Product differentiation

In the pharmaceutical industry, product differentiation generally describes a drug that offers some benefit not offered by any other currently available drugs. However, there are degrees of product differentiation. Naturally, a drug introducing a completely new therapeutic class of treatment or a drug

---

[18] See Mossinghoff (1999) for more detail.

with groundbreaking therapeutic benefits would most likely be sufficiently differentiated, but differentiation might also result from a variety of other drug attributes such as dosage, frequency, or mode of treatment (e.g., a self-administered shot, IV transfusion, or simply an oral tablet).

A sufficiently differentiated drug has several advantages in the prescription drug market. First, for patients with preferences in line with this drug's differentiated attributes, demand will be relatively inelastic. Patients seeking the therapeutic benefit embodied in a particular drug may therefore be far less price sensitive, allowing for higher prices charged by individual prescription drug manufacturers. Lu and Comanor (1998), for example, estimate that drugs with sufficient therapeutic benefit as determined by the FDA were approximately 3.2 times more expensive than alternative drugs.

Differentiated products may also have a first-mover advantage, a common occurrence in many differentiated product markets.[19] Bond and Lean (1977), and more recently Berndt *et al.* (1997), both find evidence of a strong first-mover advantage in different prescription drug markets, provided the drug in question is sufficiently effective relative to previous treatments for similar diseases (e.g., there is sufficient product differentiation).

For prescription drugs, there are at least two sources of first-mover advantage, one derived from the consumer and one from the physician. The more traditional, consumer-driven first-mover advantage arises from an initial quality impression imposed by the first successful drug in a given therapeutic class. This source of first-mover advantage has been studied in a variety of industries, including yogurt (Ackerberg, 2003) and detergent (Erdem and Keane, 1996), among others. This initial quality impression may also be influenced by various DTC marketing strategies. By some estimates, when patients request specific prescriptions, physicians follow their patients' suggestions as much as 75% of the time (Huang, 2000). As such, the patient's perception of prescription drugs may play an important role in any first-mover advantage.

Coscelli and Shum (2004) provide evidence that a first-mover advantage also derives from initial physician's perceptions of a drug and may persist well after the introduction of other, potentially competing therapies. They estimate a learning model and find evidence that physicians may be reluctant to switch therapies even as alternative (and relatively comparable) treatments become available. This type of behavior introduces a variety of informational considerations – for example, to what extent do physicians even know about alternative drugs in the market, and to what

---

[19] See Urban *et al.* (1986) for a survey of empirical evidence of first-mover advantage in various markets. We use the term first-mover generally to represent any novel therapy, not necessarily the first treatment option for a given disease.

extent do they attempt to learn about new drugs once they find a treatment that they consider effective? Coscelli and Shum's results essentially imply that physicians are subject to at least some amount of incomplete information and that obtaining new information regarding new drugs is at least somewhat costly. The extent of incomplete information and the level of physician's search or switching costs have not been thoroughly addressed in the literature.

3.3.3. Regulation and price controls

Government regulation in the prescription drug industry can refer to a variety of possible controls, including price and profit controls. Sood *et al.* (2008) report that 16 of 19 countries sampled in their analysis had imposed direct price controls by 2004. In addition, five countries had imposed total budget ceilings on prescription drug manufacturers, while only a few countries had imposed profit controls. The authors find that these types of controls, especially direct price controls, can statistically significantly reduce pharmaceutical firms' revenues.

The U.S. prescription drug market remains relatively unregulated compared to other developed nations. Most forms of price controls are essentially cost controls imposed by health plans and PBMs, which indirectly also control prices, but are generally not imposed by the government (except for government-sponsored insurance). I discuss these controls in more detail in Section 4.3.

4. Consumer behavior in the pharmaceutical industry

As the previous supply chain discussion illustrates, there is a substantial amount of "interference" between prescription drug manufacturers and consumers. One initial complication is that both physicians and patients not only have independent effects on the market, but the interaction of the two also has important effects on the structure of the demand curve. Insurance and various cost controls (e.g., formularies), as well as purchasing organizations and other middlemen that deliver drugs from manufacturers to pharmacies and hospitals, are additional sources of this interference.

In addition to these complications, consumers must compile and sift through an abundance of information in order to make informed decisions regarding the type of insurance coverage they need and the specific prescription drug best for them, although patients have less control in the latter area. In the face of strict budget constraints, patients may also make trade-offs between out-of-pocket drug expenditures and compliance with prescription drug treatment.

A complete study of the above issues and their interactions is beyond the scope of this chapter. In this section, I introduce some of these important issues and complications as they relate to consumer behavior and provide a brief introduction into some of the economic research in these areas. I discuss first the trends in prescription drug consumption. I then discuss the role of the physician and patient interaction. Finally, I discuss the role of insurance and information, respectively, and various other recent considerations regarding consumers in the pharmaceutical market.

4.1. Prescription drug utilization

Despite the growing concern over increasing prescription drug prices and expenditures, relatively few authors have formally studied the utilization of prescription drugs from a patient's perspective. Since 1980, prescription drug expenditures have increased as a percentage of total health care expenditures from just over 5% to more than 10%, and as discussed above, total prescription drug expenditures now well exceed $250 billion; however, as Berndt (2002) explains, these substantial increases in prescription drug expenditures are more due to increased utilization than increases in prescription drug prices.

No doubt part of this increase in utilization is due to an aging population. From the Current Population Survey ("CPS"), there were just over 56 million people in the United States aged 55 or older in 2000. By 2008, there were 70 million people aged 55 or older – an increase of over 25%. During this same 2000–2008 time frame, the number of people aged 54 or younger increased just 5% from 218 million in 2000 to 229 million in 2008.

An aging population has a direct effect on prescription drug utilization simply because patients aged 55 or older generally consume more prescription drugs. Moxley *et al.* (2003) determined that 88% of seniors used prescription drugs in 1996, the majority of which took three or more different drugs. According to the National Health Expenditure Data collected by the CMS, people aged 55 or older accounted for approximately 51% of total U.S. prescription drug expenditures in 2004.

The physical location of a consumer's prescription drug purchase has also shifted in the past several years. Patients have purchased and still purchase the bulk of their prescription drugs from retail pharmacies; however, a growing trend in the prescription drug industry has been to import prescription drugs (often from Canada) straight to the consumer's door. In 2003, patients in the United States purchased approximately $700 million worth of (unapproved) prescription drugs from Canada (United States Department of Health and Human Services, 2004). Although drug importation of non-FDA-approved drugs or drugs manufactured in non-FDA-approved plants is illegal as of the writing of this chapter, the FDA's Personal Importation Policy allows a large degree of leeway for imported drugs intended for individual patient use, so long as these drugs do not pose any substantial safety risks (Feder, 2004).

4.2. Demand elasticity

Several authors have estimated the overall price elasticity of demand for prescription drugs. Using co-payment amounts and prescription drug usage reported in Harris *et al.* (1990), Ringel *et al.* (2005) estimated own price elasticity for prescription drugs to be between −0.05 and −0.08. Other estimates in the literature range from −0.10 (Smith, 1993) to −0.33 (O'Brien, 1989). There are several reasons for this inelasticity. First, as mentioned in the introduction, patients perceive prescription drugs as "negative goods." The decision to purchase a prescription drug is therefore driven largely by necessity due to some preexisting condition.

Second, the percentage of out-of-pocket drug expenditures has decreased over the past several years, as discussed in more detail in Section 4.5. This implies that patients have become more reliant on insurance coverage in making their prescription drug payments. A patient with insurance coverage is generally less price elastic than a patient without insurance coverage in part because the effect of a change in price is offset by the extent of their coverage. For example, Newhouse and the Insurance Experiment Group (1993) estimated per person prescription drug expenditures approximately two times higher for patients with full coverage relative to patients with a 95% coinsurance requirement. This intuition applies both to the pharmaceutical industry and to the medical services industry in general.[20]

Although empirical studies consistently find that the overall demand for prescription drugs is inelastic, the degree of inelasticity varies largely across drugs and patients.[21] First, elasticity for a given drug differs depending on the number of appropriate substitutes available. For example, a brand name drug will generally be more inelastic than a generic drug (all else equal) simply because the generic drug is subject to more competition, and hence more substitutes. The degree of competition for a given drug also depends on the drug's therapeutic class and the treatment indicated for that drug. Drugs prescribed for less painful symptoms and diseases may have a higher price elasticity of demand than that of drugs used for treatment of less painful diseases.

Various patient characteristics can also influence a given patient's elasticity for prescription drugs. For example, elderly patients are more likely to be actively taking multiple prescription drugs and other treatments. At some point, their total cost of treatment may become prohibitively high, so that even small price increases can deter the use

[20] As discussed above, increased advertising expenditures might also explain decreases in price elasticity (Rizzo, 1999).

[21] See Kolassa (1997) for more detail.

of a given drug (and alter the use of all relevant drugs for a given patient).[22]

Patients' switching costs also influence elasticity for prescription drugs. In this case, switching costs represent expenses incurred by patients in switching from one drug to another, such as the time and energy spent learning a new drug's side effects, dosing schedule, and differences in administration (e.g., tablet vs. an at-home shot). Switching costs can vary both by drug and by patient, but in either case, higher switching costs intuitively yield more inelastic demand for a given patient or a given drug, although the size and effect of patients' switching costs on demand for prescription drugs have not been addressed in the literature.

4.3. Physicians

One of the more interesting aspects of the health care market, in general, is that the consumers are not solely responsible for their consumption decision. For prescription drugs, consumers rely on physicians in determining either: (1) the specific drug they will use or (2) the therapeutic class of drugs to be used, where the specific drug used may involve both patient and physician input.

As discussed previously, physicians tend to follow their patients' prescription drug suggestions approximately 75% of the time. Of course, many patients may not have any suggestions, in which case the overall influence patients have on general prescribing behaviors may be relatively low. Nonetheless, this illustrates a clear interaction between patients and physicians, implying that the patient/physician relationship may be less of a principal/agent relationship and more of an even partnership.

The interaction between physicians and patients also affects the patients' compliance with a given treatment (e.g., by instilling a sense of control and ownership to the patient over the final decision). Compliance plays an interesting role in the prescription drug market, specifically in understanding increases in prescription drug utilization. Kolassa (1997) argues that compliance decreases as total prescription drug expenditures increase. Non-compliance could include reduced dosage frequency or simply failure to use one of possibly many drugs intended to complement some other drug. Either way, non-compliance could yield significant increases in total prescription drug expenditures (and health care in general), as patients may not realize any medical benefit from the drug or "basket" of drugs.

---

[22] Studies such as Safran *et al.* (2002) and Piette *et al.* (2004) find evidence of patients not taking medications or not refilling prescriptions due to cost burdens.

4.4. Consumer information

In the introductory economics world, consumers can obtain any and all information necessary to compare any two or more products. In this way, consumer behavior ensures that prices remain relatively competitive among a similar class of products. However, several attributes of the prescription drug market prohibit this textbook economic scenario, and these deterrents to consumer information may negate the consumer's role in driving prices down.

First, the idea of an individual patient making, independently, a completely informed prescription drug decision seems unlikely, at least for a patient not involved in the medical profession. Not only are the details of a given drug difficult to understand for an average patient, but the details of the patient's illness are also complicated. Patients' educational background and other considerations may further complicate their ability to accurately assess alternative treatments.

Another deterrent to consumer information for prescription drugs is the fact that prescription drugs are partly "experience goods" rather than pure "search goods." This distinction goes back to the seminal search models set forth in Stigler (1961). Nelson (1970), in extending Stigler's works, made more clear the distinction between experience and search goods, defining experience goods as those with at least some characteristics not ascertainable by buyers prior to making their purchase.[23]

With pure search goods, physicians and patients can learn all of the relevant information prior to making a purchase. Sorensen (2000) provides empirical evidence that observed retail prescription drug prices are consistent with the standard consumer search environment, although Sorensen (2001) also finds that search intensity is relatively low. In both papers, Sorensen considers search at the retail pharmacy level, where patients essentially search for the best price for the same drug across different pharmacies. However, patients and particularly physicians may also search over several different drugs (e.g., when deciding which drug to take or which drug to prescribe). This "experience" element of prescription drugs further prohibits a consumer's ability to make fully informed decisions in this market.

Despite the above barriers to information, there are several avenues by which consumers can make more informed prescription drug decisions. One of the more important (albeit required) sources of information for consumers is the physician. Especially, since prescription drugs are partly experience goods, physicians can help improve a patient's *ex ante*

---

[23] See also, Laband (1991) for a theoretical discussion regarding the differences between search and experience goods.

understanding of the costs and benefits of a given drug, without having to physically use the drug. If consumers engage in costly search when making their prescription drug decisions, the cost of a physician's services may also be considered as part of a consumer's search cost.

Time and peer interaction can also improve a patient's *ex ante* information structure. Ching (2008), for example, finds evidence that consumer learning (which occurs both over time and through a patient's interaction with physicians) may help explain the relatively slow diffusion of generic drugs after patent expiration. Berndt *et al.* (2003) find evidence of consumption externalities in the antiulcer prescription drug market, whereby one patient's use of a drug influences another patient's use and finds that these externalities may influence both consumers' valuations of a given drug and the rate at which a given drug is accepted in the market.

4.5. Insurance coverage

Insurance coverage has important effects on consumer behavior, in part because coverage separates prices paid and the risk borne by consumers and the true cost and risk of services rendered. This separation leads to, among other things, a moral hazard problem whereby patients may utilize more health care services and hence require more insurance expenditures than would be preferred from the insurer's perspective.

Insurance coverage is particularly important in the prescription drug market as the share of prescription drug expenditures has shifted dramatically from consumer out-of-pocket expenditures to private and government-sponsored expenditures. For example, in 1980, roughly 70% of all prescription drug expenditures were out of pocket. By 2007, this figure reduced to approximately 21%. During this same time period, private insurance and Medicare/Medicaid insurance expenditures as a percent of total prescription drug expenditures increased from 26% to 73%.[24]

The extent of medical and prescription drug coverage a patient receives depends largely on the form of insurance obtained. Essentially, two forms of insurance exist – private third-party insurance (including employer-provided coverage) and government-sponsored insurance. The two largest government-sponsored insurance options are Medicaid and Medicare.

Medicaid began in 1965 and is a state-administered program financed by state and federal funds. It is available only for low-income individuals and

---

[24] Despite this increase in allocation of prescription drug expenditures, overall insurance coverage rates (e.g., the percentage of the U.S. population with heath care) have slightly decreased over the past several years for persons aged 18–64 years and have slightly increased for persons aged 65 or older. See Cohen *et al.* (2009) for more detail regarding general health insurance trends.

families in every state in the United States and the District of Columbia, although each state sets its own specific guidelines and eligibility requirements. Medicaid coverage is free for all eligible beneficiaries and generally includes prescription drug coverage. According to the Office of the Inspector General 2009 report on pharmaceutical reimbursement ("the OIG report"), Medicaid prescription drug expenditures totaled approximately $21 billion in 2006 (United States Office of the Inspector General, 2009).

Medicare also began in 1965 as a government-sponsored health insurance program for people aged 65 or more.[25] Until 1982, the only coverage offered under Medicare was a basic fee-for-service ("FFS"). The FFS option (also termed Original Medicare) is still available in today's current Medicare structure and consists of two parts. All beneficiaries are automatically enrolled in Part A, which covers hospital stays and skilled nursing facility care. Most beneficiaries also enroll in Part B, which is a voluntary supplemental program (often requiring an additional premium) that covers physician services, medical equipment, and most outpatient hospital services. Medicare Parts A and B do not include any formal prescription drug coverage.[26]

The Balanced Budget Act of 1997 ("BBA") set forth formal guidelines for additional supplemental insurance options for Medicare beneficiaries, termed Medicare + Choice ("M + C") plans. These plans supplemented Original Medicare and were provided by private companies who contracted with CMS yearly. The Medicare Modernization Act of 2003 ("MMA") revised the structure of M + C, and essentially replaced the M + C program with the Medicare Advantage program in 2004.

Beginning in 2006, the MMA also provided additional prescription drug coverage (at an additional premium) for all Medicare beneficiaries under Medicare Part D. Therefore, since 2006, Medicare beneficiaries can obtain prescription drug coverage through two avenues: (1) stand-alone prescription drug coverage as part of Medicare Part D or (2) some other form of coverage under Medicare Advantage supplemental insurance options, where Medicare Advantage supplemental insurance options must offer at least the same level of benefits as those offered under Medicare Part D. According to the OIG report, total Part D prescription drug expenditures totaled approximately $49 billion in 2007, with 25 million enrolled beneficiaries as of January 2008.

---

[25] People younger than 65 may also be eligible for Medicare coverage under certain conditions.

[26] To the extent that certain drugs are considered a medical benefit rather than a pharmacy benefit (e.g., drugs administered by a physician), these prescription drugs may still be covered under Medicare Part B.

A consumer's choice of an individual insurance plan is a result of a broad range of medical considerations, heterogeneities in risk aversion, and several other factors. As such, one's choice of coverage can hardly result purely from prescription drug considerations. Nonetheless, once a consumer chooses a particular plan and coverage, this coverage effects consumer behavior in the prescription drug market in several ways, largely through the PBM in which the insurance plan participates.

4.5.1. Pharmacy benefit managers

PBMs are private companies that administer and manage prescription drug benefits for various insurers, including employers, unions, managed care organizations, and other groups. PBMs are responsible for managing an insurer's formulary, administering claims, and negotiating prices between drug manufacturers and the PBM's network of pharmacies. Although PBMs generally do not physically possess any prescription drugs, they are still involved in multiple stages of the supply chain.[27]

An example of how PBMs interact with patients, pharmacies, insurance companies, and drug manufacturers is as follows (not necessarily in chronological order):

1. The PBM draws up a formulary that lists the PBM's preferred drugs in each therapeutic class of drugs. The formulary may also set different co-payment or coinsurance amounts for different drugs.
2. The PBM contracts with their clients (health care plans) to provide various services, such as formulary management, claims administration, formal record-keeping of prescription drug utilization, and disease management.
3. The PBM establishes a network of retail pharmacies by negotiating payments (i.e., reimbursement rates) for prescription drugs purchased by the associated health plans' patients. This effectively ensures some base level of sales for both the drugs covered under the PBM's formulary and the pharmacies that are part of the PBM's network. Many states have laws prohibiting the extent to which PBMs can exclude pharmacies from their network; however, in cases where such restrictions are an option, PBMs may be able to achieve higher cost savings. Wyeth-Ayerst (1999), for example, found that restricted networks obtained on average a lower reimbursement rate relative to broader networks. Pharmacists may be willing to accept this lower

[27] For a more detailed explanation of PBMs and their role in the prescription drug market, see Cook *et al.* (2000) and Atlas (2004), among others.

reimbursement since, as part of the restricted network, they are subject to less competition.

4. The PBM negotiates prices and rebates with the drug manufacturers. Deskin (1998) and others note that these negotiations hinge on the PBM's ability to enforce formulary compliance among its beneficiaries (i.e., the patients covered by a health care plan that has entered into a contract with the PBM).
5. The PBM communicates with its beneficiaries regarding the prescription drug benefits of their plan. The PBM also interacts with beneficiaries in other ways, including operating customer service telephone lines. In a 2000 study of PBMs on behalf of the Kaiser Family Foundation, Cook *et al.* (2000) note that PBMs consider beneficiary education as one of their critical roles.

The most dominant source of a PBM's income is through fees collected from health care plans for the PBM's various services. Other sources of income include manufacturer rebates and additional fees such as those collected from drug manufacturers in exchange for contacting doctors regarding their prescribing practices. Recently, the magnitude of PBMs' rebates has come under question, with some parties alleging that PBMs secretly (and illegally) obtain a portion of the rebates that they are otherwise obligated to pass through to their clients. Lawsuits also claim that PBMs have received kickbacks from drug manufacturers for recommending more expensive drugs.[28]

PBMs have become a dominant and concentrated player in the prescription drug market. For example, Atlas (2004) estimates that just three PBMs manage more than one-third of all retail prescription drug sales. Cook *et al.* (2000) estimate that the top 20 PBMs managed just over 70% of all retail prescription drug sales covered by a private third-party payor. These percentages are most likely higher today since some Medicare beneficiaries' prescription drug plans through Medicare Part D may also be managed by a PBM.

The growing role of PBMs has also generated public and regulatory concern over who actually owns a given PBM. For example, many PBMs actually started as health plans or retail pharmacies. Currently, drug manufacturers and retail pharmacies each own PBMs, and PBMs also own most of the mail-order pharmacies. In 1999, each of the top five retail pharmacies also owned a PBM. These ownership stakes may generate conflicts of interest among PBMs, pharmacies, drug manufacturers, and health care plans. For example, drug manufacturers who also own PBMs

---

[28] See, for example, "Drug manager sued over rebates, prices", *Drug Week*, *NewsRX*, February 6, 2004.

have a natural incentive to place their own drugs on the formulary and discourage use of a competing drug either by outright formulary restriction, additional cost sharing, or some other means.

As discussed above, third-party prescription drug expenditures have increased drastically over the past several years, and this has spurred several methods by which insurance companies attempt to control these rising costs. As a service to its clients, PBMs have therefore initiated several cost-control mechanisms and various other methods to influence a patient's prescription drug utilization and expenditure. These cost-control mechanisms include adjusting reimbursement rates, adopting formularies and tiered reimbursement structures, providing alternative reimbursement rates for mail-order prescription drugs, adopting alternative cost-sharing structures such as increasing co-payments and coinsurance rates, and negotiating rebates from drug manufacturers. I discuss each of these mechanisms in more detail in the following sections.

4.5.1.1. Reimbursement procedures

Third-party payors adopt different and somewhat complicated reimbursement formulas that can have important effects on drug prices and consumer behavior. Below, we discuss generally the reimbursement structure and then discuss specific reimbursement procedures among each of three major third-party payors (private third-party payors, Medicaid, and Medicare).

When purchasing prescription drugs from a neighborhood pharmacy, patients rarely understand or consider (aside from co-payments) how that pharmacy receives reimbursements. All third-party payors essentially reimburse pharmacies based on negotiated prices. The OIG report defines a negotiated price as the point-of-sale price to an individual patient or beneficiary, less any discounts passed through by the wholesaler or PBM, plus dispensing fees. In the end, these negotiated prices are often based on AWP less some percentage, plus dispensing fees, and include two primary components: (1) an ingredient cost, intended to reimburse the actual cost to make a drug and (2) dispensing fees, intended to compensate the pharmacy for any transferring and storing costs.

For most patients with private third-party insurance or Medicare Part D, their prescription drug purchases are managed by a PBM. In exchange for the large volume of sales for which they manage, PBMs can negotiate lower prices for pharmacies (and thus offer lower reimbursement rates) as a form of volume discounts. As discussed above, in cases where PBMs can restrict pharmacy access to its network, additional cost savings may be achieved through even lower reimbursement rates. For example, Cook *et al.* (2000) report ingredient cost reimbursement rates of, on average, AWP less 13% for PBMs without any pharmacy network restrictions. PBMs who can restrict pharmacy access can offer reimbursement rates from 1% to 3% lower than PBMs who cannot restrict access. Interestingly, the authors also report that lower reimbursement rates may increase dispensing errors and lead to poorer customer service on behalf of the PBM's pharmacy.

Prices negotiated by PBMs are generally substantially lower than those negotiated by Medicaid. Moreover, unlike most private third-party payors and Medicare, Medicaid fully reimburses its patients. Due to this increased exposure to drug costs and risk of higher expenditures, Medicaid's reimbursement structure is much more complicated than Medicare and most private third-party insurers. First, there are federal limits on each state's aggregate Medicaid reimbursement expenditures, which according to the OIG report are based on the lower of (1) the estimated total acquisition cost for drugs plus dispensing fees or (2) the provider's usual charge to the public for drugs. Second, Medicaid estimates the actual ingredient cost of a drug based on an estimated acquisition cost. Usually, this estimated acquisition cost derives from AWP less some percentage, but some generic drugs are subject to additional federal or state upper limits.

Both state and federal upper limits essentially set price ceilings on certain generic drugs based on drugs with comparable therapeutic effects. State limits are state specific and therefore vary largely by state, and federal upper limits are currently in a transition period. In the past, these limits were set at 150% of the lowest price for therapeutically equivalent drugs. The Deficit Reduction Act of 2005 ("DRA") adjusted to the federal upper limit calculation to be based on 250% of the lowest AMP for each drug. However, federal court rulings as well as the Medicare Improvements for Patients and Providers Act of 2008 ("MIPPA") have prohibited federal limit calculations based on AMP as well as making AMP data publicly available to each state's Medicaid program. These prohibitions were set to expire on October 1, 2009.

As the above discussion illustrates, negotiated prices (and thus reimbursement amounts) are based largely on AWP. Previous OIG reports have found that AWP is generally much higher than the actual acquisition price of a drug. In 2008, for example, the OIG determined that Medicare Part D reimbursements exceeded a pharmacy's drug acquisition cost by approximately 18%. In 2004 and 2005, the OIG also found that the federal upper limit amounts for Medicaid (which were based on AWP) were as much as five times larger than the average AMP (United States Office of the Inspector General, 2009).

Recently, the reimbursement process and particularly the use of AWP have come under intense scrutiny by consumers and various regulatory agencies. In 2006, for example, the *Wall Street Journal* issued a front-page story regarding AWP and its determinants, describing the still relatively unknown fact that AWP was not determined by actual prices charged by wholesalers. Since then, prescription drug manufacturers' use of AWP has been the subject of several lawsuits. The essential claim, among others, is that prescription drug manufacturers inflate AWP and increase the spread between the actual price paid by the pharmacy and the AWP. Drug manufacturers then push drugs for which this spread is the highest, whereby the drug manufacturer can earn a higher price and the pharmacy can receive higher reimbursements. In 2007, a federal U.S. District Court agreed that certain prescription drug manufacturers had inflated AWP in order to establish markups well above standard industry markups.[29]

Despite the above considerations, Medicare and Medicaid have been reluctant to switch to AMP-based negotiated prices and reimbursements. This is of particular concern for Medicaid, whose reimbursement amounts substantially exceed those of Medicare Part D for generic drugs (United States Office of the Inspector General, 2009).

One concern over the use of AMP to set reimbursements is that AMP is, by nature, a retrospective price. AMP is also an average, which necessarily implies that some pharmacies pay more than AMP. For such pharmacies, any reimbursement at or below AMP would yield a negative profit margin. As prescription drug expenditures continue to increase, the reimbursement process and guidelines will no doubt remain a highly debated topic.

4.5.1.2. Formularies and tiered reimbursements

The use of formularies has become a common cost-control mechanism. Initially, formularies were developed by the Pharmacy and Therapeutics ("P&T") committee as a mechanism for evaluating and controlling the use of pharmaceuticals in the health care system. A P&T Committee has been required for every hospital since 1965 by the Joint Commission on Accreditation of Hospitals ("JCAH"). Formularies were not originally designed as a mechanism to control costs; however, as expenditures have increased, PBMs (on behalf of their clients) now use formularies more as a cost-control mechanism than as a pure drug evaluation mechanism.[30]

Formularies are essentially lists of approved drugs issued by third-party payors and help insurance companies keep costs down by influencing patients toward lower price drugs. PBMs therefore use formularies essentially to adjust patient drug utilization more toward generic drugs. Most studies find that, in this sense, formularies have been successful. PBMs also use formularies to exude downward price pressure on drug manufacturers, refusing to place a drug on its formulary or requiring a high co-payment without some form of rebate and chargeback.[31] However, Hellerstein (1998) illustrates that this latter intention has been somewhat

---

[29] See *In Re: Pharmaceutical Industry Average Wholesale Price Litigation* and Rubenstein and Curtiss (2007) for more detail.

[30] See Rucker and Schiff (1990) and Kolassa (1997) for a more thorough discussion on the history of formularies.

[31] See Berndt (2002) for more detail.

hampered by insurers' inability to sufficiently control physicians' prescribing behavior.

There are essentially two ways that PBMs can use formularies to adjust prescription drug use: (1) adopting a closed formulary that explicitly does not cover certain drugs and (2) adopting a tiered formulary that may cover additional drugs but require larger co-payments. Jang (1988) and Horn *et al.* (1996) find that closed formularies may incentivize patients to use alternative, perhaps less effective, treatments. But still, a large portion of PBMs maintain some form of closed formulary. More recently, PBMs and health care plans have moved toward a tiered formulary structure, by which more drugs are covered but at different rates. A basic two-tier formulary, for example, divides drugs into generic and brand name, requiring lower co-payments for generic drugs than for brand name drugs in the same therapeutic class.

The tiered formulary structure has expanded since the early 1990s. Generic drugs generally remain in the first tier, but PBMs have created additional tiers to further segment co-payments among brand name drugs. For example, three-tier formularies divide brand name drugs into "preferred" and "nonpreferred" brands. More recent four- and five-tier formularies have also emerged, and the price of drugs can vary drastically from one tier to the next. A *Takeeda-Lilly* survey in 2000 found average retail co-payments for first tier generic drugs, second tier preferred brand name drugs, and third tier nonpreferred brand name drugs of \$7.17, \$14.14, and \$27.35, respectively. Across each tier, these average prices represented increases of 17%, 27%, and 56% from average prices in 1998.

Tiered formularies also result in an increased cost burden on patients. Kolassa (1997) notes that strict formularies and increased cost burdens may actually lead to underutilization of drugs, which may increase health care costs overall. I discuss this area in more detail in Section 4.5.2.

4.5.1.3. Mail-order prescription drugs

Takeeda-Lilly (2001) finds that dispensing fees per prescription for mail-order prescription drugs are around half the dispensing fees for retail pharmacies. To take advantage of this more favorable reimbursement environment, PBMs and health care plans have recently offered more generous co-payments for mail-order prescription drug purchases. Mail-order prescription drugs can also be more convenient for the patient and allow patients to purchase in larger quantities, thereby achieving some economies of scale at the patient level.

Although PBMs continue to encourage mail-order prescription drug use, the appropriateness of this strategy from a medical and patient satisfaction perspective is unclear. Studies such as Ghoshal (1997) and Hadzija and Shrewsbury (1999) cite a potential loss of integrity of mail-order drugs, poorer customer service and patient consultation, and delays in receipt of medication, among other potential problems. However,

Johnson *et al.* (1997) find that patients are generally satisfied with services received from mail-order pharmacies.

4.5.1.4. Increased cost sharing, co-payments, and coinsurance

Aside from the potential increase in cost sharing due to tiered and/or closed formularies, PBMs and health care plans can also adjust their coverage schemes so as to explicitly increase patient cost-sharing requirements, thereby reducing the health care plan's prescription drug expenditures. Increasing cost sharing, while providing a short-term reduction to health plan expenditures, may actually increase total prescription drug expenditures. For example, patients will intuitively make more informed decisions when faced with higher cost burdens for prescription drugs and health care in general. However, the RAND health insurance experiment, based off of data from 1974 through 1982, found evidence that increased cost sharing did not influence patients to make more informed decisions than patients with lower cost burdens.[32]

There are essentially two methods of cost sharing employed by most health care plans – co-payments and coinsurance. Co-payments are a set fee paid by the patient for each prescription. For example, patients may pay a flat $5.00 fee for a generic drug, and the health care plan then pays the remaining amount for the prescription. Co-payments have increased for certain drugs over time due largely to the adoption of tiered formularies, which require higher co-payments for nonpreferred brand name drugs relative to co-payments for generic drugs. With coinsurance, patients pay a percentage of the prescription cost rather than a flat dollar fee, which means patients pay more out of pocket for a more expensive drug. In this sense, coinsurance can shift some of the risk of prescription drug use from the health care plan to the patient, thereby reducing the extent of moral hazard.

4.5.1.5. Rebates

Because PBMs can ensure (or at least decrease uncertainty for) a certain level of sales volume, drug manufacturers are willing to dispense rebates to PBMs in exchange for being listed on the PBMs' formularies. Rebates are not unconditional, however, as manufacturers may require visible increases in market share before dispensing any rebates. As mentioned above, Medicaid actually requires that participating drug manufacturers provide rebates.

The extent to which rebates actually decrease prices, however, is relatively unclear. For example, the largest rebates are usually offered for newer, brand name drugs. Kreling (2000) explains that these newer drugs

---

[32] See Newhouse and the Insurance Experiment Group (1993) for more detail.

are usually priced high enough so that, even with the rebate, the drug may be substantially more expensive than an alternative and effective generic substitute. In this sense, rebates may actually increase overall prescription drug expenditures.

4.5.2. Substitutability

Several studies estimate the effect of prescription drug coverage on consumers' utilization of other forms of health care. As discussed above, Safran *et al.* (2002) and Piette *et al.* (2004) each find evidence that patients do not fully comply with their prescription drug treatments (e.g., not filling their prescriptions or skipping doses). Among other things, this type of behavior may have important effects on a patient's general health status, as well as hospitalization rates and nursing home utilization. Heisler *et al.* (2004), for example, find that elderly patients who have reduced prescription drugs due to cost concerns are also more likely to report lower health status and more likely to suffer from various heart problems. Tamblyn *et al.* (2001) also find that elderly patients with increasing prescription drug cost burdens have higher mortality, hospitalization, and nursing home admission rates.

5. *Conclusion*

This chapter presents an overview of the economics of the U.S. pharmaceutical industry. I discussed a standard product life cycle, overall industry statistics regarding sales and patient expenditures, R&D, and marketing, and various regulatory procedures affecting a drug's adoption in the market and the movement from being introduced as a brand name drug to becoming a generic drug. This chapter also introduces some of the underlying price determinants and many of the constraints on consumer information in this market. Throughout this chapter, I have attempted to introduce some of the economic literature relevant to these areas.

The breadth of research on the prescription drug industry is expansive, with entire books covering prescription drug prices, utilization, insurance coverage, and a variety of other issues. As public and government concern rises over prescription drug expenditures, prices, and insurance coverage, the market will no doubt undergo some major policy changes in the coming years. I suspect that much of the proposed policy changes will center around one or more of the following areas: (1) direct price or profit controls on prescription drug manufacturers; (2) more strict regulation of DTC advertising; (3) transparency of the AWP, AMP, and WAC; (4) the role and interaction of PBMs, prescription drug wholesalers, and health care plans; and (5) the specific role of Medicare and Medicaid and the government's growing expenditures in these areas. This chapter will hopefully inspire future research into these areas and the effects of any such policy changes.

References

Ackerberg, D. (2003), "Advertising, learning, and consumer choice in experience good markets: a structural empirical examination", *International Economic Review*, Vol. 44(3), pp. 1007–1040.

Atlas, R. (2004), "The role of PBMs in implementing the Medicare prescription drug benefit", *Health Affairs*, Vol. 23 (Web Exclusive), pp. W4504–W4515.

Azoulay, P. (2002), "Do pharmaceutical sales respond to scientific evidence?", *Journal of Econometrics and Management Strategy*, Vol. 11, pp. 551–594.

Berndt, E. (2002), "Pharmaceuticals in U.S. health care: determinants of quantity and price", *Journal of Economic Perspectives*, Vol. 16(4), pp. 45–66.

Berndt, E., L. Bui, D. Reiley and G. Urban (1995), "Information, marketing and pricing in the U.S. anti-ulcer drug market", *American Economic Review*, Vol. 85(2), pp. 100–105.

Berndt, E., L. Bui, D. Reiley and G. Urban (1997), "The roles of marketing, product quality and price competition in the growth and composition of the U.S. anti-ulcer drug industry", in: T. Bresnahan and R. Gordon, editors, *The Economics of New Goods*, Chicago, IL: University of Chicago Press.

Berndt, E., R. Pindyck and P. Azoulay (2003), "Consumption externalities and diffusion in pharmaceutical markets: anti-ulcer drugs", *The Journal of Industrial Economics*, Vol. 51(2), pp. 243–270.

Bhattacharyya, A. (2005), "Advertising in specialized markets: example from the U.S. pharmaceutical industry", Working Paper no. 610, Boston College.

Bond, R. and D. Lean (1977), "Sales, promotion and product differentiation in two prescription drug markets", Staff Report of the Bureau of Economics of the Federal Trade Commission, Washington, DC.

Bradford, D., A. Kleit, P. Nietert, T. Steyer, T. Mcllwain and S. Ornstein (2006), "How direct-to-consumer television advertising for osteoarthritis drugs affects physicians' prescribing behavior", *Health Affairs*, Vol. 25(5), pp. 1371–1377.

Bradford, D., A. Kleit, P. Neitert and S. Ornstein (2010), "The effect of direct to consumer television advertising on the time of treatment", *Economic Inquiry*, Vol. 48(2), pp. 306–322.

Brekke, K. and M. Kuhn (2005), "Direct-to-consumer advertising in pharmaceutical markets", CESifo Working Paper No. 1493.

Calfee, J. (2003), "What do we know about direct-to-consumer advertising of prescription drugs?", *Health Affairs* (Web Exclusive), pp. W3116–W3119.

Carpenter, D. (2004), "The political economy of FDA drug review: processing, politics, and lessons for policy", *Health Affairs*, Vol. 23(1), pp. 52–63.

Causey, L. (2009), "Nuts and bolts of pharmacy reimbursement: why it should matter to you", *Health Law Perspectives* (http://www.law.uh.edu/healthlaw/perspectives/homepage.asp). Retrieved on April 2010.

Ching, A. (2008), "Consumer learning and heterogeneity: dynamics of demand for prescription drugs after patent expiration", Munich Personal RePEc Archive, Working Paper No. 7265.

Cohen, R., D. Makuc, A. Bernstein, L. Bilheimer and E. Powell-Griner (2009), "Health insurance coverage trends, 1959–2007: estimates from the national health interview survey", National Health Statistics Reports, No. 17.

Cook, A., T. Kornfield and M. Gold (2000), "The role of PBMs in managing drug costs: implications for a Medicare drug benefit", The Kaiser Family Foundation.

Coscelli, A. and M. Shum (2004), "An empirical model of learning and patient spillovers in new drug entry", *Journal of Econometrics*, Vol. 122, pp. 213–246.

Danzon, P. (1997), "Price discrimination for pharmaceuticals: welfare effects in the U.S. and the E.U.", *International Journal of the Economics of Business*, Vol. 4(3), pp. 302–321.

Danzon, P. (2000), "Making sense of drug prices", *Regulation*, Vol. 23(1), pp. 56–63.

Danzon, P. and L. Chao (2000), "Cross-national price differences for pharmaceuticals: how large, and why?", *Journal of Health Economics*, Vol. 19(2), pp. 159–196.

Deskin, M. (1998), *The Managed Pharmacy Benefit Market*, Scottsdale, AZ: Pharmacy Benefit Management Institute, Inc.

Donahue, J., M. Cevasco and M. Rosenthal (2007), "A decade of direct-to-consumer advertising of prescription drugs", *New England Journal of Medicine*, pp. 673–681.

"Drug manager sued over rebates, prices", *Drug Week*, *NewsRX*, February 6, 2004.

Erdem, T. and M. Keane (1996), "Decision-making under uncertainty: capturing dynamic brand choice processes in turbulent consumer goods markets", *Marketing Science*, Vol. 15, pp. 1–20.

Feder, J. (2004), "Prescription drug importation and internet sales: a legal overview", Congressional Research Service Report for Congress.

Frank, R. (2001), "Prescription drug prices: why do some pay more than others do?", *Health Affairs*, Vol. 20(2), pp. 115–128.

Ghoshal, S. (1997), "Mail-order pharmacy: good or evil?", *Canadian Pharmaceutical Journal*, Vol. 129, pp. 11–15.

Giaccotto, C., R. Santerre and J. Vernon (2003), *Explaining Pharmaceutical R&D Growth Rates at the Industry Level: New Perspectives and Insights*, Washington, DC: Brookings Joint Center for Regulatory Studies.

Gonul, F., F. Carter, E. Petrova and K. Srinivansan (2001), "Promotion of prescription drugs and its impact on physicians' choice behavior", *Journal of Marketing*, Vol. 65, pp. 79–90.

Grabowski, H. and J. Vernon (1986), "Longer patents for lower imitation barriers: the 1984 Drug Act", *American Economic Review*, Vol. 76(2), pp. 195–198.

Grabowski, H. and J. Vernon (1992), "Brand loyalty, entry, and price competition in pharmaceuticals after the 1984 Act", *Journal of Law and Economics*, Vol. 35(2), pp. 331–350.

Grossman, G. and C. Shapiro (1984), "Informative advertising with differentiated products", *Review of Economic Studies*, Vol. 51, pp. 529–546.

Hadzija, B. and R. Shrewsbury (1999), "Stability of four commercial products delivered by mail order", *International Journal of Pharmaceutical Compounding*, Vol. 3, pp. 59–63.

Harris, B., A. Stergachis and L. Ried (1990), "The effect of drug copayments on utilization and cost of pharmaceuticals in a health maintenance organization", *Medical Care*, Vol. 28(10), pp. 907–917.

Heisler, M., K. Langa, E. Eby, A. Fendrick, M. Kabeto and J. Piette (2004), "The health effects of restricting prescription medication because of cost", *Medical Care*, Vol. 42, pp. 626–634.

Hellerstein, J. (1998), "The importance of the physician in the generic versus trade-name prescription decision", *RAND Journal of Economics*, Vol. 28(3), pp. 108–136.

Hertzendorf, M. (1993), "I'm not a high-quality firm – but I play one on TV", *RAND Journal of Economics*, Vol. 24, pp. 236–247.

Horn, S., D. Sharkey, D. Tracy, C. Horn, B. James and F. Goodwin (1996), "Intended and unintended consequences of HMO cost-containment strategies: results from the managed care outcomes project", *American Journal of Managed Care*, Vol. 2, pp. 253–264.

Huang, A. (2000), "The rise of direct-to-consumer advertising of prescription drugs in the United States", *Journal of the American Medical Association*, Vol. 284, p. 2240.

Jang, R. (1988), "Medicaid formularies: a critical review of the literature", *Journal of Pharmaceutical Marketing and Management*, Vol. 2, pp. 39–61.

Johnson, J., S. Coons, R. Hays, D. Sabers, P. Langley and P. Jones (1997), "Comparison of satisfaction with mail versus traditional pharmacy services", *Journal of Managed Care Pharmacy*, Vol. 3, pp. 327–337.

Keith, A. (1995), "Regulating information about aspirin and the prevention of heart attack", *American Economic Review*, Vol. 85(2), pp. 96–99.

King, C. (2000), *Marketing, Product Differentiation, and Competition in the Market for Anti-Ulcer drugs*, Mimeo: Harvard University.

Kolassa, E. (1997), *Elements of Pharmaceutical Pricing*, Birmingham, NY: Pharmaceutical Products Press.

Kreling, D. (2000), "Cost control for prescription drug programs: Pharmacy Benefit Manager (PBM) efforts, effects, and implications", Department of Health and Human Services' Conference on Pharmaceutical Pricing Practices. Washington, DC.

Laband, D. (1991), "An objective measure of search versus experience goods", *Economic Inquiry*, Vol. 29, pp. 497–509.

Lu, J. and W. Comanor (1998), "Strategic pricing of new pharmaceuticals", *Review of Economics and Statistics*, Vol. 80(1), pp. 108–118.

Masson, A. and P. Rubin (1985), "Matching prescription drugs and consumers: the benefits of direct advertising", *New England Journal of Medicine*, Vol. 313(8), pp. 513–515.

McFadden, D. (2006), "Free markets and fettered consumers", *American Economic Review*, Vol. 96(1), pp. 3–29.

Mossinghoff, G. (1999), "Overview of the Hatch-Waxman Act and its impact on the drug development process", *Food Drug and Law Journal*, Vol. 54(2), pp. 187–194.

Moxley, E., J. O'Connor, K. Noveielli, S. Teutsch and D. Nash (2003), "Prescription drug use in the elderly: a descriptive analysis", *Health Care Financing Review*, Vol. 24, pp. 127–141.

NACDS Foundation Chain Pharmacy Industry Profile (2007), National Association of Chain Drug Stores: Alexandria, VA.

Nelson, P. (1970), "Information and consumer behavior", *Journal of Political Economy*, Vol. 83, pp. 729–754.

Newhouse, J. and The Insurance Experiment Group (1993), "New estimates of price and income elasticities", in: R. Rosett, editor, *The Role of Health Insurance in the Health Services Sector*, New York: National Bureau of Economic Research.

O'Brien, B. (1989), "The effect of patient charges on the utilization of prescription medicines", *Journal of Health Economics*, Vol. 8(1), pp. 109–132.

Patented Medicine Prices Review Board (2008), Annual report, Canada.

PhRMA (2008), *Pharmaceutical Industry Profile*, Washington, DC: Pharmaceutical Research and Manufacturers of America.

PhRMA (2009), *Pharmaceutical Industry Profile*, Washington, DC: Pharmaceutical Research and Manufacturers of America.

Piette, J., M. Heisler and T. Wagner (2004), "Cost-related medication underuse: do patients with chronic illnesses tell their doctors?", *Archives of Internal Medicine*, Vol. 164, pp. 1749–1755.

Ringel, J., S. Hosek, B. Vollaard and S. Mahnovski (2005), "The elasticity of demand for health care: a review of the literature and its application to the military health system", National Defense Research Institute, RAND Health.

Rizzo, J. (1999), "Advertising and competition in the ethical pharmaceutical industry: the case of anti-hypersensitive drugs", *Journal of Law and Economics*, Vol. 42, pp. 89–116.

Rosenthal, M., E. Berndt, J. Donohue, A. Epstein and R. Frank (2003), "Demand effects of recent changes in prescription drug promotion", in: M. Cutler and A. Garber, editors, *Frontiers in Health Policy Research*, Vol. 6, Cambridge, MA: MIT Press.

Rubenstein, E. and F. Curtiss (2007), "How much 'spread' in AWP pricing is unlawful?", *Journal of Managed Care Pharmacy*, Vol. 13(6), pp. 515–516.

Rucker, T. and G. Schiff (1990), "Drug formularies: myths-in-formation", *Medical Care*, Vol. 28, pp. 928–942.

Safran, D., P. Neuman, C. Schoen, J. Montgomery, W. Li, I. Wilson, M. Kitchman, A. Bowen and W. Rogers (2002), "Prescription drug coverage and seniors: how well are states closing the gap?", *Health Affairs* (Web Exclusive), pp. W253–W268.

Scherer, F.M. (2001), "The link between gross profitability and pharmaceutical R&D spending", *Health Affairs*, Vol. 20(5), pp. 216–220.

Schmalensee, R. (1986), "Advertising and market structure", in: J. Stiglitz and F. Mathewson, editors, *New Developments in the Analysis of Market Structure*, Cambridge, MA: MIT Press.

Simmons, W. (2010), "Biosimilars pathway: a far cry from Hatch-Waxman", *IP Law*, Vol. 360.

Smith, D. (1993), "The effects of copayments and generic substitution on the use and costs of prescription drugs", *Inquiry*, Vol. 30, pp. 189–198.

Sood, N., H. de Vries, I. Gutierrez, D. Lakdawalla and D. Goldman (2008), "The effect of regulation on pharmaceutical revenues: experience in nineteen countries", *Health Affairs*, (Web Exclusive), pp. W125–W137.

Sorensen, A. (2000), "Equilibrium price dispersion in retail markets for prescription drugs", *Journal of Political Economy*, Vol. 108(4), pp. 833–850.

Sorensen, A. (2001), "An empirical model of heterogeneous consumer search for retail prescription drugs", NBER Working Paper No. 8548.

Spence, M. (1980), "Notes on advertising, economies of scale, and entry barriers", *Quarterly Journal of Economics*, Vol. 95, pp. 493–508.

Stigler, G. (1961), "The economics of information", *Journal of Political Economy*, Vol. 69(3), pp. 213–225.

Takeeda-Lilly (2001), *Takeeda-Lilly Prescription Drug Benefit Cost and Plan Design Survey Report*, Scottsdale, AZ: Pharmacy Benefit Management Institute, Inc.

Tamblyn, R., R. Laprise, J. Hanley, M. Abrahamowicz, S. Scott, N. Mayo, J. Hurley, R. Grad, E. Latimer, R. Perreault, P. McLeod, A. Huang, P. Larochelle and L. Mallet (2001), "Adverse events associated with prescription drug cost-sharing among poor and elderly persons", *Journal of the American Medical Association*, Vol. 285, pp. 421–429.

"The FDA's drug review process: ensuring drugs are safe and effective", *FDA Consumer Magazine*, September 2005 (http://www.fda.gov/fdac/features/2002/402_drug.html). Retrieved on January 2010.

Thomaselli, R. (2009), "Pharma drops search advertising after FDA warning", *Advertising Age*.

Tirole, J. (2003), *The Theory of Industrial Organization*, Cambridge, MA: MIT Press.

United States Congressional Budget Office (2006), *Research and Development in the Pharmaceutical Industry*, Washington, DC: U.S. Government Printing Office.

United States Congressional Budget Office (2007), *Prescription Drug Pricing in the Private Sector*, Washington, DC: U.S. Government Printing Office.

United States Department of Commerce (2004), *Pharmaceutical Price Controls in OECD Countries*, Washington, DC: U.S. Government Printing Office.

United States Department of Health and Human Services (2004), Report on Prescription Drug Importation. U.S. Government Printing Office, Washington, DC.

United States Office of the Inspector General (2009), Comparing Pharmacy Reimbursement: Medicare Part D to Medicaid. U.S. Government Printing Office: Washington, DC.

United States Office of Technology Assessment (1993), *Pharmaceutical R&D: Costs, Risks and Rewards*, Washington, DC: U.S. Government Printing Office.

Urban, G., T. Carter, S. Gaskin and Z. Mucha (1986), "Market share rewards to pioneering brands: an empirical analysis and strategic implications", *Management Science*, Vol. 32, pp. 645–659.

Wyeth-Ayerst (1999), *The Wyeth-Ayerst Prescription Drug Benefit Cost and Plan Design Survey Report*, Scottsdale, AZ: Pharmacy Benefit Management Institute, Inc.

CHAPTER 11

The Indirect Impacts of Smoking Bans in Gaming Venues

Joseph G. Hirschberg* and Jeanette N. Lye

Abstract

Recent changes in smoking laws have influenced gambling behaviour at electronic gaming machine (EGM) venues. In this chapter, we review the literature that examines the interrelationship between gambling, problem gambling, and smoking in order to gauge the indirect effects of smoking bans in gaming venues. We then perform an analysis on the consequences of a smoking ban in Victoria, Australia, that was instituted on 1st September 2002. This analysis investigates the nature of the pattern of drops in local EGM revenue and the impact on the state tax revenue.

Keywords: slot machines, smoking ban, tax revenue, smoking ban, border effects

JEL classifications: L83, H27, I18

1. Introduction

The stated objectives for smoking bans in public places are primarily defined from a public health perspective. They are to reduce exposure to

---

* Corresponding author.

CONTRIBUTIONS TO ECONOMIC ANALYSIS
VOLUME 290 ISSN: 0573-8555
DOI:10.1108/S0573-8555(2010)0000290014

second-hand smoke and to discourage smoking in general. However, when a government institutes these bans in a gambling venue, they have a combination effect.

The direct consequences are to the environment in the venue. Employees and patrons are exposed to less smoke. Smoking is shifted away from the proximity of the gaming machines. However, there may be secondary influences that require examination as well. It has been found that smokers are no more likely to play gaming machines than non-smokers (Pritsos *et al.*, 2008); if smokers do play, they spend over twice as much (Harper, 2003). Furthermore, smoking has been linked to problem gambling (Rodda *et al.*, 2004). The introduction of a smoking ban may interrupt the behaviour of these gamblers. This may result in reducing attendances and revenue at gaming venues.

In this chapter, we examine the impacts of such a ban in the Australian state of Victoria. In Victoria, as in most of the Australian states that allow gambling, a large portion of the state's revenues are generated by taxes on the gaming industry, and in particular electronic gaming machines (EGMs).[1] Thus, any policy that changes the patterns of gambling may have significant budgetary impact. The contributing factors to this shift in gambling behaviour are the potential flight of local gamblers to an adjacent state where smoking bans have not been enacted and the socio-economic characteristics of the communities in which they are located.

In this chapter, we examine the relationship between smoking and EGM gambling and the consequences of a smoking ban. The rest of the chapter proceeds as follows. Section 2 of this chapter discusses characteristics of EGM gambling. Section 3 examines the relationship between smoking and gambling. Section 4 reviews previous research on the effects of a smoking ban in gaming establishments. In Section 5, we look at the characteristics of the associated fall in gaming expenditure related to the smoking ban imposed on the 1st of September 2002 by the Victorian Government in Australia.[2] In particular, we look at the relationship between the associated fall in gaming expenditure and socio-economic status of the locality in which the gaming venue is located and if there is evidence of a greater drop for those areas that border New South Wales (NSW), where there was no smoking ban in gaming areas at this time. We also examine the impact on state tax revenue. Finally, Section 6 presents conclusions.

---

[1] The Australian state of Western Australia is the only state where such gambling outside of a casino is not allowed.

[2] In Australia, gaming expenditure refers to gross profits of gambling operators (prior to fees and taxes). In US studies, this term is often referred to as gaming revenue. We use both of these terms.

2. *Electronic gaming machines*

Worldwide there are a range of different types of gaming machines. These machines can be classified as pachinko machines, amusement machines with prizes and EGMs (e.g. slots, video lottery terminals, poker machines, pokies). Pachinko machines and amusement machines with prizes have a low maximum spending per game and slow speed of play. EGMs are high-intensity gaming machines and are characterized by high maximum spending per game and fast speed of play. Because they are computers, EGMs can be designed to have more gambling-inducing structural characteristics than for other forms of gambling. Such structural characteristics include: a high number of near-winning situations, the use of light and colour effects, sound effects and the inclusion of interesting payment features. In 2008, the worldwide total number of gaming machines was estimated as 7,678,528 (TNS, 2008), where 14% were EGMs (Dowling *et al.*, 2005).[3]

Playing EGMs is the form of gambling most strongly linked to 'problem gambling' (Dowling *et al.*, 2005; Lund, 2006). The term 'problem gambling' is often used to describe interfering patterns of excessive or destructive gambling.[4] Previous research has linked 'problem gambling' with increased accessibility to gambling opportunities, poverty, low socio-economic status and substance abuse (Marshall and Wynne, 2004). In particular, problem gambling tends to occur more among men, those with low income, low education and from ethnic minorities (Lund, 2006).

It has been estimated that 75%–80% of gambling-related problems are associated with EGMs (Delfabbro and Le Couteur, 2007). Furthermore, problem gamblers are thought to account for a disproportionate amount of the total expenditure on EGMs. In 2009, the Australian Productivity Commission estimated that problem gamblers account for around 40% of the total gaming machine expenditure (Productivity Commission 2009). Williams and Wood (2007) estimate that up to 61% of revenue from gaming machines in the Canadian province of Ontario may come from problem gamblers.

---

[3] It is thought that the actual total may be larger due to the existence of unregistered and illegal machines. The actual numbers of these could not be verified.

[4] In the literature, the term problem gambling is commonly used to include pathological gambling. Pathological gambling has been formally recognized as a medical disorder of impulse control by the American Psychiatric Association (APA) since 1980 (Lesieur and Rosenthal, 1991). It is a progressive disease with elements of addiction similar to alcohol and drug addiction. According to the APA, clinicians identify the presence of a gambling disorder by confirming at least 5 out of 10 Diagnostic Statistical Manual (DSM) criteria. Each criterion carries equal weight. In addition, clinicians must determine that the pattern of excessive gambling is not caused by a manic disorder.

It is widely believed that greater gambling availability leads to increased gambling participation. Two recent studies that highlight the relationship between problem gambling and EGM density include Storer *et al.* (2009) and Lund (2009). By examining 34 problem gambling surveys that were conducted in Australia and New Zealand since 1991, Storer *et al.* (2009) conclude that the prevalence of problem gambling increases with increasing density of EGMs. This is estimated to be at a rate of approximately 0.8 problem gamblers per EGM. Furthermore, they found no evidence of a plateau in the relationship between problem gambling prevalence and increasing density of EGMs. Lund (2009) examined the Norwegian ban on EGMs from 1st July 2007.[5] Prior to the ban, there had been no restrictions specifying where such machines could be placed. In 2003, it was estimated that there was approximately one machine per 250 people, and the most common type of gambling for problem gamblers was playing on EGMs (Lund, 2006). Many of these EGMs were located in easily accessible areas such as shopping centres and railway stations. Lund (2009) shows that after the ban, gambling participation, gambling frequencies and gambling problems all declined. In particular, she found no indication that there was any substitution of EGMs with other types of gambling.

A number of studies have noted a tendency for EGMs to be located in more socio-economically disadvantaged regions. Marshall and Baker (2001) found the distribution of EGMs to be skewed towards less advantaged regions in Melbourne which were characterized by higher levels of population from non-English-speaking backgrounds and high unemployment. Gilliland and Ross (2005) found a similar spatial distortion of EGMs and socio-economic conditions in Montreal and Laval.

In sum, EGMs appear to be responsible for higher levels of 'problem gambling'. They do not appear to be strong substitutes for other forms of gambling. Also, that the most profitable locations for EGMs appear to be in the lower socio-economic neighbourhoods.

3. *The relationship between gambling and smoking*

Tobacco smoking is identified with a range of adverse health effects. It is the main known cause of cancer-related death worldwide (Sasco *et al.*, 2004) and has been linked to 13 different cancers (WHO, 2008). It has also been identified as a major cause of heart disease and stroke (Mattsom

[5] This ban excluded Bingo Automats although 99.7% of adults in 2007 reported that they did not use or seldom used them.

et al., 1987). Worldwide it is estimated that there are 1.3 billion smokers. In 2000, it was estimated that 21% of total global cancer deaths were caused by smoking. Furthermore, smoking was shown to be an important determinant of cancer mortality for men in all regions and for women in industrialized countries (Ezzati *et al.*, 2005). On average, smokers lose 8 years of their life, which represents 4 million smoker deaths each year worldwide (Edwards, 2004). In high-income countries, low socio-economic status is associated with an increased likelihood of being a smoker and smoking more cigarettes per day. In low- and middle-income countries, men of low socio-economic status are more likely to smoke than men of high socio-economic status; and for those men from a low socio-economic status who smoke, their daily consumption of cigarettes is similar to or greater than men from a high socio-economic status who smoke (Davis *et al.*, 2007).

There are also known harmful health effects in adult non-smokers from the inhalation of other people's tobacco smoke (passive smoking, second-hand tobacco smoke). These may include irritation to the eyes, nose and throat, allergy, headache, nausea, decreased lung function, chronic airways disorders, lung cancer and emphysema (Winstanely *et al.*, 1995). Non-smokers exposed to second-hand tobacco smoke at work have a 16%–19% increase in risk of developing lung cancer (Sasco *et al.*, 2004). Smoking in workplaces and indoor public areas is a major source of second-hand smoke exposure. Globally, about one-third of adults are regularly exposed to second-hand smoke (WHO, 2009).

There appears to be a high degree of complementarity between tobacco use and gambling. A number of studies have found high rates of tobacco use among gamblers (McGrath and Barrett, 2009). In particular, a higher rate of smoking has been observed in gamblers undergoing treatment. Estimates of daily tobacco use among problem gamblers range from 41%–69% (Grant *et al.*, 2008). Rodda *et al.* (2004) identify higher rates of tobacco dependence and anxiety among problem EGM players. Similarly, Grant and Potenza (2005) note that daily tobacco use in pathological gamblers who seek treatment is common and appears to be associated with the greater urge to gamble. This relationship also appears in the research by Petry and Oncken (2002) who found that of the gamblers seeking treatment, those who smoked on a daily basis gambled on more days and spent more money per month than gamblers who did not smoke on a daily basis. In Victoria, Australia, it was found that smokers were no more likely to play EGMs than non-smokers. However, if smokers did play, they spent over twice as much (Harper, 2003).

Thus, we can conclude that the literature shows a strong link between smoking and detrimental health effects both for the smoker and the passive smoker. There is also a strong association between smoking and 'problem-gambling' behaviour that may well act as the mechanism by which smoking bans influence gambling behaviour.

4. Smoking bans – a review of previous literature

To improve health outcomes for both workers and patrons by reducing exposure to environmental tobacco smoke, smoking bans have been introduced in a number of gaming establishments worldwide. However, these bans may also break the '*trance-inducing rituals*' associated with gambling by requiring players who smoke to interrupt their play to go outdoors to smoke (Harper, 2003). Thus, smoking bans may act as a method of harm minimization for some gamblers. It may also have implications for gaming revenue, admissions and tax revenue.

A number of studies have examined the effect of the smoke-free laws introduced in the US state of Delaware implemented on 27th November 2002. Mandel *et al.* (2005) and Glantz and Alamar (2005) concluded that there was no change in gaming revenue for the EGMs in the state's three racetracks. However, after correcting data errors in these earlier studies and also adopting a more robust methodology, Pakko (2006) found that there was a revenue loss of 13% compared to the year preceding the smoking ban. In a further study, Pakko (2008) found that the Delaware casinos differed in the magnitudes of percentage losses. The casino with the largest proportionate loss due to the smoking ban faced the most direct competition from alternative gaming facilities in Atlantic City, New Jersey, that were not subject to smoking bans. Thalheimer and Ali (2008) estimate a system of EGM demand equations for each of the three Delaware casinos. Across the three Delaware casinos, the falls in gaming demand varied between 12.7%–17.8%. However, it was found that these amounts were not significantly different across the three casinos. Thus, it was concluded that the smoking ban reduced gaming demand by 15.9%.

Two other studies have looked at the introduction of smoking bans using the experiences in the Australian state of Victoria and the US state of Illinois. Using data from the Victorian experience, Lal and Siahpush (2008) concluded that the smoke-free policy on all EGM locations instituted on 1st September 2002 led to a sudden 14% sustained drop in the mean level of state-level monthly EGM expenditure. Garrett and Pakko (2009) examine the effect of a smoking ban in all Illinois casinos on 1st January 2008 on both casino revenue and attendance. Results indicated that casino revenue declined by more than 20% and total admissions fell by 10%. A further implication was substantial losses in tax revenue for the state and local communities that host the casinos. Total Illinois tax revenue was down by $200 million.

In these three cases, the imposition of smoking bans in gaming facilities has reduced gambling by substantial amounts. In the next section, we will re-examine the evidence from the Victorian smoking ban and try to establish why the ban varied regionally in its impact on gaming revenues.

5. *Smoking ban in Victoria, Australia*

In 1991, the Victorian legislature allowed the introduction of EGMs into selected hotels and clubs licensed to serve alcohol.[6] Two corporations, Tattersalls and Tabcorp, are licensed to own and lease gaming machines to approved clubs and hotels. Each corporation is permitted to operate 50% of the maximum permissible number of these gaming machines.[7] Victoria has imposed a statewide cap of 27,500 machines in hotels and clubs. From the 1st of September 2002, the Victorian Government imposed a ban on smoking in gaming areas of licensed premises. No smoking was permitted in venues with gaming machines that consisted of only one room and gambling rooms in venues that had two or more rooms. For the first time since EGMs were introduced into Victoria, expenditure on the machines dropped in 2002–2003. There was also a reduction in problem gamblers seeking help with statewide counselling numbers falling from 5,309 in 2001 to 3,508 in 2003 (Abbott, 2006).

5.1. *The local impacts of the smoking ban*

First, we investigate how the Victorian bans had a differential impact on different regions depending on the proximity to the border with NSW, where there were no smoking bans in effect at the time. We also investigate how the local socio-economic conditions influenced the degree of the impact of the ban. Then, we determine the impact of the bans on the Victorian state tax revenues.

Victoria is subdivided into a number of local government areas (LGAs) that can be defined as being metropolitan, regional or rural. The Victorian Commission for Gambling Regulation reports LGA-level annual data on EGM expenditures and the number of EGMs. Using the annual expenditure on EGMs per LGA for the years 2002–2003, we construct the variable *%Change in EGM Expenditure 2002–2003*, in $2002 (*%ΔExpend*). Also, for these years we construct a variable that reflects the percentage change in EGM numbers within the LGAs (*%ΔEGM numbers*). As a measure of socio-economic status, for each LGA we use the Index of Relative Socio-Economic Disadvantage (*IRSED*) produced by the Australian Bureau of

---

[6] The term hotel in Australia is used to refer to establishments that may only have a bar or pub. Most do not have accommodations for sleeping and many also provide live music. They are usually privately owned. Clubs are also public bars and pubs but they are owned by an organization such as a veterans association and sports club.

[7] There is also a casino in Melbourne. It was opened on 30th June 1994 and has a cap of 2,500 machines. With the introduction of the smoking ban, the casino was also required to be smoke free, except in TAB rooms, bar areas and high roller rooms that were exempted by the Minister of Health. The data for the casino is not included in the analysis presented here.

Table 1. Summary statistics

Variable		Border	No border
%ΔExpend	Mean	−15.8	−12.4
	Minimum	−25.1	−19.8
	Maximum	−8.9	−2.2
IRSED	Mean	993.2	1015.2
	Minimum	976.7	876.9
	Maximum	1033.7	1122.2
%ΔEGM numbers	Mean	0.294	−0.296
	Minimum	0.000	4.688
	Maximum	2.643	−6.749
Observations		9	51

Statistics. This measure is derived from a weighted average of a number of Census attributes that reflect socio-economic status. These include low income, low educational attainment, high unemployment and a greater proportion of the local workforce in relatively unskilled occupations. The *IRSED* is scaled across Australia so that the average score is 1000. The higher the score the lower the level of disadvantage in the LGA. Scores lower than 1000 indicate relatively disadvantaged areas (Victorian Government Department of Human Services, 2003). We also identify the LGAs that border the state of New South Wales (NSW) by defining a dummy variable *border*.[8]

Table 1 reports the summary statistics of these variables categorized as to whether the LGA is located on the border of NSW or not. Out of a total of 60 LGAs, 9 are defined as bordering NSW. From Figure 1, one can note that the impact of the smoking ban in Victoria differed across LGAs.[9] On average, the fall was larger for those LGAs that bordered NSW. Note that all the LGAs that border NSW are either classified as regional or rural. This is reflected in the statistics for *IRSED* where the values are more similar for those LGAs on the border than those for the rest of Victoria which are made up of metropolitan, regional and rural LGAs. This can be viewed in Figure 2 which compares the box plots of *IRSED* by the border location of the LGA. The distribution for those on the border is more compact indicating the homogeneity of the mainly rural LGAs along the

[8] These LGAs include Greater Shepparton, Mildura, Swan Hill, Wangaratta, Wodonga, East Gippsland, Moira, Indigo, Towong and Campaspe. Note the LGA of Gannawarra had $0 expenditure and was not included in the sample. Also, note that due to confidentiality requirements, only the combined expenditures are reported for Indigo and Towong.

[9] The box plots show both the median and mean. The median is depicted using a line through the centre of the box, while the mean is illustrated with a dot.

Figure 1. Comparison of the change in EGM Expenditure 2002–2003 ($2002)

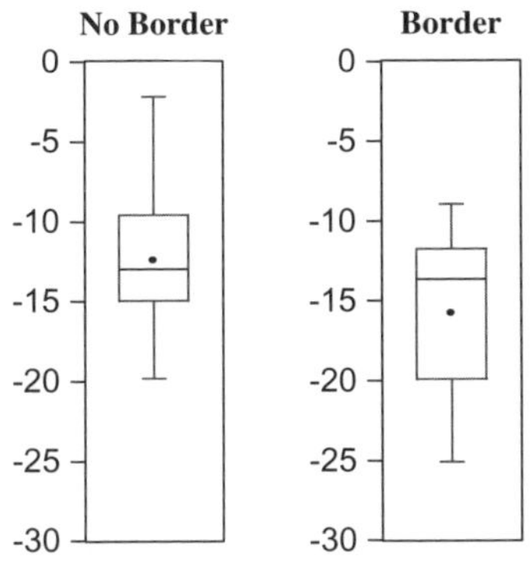

***Figure 2. Comparison of* IRSED**

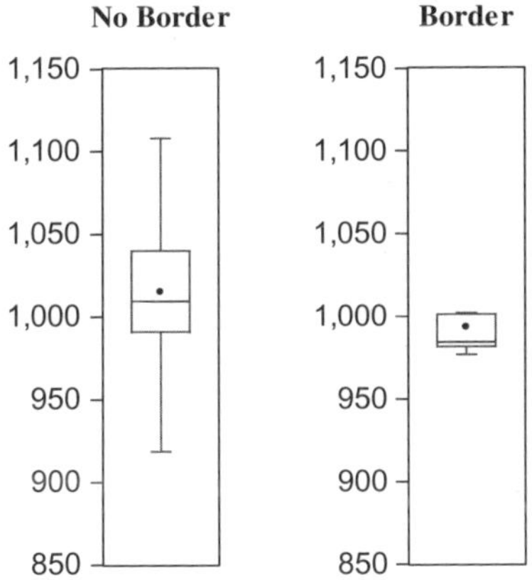

border. Another feature of the data that can be noted in Table 1 is the small variation in the number of EGMs between the two years.

Table 2 presents the results of a regression in which *%ΔExpend* is the dependent variable and *IRSED*, *%ΔEGM* numbers and *border* are explanatory variables. The small number of EGMs moved between venues during 2002–2003 is accounted for by including *%ΔEGM* numbers as a regressor.

The estimated coefficient on *border* is negative and statistically significant. This implies that conditioned on the level of *IRSED* for the LGA, the fall in the expenditure after the introduction of the smoking ban was 4.4% greater for those LGAs that bordered the state of NSW, where there was no

Table 2. Estimation results

Variable	Coefficient	t-statistic	P value
Dependent Variable: *%Change in EGM Expenditure 2002–2003* ($2002)			
Intercept	23.441	2.028	0.047
%ΔEGM numbers	0.5034	2.678	0.010
IRSED	−0.0352	−3.121	0.003
Border	−4.4454	−2.421	0.020
$R^2 = 0.232$		F-Stat = 5.653	

Note: Number of observations = 60. *t*-statistics based on White Heteroscedasticity-Consistent Standard Errors.

smoking ban at that time. This finding supports the claim in a newspaper article (Ryan, 2003) where it was noted that '*Smoking punters have crossed the border where they are gleefully greeted by NSW club managers* ...' To counter the '*massive*' revenue falls occurring at Victorian venues on the border, the state opposition party proposed a 'buffer zone', that is an exemption to the smoking ban in Victorian gaming venues that were within about 10 kilometres of the border (Gray, 2003). However, this proposal was rejected by the health minister who argued that the '*bans are a good idea for the health of human beings and that's my primary concern*' (Warner, 2003).

Given that problem gamblers are more likely to smoke, it was thought that the introduction of the smoking ban may significantly impact upon the behaviour of problem gamblers acting as a harm minimization strategy. However, the estimated coefficient of *IRSED* is negative and statistically significant. This indicates that the smoking ban was associated with greater falls in expenditure for those gaming venues located in the more advantaged LGAs. It has been found that the more advantaged areas are associated with lower smoking prevalence (Siahpush *et al.*, 2005). Furthermore, problem gamblers are linked to low socio-economic or more disadvantaged areas (Marshall and Wynne, 2004). Thus, this result may suggest that problem gamblers were less influenced by the smoking ban than non-problem gamblers. According to a survey of gaming venue managers, they reported that the smoking ban had most significantly impacted on non-problem gamblers (Rodda and Cowie, 2005). One manager commented that prior to the smoking ban, the gaming rooms used to attract business from diners at the bistro who '*used to put money in while having a cigarette break from dinner*' (Rodda and Cowie, 2005, Section 3, p. 29).[10] Marshall (2003) concludes that while there was a clearly

[10] Smoking in restaurants and cafes was prohibited in Victoria in July 2001.

identifiable drop in expenditure, there is no evidence that the smoking ban changed the behaviour of problem gamblers.

This analysis demonstrates that a number of factors influenced the impact of the smoking ban. The percentage fall in revenue was the greatest for those gaming venues in more advantaged areas and for those that were closest to the NSW border. In the next section, we investigate the statewide impact of the smoking ban in terms of state tax revenue.

5.2. The tax revenue impacts of the smoking ban

To investigate how the smoking ban influenced the state tax revenues, we present the evidence on how the EGM revenues changed in the years after the introduction of the ban.

Figure 3 compares the actual and forecast tax revenue from EGM gambling over the period 1998–2007 obtained from Victorian State Budget papers.[11] Tax revenue from EGM gambling constituted between 8%–10% of total state tax revenue. In addition, this time period was not

Figure 3. Actual and forecasted tax revenue from EGMs for Victorian Government (hundreds of millions $2002)

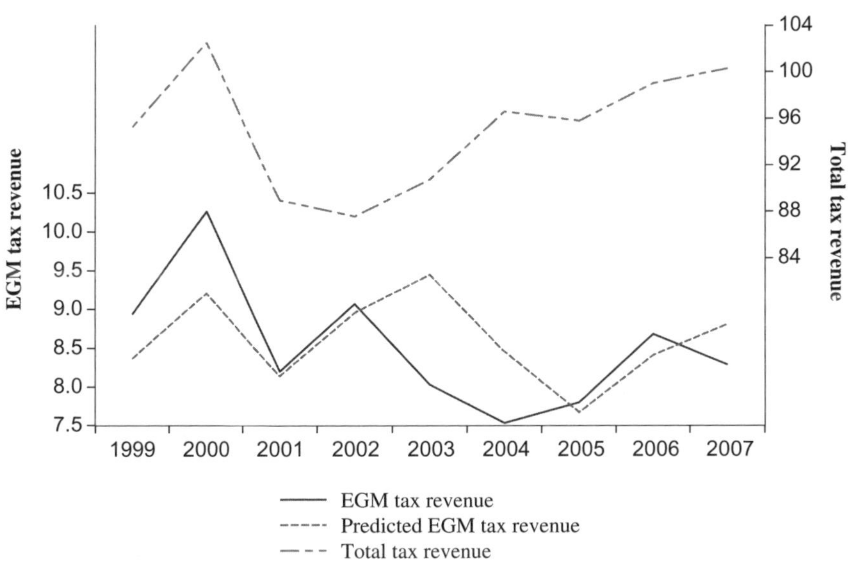

[11] These are available at http://www.dtf.vic.gov.au.

Figure 4. Components of real gambling expenditure in Victoria ($2002 millions)

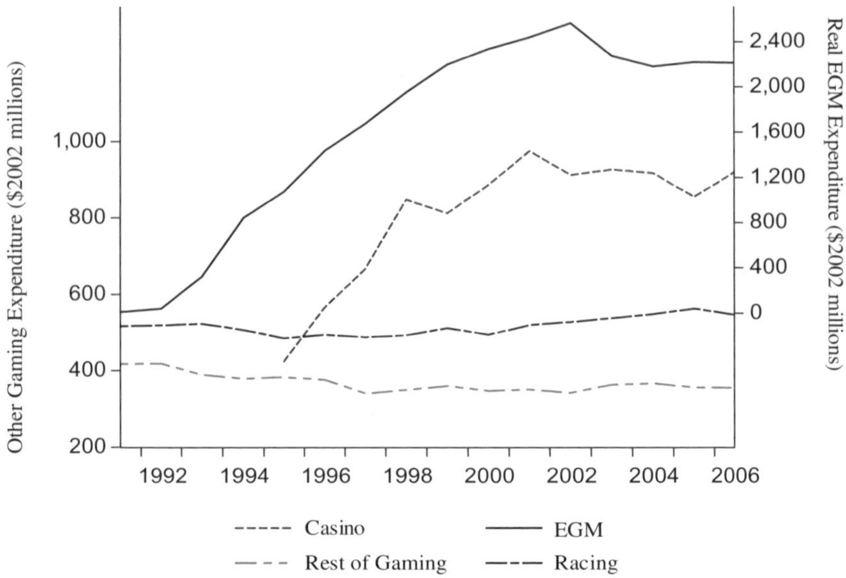

associated with an economywide downturn (Gillitzer *et al.*, 2005). Figure 3 illustrates that total state revenue was generally increasing over this period. There was a dip in 2001 due to the introduction of a federal goods and services tax, which resulted in a change in state tax revenue when a number of state-based taxes were removed and a federal sales tax was imposed. When EGMs were first introduced, the forecasted state tax revenue was well below the actual revenue collected. This was reversed with the introduction of the smoking ban with the actual being less than the forecasted over 2003–2004 by approximately $234 million ($2002) or 1.2% of total tax revenue for this period. This loss was commented on by Australian Hotels Association chief executive Alan Giles who claimed that the smoking ban was '*... unlikely to help with problem gambling and all it has done is take $200 million out of Government taxes that could have gone into the health system ...*' (Baker, 2003).[12]

There was only a minor impact of the smoking ban on other types of gambling in Victoria. Figure 4 is a plot of the real expenditure for the main

[12] A substantial proportion of gambling tax revenue in Victoria is earmarked for the State Hospitals and Charities Fund and Communities Support Fund.

components of gambling in Victoria. The dip in real EGM expenditure coincides with the smoking ban. Prior to the smoking ban, there had been a dip in casino real expenditure, which was due to a fall in the 'high roller' business (Power, 2002) and thereafter, until 2004, there was only moderate increases. The casino was not affected as much by the smoking ban as were the EGMs located in hotels and clubs. This may be due to the close proximity of smoking areas in the casino to the EGMs. Furthermore, at that time, in the casino, a player could interrupt his or her play and transfer credit to a card, whereas in hotels and clubs, cards were less likely to be used (SACES, 2005). Both racing and the rest of gaming showed minor increases in real expenditure.[13] As a consequence, there was an increase in state revenue associated with taxes from racing and private lotteries. For the two fiscal years following the implementation of the smoking ban, the increase due to racing and private lotteries in state revenue was around $39 million ($2002) or only about 27% of the actual fall in state revenue due to EGMs. There was another side-effect of the smoking ban to the racing industry though as they received a 25% share of Tabcorp's revenue from EGMs (Bourke, 2002).

6. *Conclusions*

It has been estimated that 75%–80% of gambling-related problems are associated with EGMs (Delfabbro and Le Couteur, 2007). A link has also been established between tobacco use and problem EGM gamblers (Rodda *et al.*, 2004). It has also been shown that if smokers do play EGMs, they spend over twice as much as non-smokers. Recently, a number of gaming establishments have introduced smoking bans.

One reason for these types of bans is to reduce exposure to second-hand smoke for workers and patrons. However, smoking bans may also act as a method of harm minimization for gambling. This is because it is thought that bans may require gamblers to interrupt their play to have a smoke outside and hence break the '*trance-inducing rituals*' associated with gambling (Harper, 2003). A review of previous research indicates that these smoking bans do result in substantial drops in revenue and demand for gaming. Another implication is that tax revenue can fall dramatically.

From 1st September 2002, the Victorian Government introduced a ban on smoking in gaming areas of licensed premises, which resulted in a fall in EGM expenditure. An analysis of the percentage fall over LGA showed that the fall in expenditure was greater in less disadvantaged regions. However, both smoking prevalence and problem gamblers are linked to

[13] Rest of gaming includes Keno, instant lottery, Lotteries, Lotto and Pools.

more disadvantaged areas. The percentage fall in expenditure was also greater for those LGAs that border NSW, which did not impose a smoking ban at this time. This is similar to the experience in the United States where bars subject to bans have reported losing customers to nearby communities where bans are not imposed (McCormick-Jennings, 2007). In a study of 239 towns in Massachusetts, Bartosch and Pope (2002) found a significant positive effect for towns bordered by those with a highly restrictive restaurant smoking policy. The ban also resulted in a tax revenue shortfall of $234 million dollars over the period 2003–2004.

References

Abbott, M. (2006), "Do EGMS and problem gamblers go together like a horse and carriage?", *Gambling Research*, Vol. 18, pp. 7–38.

Baker, R. (2003), "Gambling losses fall by $220", *The Age*, 8 August.

Bartosch, W. and G. Pope (2002), "Economic effect of restaurant smoking restrictions on restaurant business in Massachusetts, 1992 to 1998", *Tobacco Control*, Vol. 11, pp. 38–42.

Bourke, T. (2002), "Smoking bans prove to have costly side-effects", *The Age*, 14 December.

Davis, R., M. Wakefield, A. Amos and P. Gupta (2007), "The Hitchhiker's guide to tobacco control: a global assessment of harms, remedies, and controversies", *Annual Review of Public Health*, Vol. 28, pp. 171–194.

Delfabbro, P. H. and A. Le Couteur (2007), "A decade of gambling research in Australia and New Zealand: implications for policy, research and harm minimization", Report prepared for the Independent Gambling Authority of South Australia.

Dowling, N., D. Smith and T. Thomas (2005), "Electronic gaming machines: are they the 'crack-cocaine' of gambling?", *Addiction*, Vol. 100, pp. 33–45.

Edwards, R. (2004), "ABC of smoking cessation: the problem of tobacco smoking", *British Medical Journal*, Vol. 328, pp. 217–219.

Ezzati, M., J. Henley, A. Lopez and M. Thun (2005), "Role of smoking in global and regional cancer epidemiology: current patterns and data needs", *International Journal of Cancer*, Vol. 116, pp. 963–971.

Garrett and Pakko (2009), "Casino revenue and the Illinois smoking ban", Federal Reserve Bank of St. Louis, Working Paper No. 2009-027A.

Gilliland, J. and N. Ross (2005), "Opportunities for video lottery terminal gambling in Montreal: an environmental analysis", *Canadian Journal of Public Health*, Vol. 96, pp. 55–59.

Gillitzer, C., J. Kearns and A. Richards (2005), "The Australian business cycle: a coincident indicator approach", Research Discussion Paper 2005-07, Reserve Bank of Australia.

Glantz, S. and C. Alamar (2005), Erratum to Mandel, L., C. Alamar and S. Gantz (2005), "Smoke-free law did not affect revenue from gaming in Delaware Tobacco Control", 14, pp. 10–12. Tobacco Control On-Line (Electronic Letter) 23 May.

Grant, J. and M. Potenza (2005), "Tobacco use and pathological gambling", *Annals of Clinical Psychiatry*, Vol. 17, pp. 237–241.

Grant, J., M.S. Kim, B. Odlaug and M. Potenza (2008), "Daily tobacco smoking in treatment-seeking pathological gamblers: clinical correlates and co-occurring psychiatric disorders", *Journal of Addiction Medicine*, Vol. 2, pp. 178–184.

Gray, D. (2003), "Smoking bans drive gamblers into NSW", *The Age*, 7 March.

Harper, T. (2003), "Smoking and gambling: a trance inducing ritual", *Tobacco Control*, Vol. 12, pp. 231–233.

Lal, A. and M. Siahpush (2008), "The effect of smoke-free policies on electronic gaming machine expenditure in Victoria, Australia", *Journal of Epidemiology and Community Health*, Vol. 62, pp. 11–15.

Lesieur, H. and R. Rosenthal (1991), "Pathological gambling: a review of the literature", *Journal of Gambling Studies*, Vol. 7, pp. 5–39.

Lund, I. (2006), "Gambling and problem gambling in Norway: what part does the gambling machine play?", *Addiction Research and Theory*, Vol. 14, pp. 475–491.

Lund, I. (2009), "Gambling behaviour and the prevalence of gambling problems in adult EGM gamblers when EGMs are banned. A natural experiment", *Journal of Gambling Studies*, Vol. 25, pp. 215–225.

Mandel, L., C. Alamar and S. Glantz (2005), "Smoke-free law did not affect revenue from gaming in Delaware", *Tobacco Control*, Vol. 14, pp. 10–12.

Marshall, D. (2003), "EGM gambling patterns in Victoria: continuity and change", in: G. Coman, editor. Proceedings of the 13th Annual Conference of the National Association for Gambling Studies, Canberra, ACT, pp. 144–160.

Marshall, D. and R. Baker (2001), "Clubs, spades, diamonds and disadvantage: the geography of electronic gaming machines in Melbourne", *Australian Geographical Studies*, Vol. 39, pp. 17–33.

Marshall, K. and H. Wynne (2004), "Against the odds: a profile of at-risk and problem gamblers", *Canadian Social Trends*, Vol. 73, pp. 25–29.

Mattsom, M., E. Pollack and J. Cullen (1987), "What are the odds that smoking will kill you?", *American Journal of Public Health*, Vol. 77, pp. 425–431.

McCormick-Jennings, R. (2007), "Smoking ban has them fuming", *Business Journal of Milwaukee*, 2 February, 2007.

McGrath, D. and S. Barrett (2009), "The comorbidity of tobacco smoking and gambling: a review of the literature", *Drug and Alcohol Review*, Vol. 28, pp. 676–681.

Pakko, M. (2006), "Smoke-free law did affect revenue from gaming in Delaware", *Tobacco Control*, Vol. 15, pp. 68–69.

Pakko, M. (2008), "No smoking at the slot machines: the effect of a smoke-free law on Delaware gaming revenues", *Applied Economics*, Vol. 40, pp. 1769–1774.

Petry, N.M. and C. Oncken (2002), "Cigarette smoking is associated with increased severity gambling problems in treatment-seeking pathological gamblers", *Addiction*, Vol. 97, pp. 745–753.

Power, B. (2002), "Crown Casino chokes on smoking ban", *The Australian Financial Review*, 5 September.

Pritsos, C., K. Pritsos and K. Spears (2008), "Smoking rates among gamblers at Nevada casinos mirror US smoking rate", *Tobacco Control*, Vol. 17, pp. 82–85.

Productivity Commission (2009), Gambling Draft Report, October, Commonwealth of Australia.

Rodda, S., S.L. Brown and J.G. Phillips (2004), "The relationship between anxiety, smoking, and gambling in electronic gaming machine players", *Journal of Gambling Studies*, Vol. 20, pp. 71–81.

Rodda, S. and M. Cowie (2005), "Evaluation of electronic gaming machine harm minimisation in Victoria", Report prepared for the Victorian Department of Justice Melbourne, Caraniche Pty Ltd.

Ryan, K. (2003), "Pokies future under a cloud", *Herald Sun*, 29 March.

Sasco, A., M. Secretan and K. Straif (2004), "Tobacco smoking and cancer: a brief review of recent epidemiological evidence", *Lung Cancer*, Vol. 45(Suppl 2), pp. S3–S9.

Siahpush, M., G. Heller and G. Singh (2005), "Lower levels of occupation, income and education are strongly associated with a longer smoking duration: multivariate results from the 2001 Australian National Drug Strategy Survey", *Public Health*, Vol. 119, pp. 1105–1110.

South Australian Centre for Economic Studies (SACES) (2005), Community Impacts of Electronic Gaming Machine Gambling Victorian Department of Justice, Melbourne.

Storer, J., M. Abbott and J. Stubbs (2009), "Access or adaptation? a meta-analysis of surveys of problem gambling prevalence in Australia and New Zealand with respect to concentration of electronic gaming machines", *International Gambling Studies*, Vol. 9, pp. 225–244.

Thalheimer, R. and M. Ali (2008), "The demand for casino gaming with special reference to a smoking ban", *Economic Inquiry*, Vol. 46, pp. 273–282.

TNS (2008), "World Count of Gaming Machines 2008" (http://www.agmma.com). Accessed on 16 February, 2010.

Victorian Government Department of Human Services (2003), "Measuring disadvantage across Victoria" (https://fac.dhs.vic.gov.au/public folder/data_statistics/DHS/community_profiles/measure-disadvantage-vic-LGA-2001.pdf) Accessed on 2 March, 2010.

Warner, M. (2003), "Push to end smoke bans", *Herald Sun*, 17 March.
WHO (2008), "World cancer report 2008", in: P. Boyle and B. Levin, editors, International Agency for Research on Cancer, France.
WHO (2009), "WHO report on the global tobacco epidemic 2009 implementing smoke-free environments", World Health Organization, France.
Williams, R. and R. Wood (2007), "The proportion of Ontario gambling revenue derived from problem gamblers", *Canadian Public Policy*, Vol. 33, pp. 367–387.
Winstanely, M., S. Woodward and N. Walker (1995), "Tobacco in Australia facts and issues 1995", Victorian Smoking and Health Program, Australia.